Tackling the
Wicked Challenge of
Strategic Change

Tackling the Wicked Challenge of Strategic Change

The story of how a University changed itself

Pamela Baker, Norman Jackson and Jane Longmore

authorHOUSE®

AuthorHouse™ UK Ltd.
1663 Liberty Drive
Bloomington, IN 47403 USA
www.authorhouse.co.uk
Phone: 0800.197.4150

Published by AuthorHouse 06/12/2014

ISBN: 978-1-4969-8288-9 (sc)
ISBN: 978-1-4969-8286-5 (hc)
ISBN: 978-1-4969-8287-2 (e)

Dedication

To every member of Southampton Solent University who contributed and gave meaning to the Strategic Development Programme

Acknowledgements

It takes courage for an organisation to open itself to research that had the potential to reveal conflicts and problems as well as stories of success in its change process. The conviction that there was nothing to hide and the only benefit comes from discovering the process of change never wavered during the twelve months that this book took to produce. I am sincerely grateful for the opportunity afforded me in the commissioning of this study and book by the leaders of the SDP project Professor Jane Longmore and Pamela Baker. Their help, encouragement and practical support was fantastic throughout the process.

This book is intended to reflect the voices of people who were involved in the Strategic Development Programme. It is a testament to individuals' commitment to the story telling process that everyone who was contacted agreed to be interviewed. Without their contribution the changes brought about by SDP would not have happened and this book would not have been written. The following people generously gave their time to be interviewed and their permission for extracts from their interview to be used to create the narrative on which this book is based:

Jenny Anderson, Georgina Andrews, Pam Baker, Les Buckingham, Chris Barlow, Julie Beattie, Laura Bond, Helen Carmichael, Philip Clarke, Sarah Daley, Paul Davies, Suzanne Dixon, Andrew Doig, Richard Elliot, Roger Emery, Anita Esser, Phil Green, Andy Hair, Sarah Hand, Ian Harris, Kevin Harris, Jeanette Harrison, Steve Hogg, Sally Holland, Israr Jan-Parker, Mark Jones, Julian Konczak, Wendy Leeks, Jane Longmore, Lisa Mann, Shirley Manzi, Ramesh Marasini, Pascal Matthias, Fiona McKichan, Alistair Monger, Maggie Moss, Oscar Mwaanga, Rebecca Myers, Suzie Norris, Gill O'Reilly, Jo Parish, Claire Pekcan, Rod Pilling, Emma Pritchard, Ann Read, Vivienne Rivis, Steve Rose, Elizabeth Selby, Alan Schechner, Martin Skivington, Julia Tucker-Blackford, Gill Tunney, Matt Weet, Lorry West, Karen Wilbraham, Kenton Wheeler, Hannah Young.

Contents

Contributors

Norman Jackson is the principal researcher for and author of this book. He is Emeritus Professor at the University of Surrey, Fellow of the Royal Society of Arts, Director of Chalk Mountain Education and Media Services and Founder of the Lifewide Education Community Interest Company. During a long career in higher education he has been a teacher, course tutor, researcher, inspector and policy developer. He has studied the theory and practice organisational change and with the Higher Education Academy he led the development of the very successful Change Academy to help universities change their practices. He has authored four books all of which tackle change in higher education. In his last university role, as Director of the Surrey Centre for Excellence in Professional Training and Education, he had first hand experience of trying to lead and accomplish educational innovation in a university.

Jane Longmore is co-editor of this book and author of the final chapter. She is Professor of Urban History and Deputy Vice-Chancellor at Southampton Solent University, a Fellow of the Royal Historical Society, a member of the Quality Assurance Agency's Advisory Committee on Degree Awarding Powers and a Trustee of Sport Solent in the Community. Her career in higher education management spans more than twenty years and she has taught in a broad range of higher education institutions in the UK since the late 1970s. Her interests in pedagogy are reflected in her long-standing involvement with the Higher Education Academy as Chair of the national Forum for History. She has published in the field of pedagogy as well as in urban history. As Project Sponsor for the Strategic Development Programme at Southampton Solent, she co-ordinated the original bid in 2007, led the programme from 2009 to 2012 and oversaw the submission of the final report to HEFCE in 2013.

Pamela Baker is Strategic Development Director at Southampton Solent University, a Chartered Management Accountant, she joined as Director of the Strategic Development Programme in 2009 from the pharmaceutical industry having previously worked for Unilever. She has held senior positions across many functional areas from finance to marketing, to IT, security, internal communications and public affairs. Common to her roles has been the need to initiate or lead change, from starting up new departments and implementing new business systems to downsizing and restructuring. Her thinking round organisational change and complexity was sparked by James Gleick's 1988 book *Chaos*, which led her to question the popular use of causal models in large scale change and to look at alternatives. She has published in the field of employee engagement as well as resource planning. Pamela has contributed to Chapters 2, 3 and 4 as well as undertaking a co-editorial role.

Sarah Campbell is a PhD student at the University of Surrey, researching music and emotion and how it could be used to facilitate neural plasticity in recovery from addictions. While an undergraduate student at the University of Surrey she has conducted a number of qualitative and quantitative research studies into the way people change through their experiences including immersive experiences. Sarah contributed to the research studies underlying chapters 5 and 13.

Foreword
Professor Van Gore

Most forewords include an expression of thanks to the people who helped to achieve something significant, especially so in the form of major institutional change; more precisely, in this case, Southampton Solent University's ambitious attempt to transform the organisational culture(s) and make a new and distinctive kind of university. Yet there were so many phases and facets to that wide and intense process of change that it is neither feasible nor fair to single out any individual. There are two important exceptions, however.

First, I should like to express our gratitude as a university to the Higher Education Funding Council for England, particularly its then Chief Executive, Professor David Eastwood, for having the vision and the courage to fund what became known as the Strategic Development Programme, here in Southampton, 2009-12.

And second to Professor Norman Jackson, the industrious main author and editor of this book. From the very outset, he was a shrewd and objective commentator on what we were trying to do. Like a bird of good omen, Norman sat quietly perched in a corner at the series of internal 'conversations' and dissemination events, head to one side, constantly observing, reflecting, assimilating and evaluating—more ethnography than ornithology, in fact. As was the experience for so many of those involved, the project seemed to really capture his attention and his imagination. We were very fortunate, as this book testifies, to have had such an independent and curious spirit on board for what was, until now, a mysterious and uncharted voyage.

The passage we embarked upon proved to be complex, challenging, sometimes frustrating but very satisfying, always a privilege and in hindsight a continuous source of stimulus and benefit for the organisation, before we even reached the distant shore. Norman brings out skilfully the value of the journey made, not in terms of targets imposed and ticked off but rather a process of holistic, collective organisational learning. He discerns a relatively unusual leadership approach at work that consciously rejected positivism and dirigisme in favour of something more fluid, risky, participatory and creative. The project engaged energetically with what he calls 'wicked problems', vital and complex organisational conundrums that, by definition, have no prescribed solution or indeed a determinate end point. Moliere's bourgeois gentilhomme was famously delighted to learn from his tutors that he had been "speaking prose all his life". With greater humility and self-awareness, we hope, the senior team here is pleased to see how its leadership instincts and behaviour have been subject to such a critical, erudite and sympathetic analysis.

But we are far more pleased by the attention that the author reserves for the literally hundreds of university colleagues who have been involved in this far-reaching and multi-layered development. The book is interesting not only for the freshness, sweep and clarity of its conceptual framework, but also its profound sensitivity to the empirical messiness of lived experience, the law of unintended consequences, the revealing mosaic of conflicting local narratives and the overriding importance for management of engaging and listening closely to the 'voice from below'.

CHAPTER 1

The Challenge of Changing a University

PURPOSE

This book is about organisational change; intentional and unintentional change that occurs inside an organisation and between an organisation and its environment. What makes this book distinctive in the extensive literature on organisational change is its focus on a single educational institution, Southampton Solent University, which engaged in an unprecedented and highly complex strategic change initiative between 2009 and 2012. Known locally as the 'Strategic Development Programme (SDP)', this initiative ran across the whole University, its structures, processes and systems

The second distinctive feature of the book is the way it considers organisational change through the people who were involved in change. Their stories reveal their contextualised knowledge and insights about how change happened in their organisation, and this knowledge provides the foundation for more theoretical interpretation, analysis and synthesis.

The third feature of this book that makes it distinctive is the holistic and integrated approach to change that was adopted by the University: an approach that promoted change across academic departments, business systems and processes and administrative practices. Such an all embracing approach is rare in universities.

'Change' is an interesting and challenging idea: few words are as rich in meaning and consequence. Everyone can relate to the idea of change because our lives are full of it and it is an important phenomenon because significant change can cause great stress and challenge our sense of identity. As adults, responding to, coping with and creating change in different parts of our lives is what most people do most of their time, it's a natural part of being and evolving in the different social contexts in which we live out our lives. In the work environment, change is a continuous process: for many people work has become synonymous with change.

> *Change is the law of life and those who look only to the*
> *past or present are certain to miss the future. John F.*
> *Kennedy*

Engaging in deliberate and systematic change is what organisations have to do when they want to shift themselves strategically in order to secure a different and hopefully better future. Every organisation is different and every organisation has to chart its own pathways through strategic change, but it helps if you can draw on the experiences of other organisations. Unfortunately, there are few comprehensive accounts with the sort of rich detail that is provided in this book, of how a university has engaged in strategic change. So the second purpose of this book is to make a contribution to the organisational change literature in the hope that it will be of value to others involved in organisational change.

The phrase 'learning organisation' is not used very often where universities are concerned. Even though research, learning and knowledge creation is what universities do, they are often not very good at learning from their own experiences of change. Here we need to make the distinction between the learning of individuals and teams which does happen, and the learning of the organisation which is embedded in its values, policies, procedures and practices. All too often the organisational learning is lost as people move on and there is no means of transferring what has been learnt to people who take on new change projects. Indeed, a number of contributors to this book raised concerns that the knowledge they had developed through their experience of bringing about change would not be visible within the organisation. They believed that there was no home within the organisation where their knowledge could be stored, shared and used in future change projects.

Producing a book during a strategic change process, is one way in which an organisation can reflect on its experiences and achievements, draw together a range of perspectives and develop a deeper understanding about how complex change was accomplished so that the organisational memory is crystallised and can be drawn upon in future change processes. The book surfaces some of this deeply buried personal knowledge and makes it more visible within the organisation. By codifying it in this way and more importantly, diffusing this knowledge through the University, there is a real possibility of enabling the knowledge to be passed on to other people who will be able to make use of it.

In making this knowledge visible there is also the potential for the University to utilise it in its own professional and leadership development activities to help people develop the awareness of what is important in engaging in strategic change. This is another way in which codified knowledge that usually sits on shelves or on a computer can be brought to bear in appropriate and relevant learning processes. So the third reason for this book is to provide the University with an asset that can be used in its own leadership and management development programmes

In publishing the book the University is also demonstrating its willingness to share what it has learnt with other people who are working in higher education. In spite of increasing competitiveness, collegiality is still important in UK higher education and Southampton Solent University's willingness to place knowledge and insights about its own change practices in the public domain is testament to this value. This spirit of collegiality underpins the fourth reason for this book.

The fifth purpose this book fulfils is to highlight and publicly honour the enormous commitment and effort that so many members of the University have made. One of the findings to emerge from this study of change is the importance participants place on feeling that their efforts and creativity had been recognised and valued by the University. This was not always clear to them and the book is intended to show the people who were involved in the SDP that their efforts were appreciated and valued by the University.

The book celebrates the achievements of the many hundreds of people, who through the adaptations and inventions they have made to their own practice, have enabled the University to develop itself so that it is in a better position to meet the new challenges and opportunities that emerge today and tomorrow.

THE 'WICKED' CHALLENGE OF CHANGING AN ORGANISATION

Wicked problems or challenges are a category of problems defined by Rittel and Webber (1973) which have innumerable causes, are tough to describe, and do not have a right answer. They're significantly different to hard but ordinary problems, which people can solve by applying standard techniques. Not only do conventional processes fail to tackle wicked problems, but they may exacerbate situations by generating undesirable consequences.

According to Richie (2011) wicked problems are ill-defined, ambiguous and associated with strong moral, political and professional issues. Since they are strongly stakeholder dependent, there is often little consensus about what the problem is, let alone how to resolve it. Furthermore, wicked problems won't keep still: they are sets of complex, interacting issues evolving in a dynamic social context. Often new wicked problems emerge as a result of trying to understand and solve one of them. Examples include: How should we fight the "War on Terrorism?" How do we get genuine democracies to emerge from authoritarian regimes? What is a good national immigration policy? and the one that this book addresses: How should our organisation develop in the face of an increasingly uncertain future? (Richie 2011: 2).

Accomplishing strategic change in an organisation is not just a tough challenge, it's a 'wicked challenge'.

> [When creating strategy] Companies tend to ignore one complication along the way: they can't develop models of the increasingly complex environment in which they operate. As a result, contemporary strategic—planning processes don't help enterprises cope with the big problems they face. Several CEOs admit that they are confronted with issues that cannot be resolved merely by gathering additional data, defining issues more clearly, or breaking them down into small problems. Their planning techniques don't generate fresh ideas, and implementing the solutions those processes come up with is fraught with political peril. That's because, I believe, many strategy issues aren't just tough or persistent—they're "wicked." (Camillus 2008:1).

Wicked problems or challenges occur in organisations when they are subjected to constant change or unprecedented challenges. Because they occur in a social context, people have different ideas about what the challenge is and how it should be tackled. It's the social complexity of wicked problems as much as their technical difficulties that make them tough to tackle, lead and manage.

Camillus (2008:2) lists five characteristics that are typical of wicked problems in the context of strategic organisational change.

- The problem involves many stakeholders with different values and priorities.
- The issue's roots are complex and tangled.
- The problem is difficult to come to grips with and changes with every attempt to address it.
- The challenge has no precedent.
- There's nothing to indicate the right answer to the problem.

Camillus (2008:3-5) provides the following suggestions for the way organisations can work with wicked challenges.

Involve stakeholders, document opinions, and communicate.

Companies can manage strategy's wickedness not by being more systematic but by using social-planning processes—involving people in discussion, brain storming, designing and implementing possible solutions. The aim should be to create a shared understanding of the problem and foster a joint commitment to possible ways of resolving it. Not everyone will agree on what the problem is, but stakeholders should be able to understand one another's positions well enough to discuss different interpretations of the problem and work together to tackle it. All planning processes are, at their core, vehicles for communication with employees at all levels and between business units. This is particularly true of processes that tackle wicked issues.

Characteristic	Southampton Solent Strategic Change Programme
A wicked problem has no proper definition or structure to it.	'organisational and cultural change is essential. The change programme *we propose is truly transformative. It will impact on every aspect of culture and systems of the University'* p3 Strategic Development Fund Business Plan The ultimate objective of the University's strategic change programme was to bring about cultural change. While the direction for strategic change was defined in terms of broad goals the details of how to achieve cultural change was not defined. Rather, the detail emerged through the process of moving in the direction of the overall strategic aims.
Wicked problems can be explained in numerous ways. The choice of explanation determines the nature of the problem's resolution.	The wicked problem of cultural change was framed by the SDP which identified directions for change but did not provide the detail of how cultural change would be accomplished. The choice of explanation was an attempt to define the problem in ways that could be understood and acted upon by the members of the organisation. But it was also a way of showing the external stakeholder who provided additional resources that there were concrete plans for tackling the challenge.
Wicked problems have no stopping rule.	The end goal is cultural change—while the strategic development programme lasted 3 years this apparent stopping rule relates only to external funding. The University continues to seek the forms of cultural change that will enable it to perform more effectively, responsively and imaginatively in an increasingly uncertain world.
Solutions to wicked problems are not true-or-false, but better or worse.	There are no right answers to these sorts of problems, rather workable answers emerge through the day to day interactions of people involved in trying to find solutions. The SDP deliberately encouraged people to create ideas and support them in implementing their ideas in the knowledge that there are many possible answers that would contribute to changes in practice and culture but the impacts of which could only be judged after they had been implemented.

Every solution is a "one-shot operation" and counts significantly.	SDP resources were committed to support an organic process of idea generation and implementation of new practices. Every aspect of the programme contributed to the whole and the process enabled new approaches and models of practice to be evaluated once they had been created.
Wicked problems do not have pre-determined solutions nor well-described resolving actions.	There is no pre-defined way to solve the challenge of cultural change—every organisation is different. While ideas and practices have been imported from other organisations and contexts—potential solutions have had to be adapted or created in and for the organisations own contexts.
Problem-solvers should realise that solutions they try out may generate unintended consequences.	Once a solution has been implemented it will undoubtedly impact on other aspects of organisational systems and practices. Areas of conflict will need to be resolved and this may lead to unanticipated effects. Many of the case studies show that SDP educational innovations frequently collided with existing institutional practices and these were often sites of tension and conflict.

Table 1.1—Some of the 'wicked' characteristics (Rittel and Webber) of strategic organisational change initiated through the Strategic Development Programme at Southampton Solent University.

Define and embody the corporate identity.

While an organisation dealing with a wicked problem has to experiment with many strategies, it must stay true to its sense of purpose. Mission statements are the foundations of strategy, but an organisation's identity, which serves as a touchstone against which it can evaluate its choices, is often a more enduring statement of strategic intent. An organization's identity, like that of an individual, comprises its

- *Values.* What is fundamentally important to the company?
- *Competencies.* What does the company do better than others do?
- *Aspirations.* What does the organisation want to become and how does it measure success in becoming its vision?

Focus on action

In a world of Newtonian order, where there is a clear relationship between cause and effect, companies can judge what strategies they want to pursue. In a wicked world of complex and shadowy possibilities, enterprises don't know if their strategies are appropriate or what those strategies' consequences might be. They should therefore abandon the convention of thinking through all their options before choosing a single one, and experiment with a number of strategies that are feasible even if they are unsure of the implications.

A 'feed-forward' orientation

Organisations design their operations on the basis of gaining feedback on their performance so they compare results with plans and take corrective actions where appropriate. Though it's a powerful source of learning, feedback has limited relevance in a wicked context. Feedback allows enterprises to refine fundamentally sound strategies; wicked problems require people to come up with novel solutions. Feedback helps people learn from the past; wicked problems arise from unanticipated, uncertain, and unclear futures and challenges which emerge during the implementation process. Feedback helps people learn in contexts that are known and understood. Wicked problems involve contexts and problems that are unfamiliar or unknown. Comprehending the challenge is the initial and ongoing problem. Wicked strategy issues don't occur according to a timetable. Companies must constantly scan the environment for the effects of what they are doing, rather than conduct periodic analyses, and adjust their efforts in real time. To forge effective approaches to wicked issues, people must explore and monitor the assumptions behind their strategies.

Feed-forward requires an organisation's systems and procedures for making decisions allocating resources to be aligned to this real-time process—a condition that a number of case studies reveal was sometimes not realised.

'Wickedness' is the challenge for any organisation involved in significant strategic change and this book documents the ways in which one university tried to work with this challenge in its particular contexts. As the story unfolds it is worth reflecting on how the organisation's strategies reflect these suggestions for working with the wicked challenge.

UNIVERSITIES AS 'WICKED' PLACES FOR CHANGE

The characteristics of universities as organisational environments for change contribute to the wickedness of the challenge. In the words of one retiring university leader:

> Universities are pluralistic institutions with multiple, ambiguous and conflicting goals. They are professional institutions that are primarily run by the profession (i.e. the academics) often in its own interests rather than those of the clients and they are collegial institutions in which the Vice—Chancellor is less a CEO who can manage by diktat and decree and more a managing partner in a professional firm who has to manage by negotiation and persuasion. Change is extremely difficult to bring about in

> an institution with these characteristics. So, a prerequisite
> for change is some pressure—often a threat from outside
> the institution—which convinces its members that change
> is necessary (Bain 2007:13)

Universities are large organisations, employing a multi-skilled professional and administrative workforce providing a complex range of services that extend well beyond their core missions of education, research and scholarship. Their managers and other employees are networked to tens of thousands of people who provide new ideas and opportunities for change. They receive directions for change from Government and its agents (like HEFCE). They comply with regulatory authorities, like the Quality Assurance Agency, Statutory and Professional Bodies. They are open to requests from businesses and global markets. They pick up ideas from competitors and from system brokers charged with diffusing ideas (like the HE Academy and Leadership Foundation). They interact with partner FE college, schools and academies. They are subjected to observations and recommendations for change from peers e.g. through quality audits, visits by representatives from Professional Bodies, External Examiners and business representatives and leaders. Their students bring with them new ways of communicating and interacting with technology and people take the changes they adopt in their daily lives into their working environments. For example, an academic might buy an ipad for personal use but very quickly start to use it in his teaching. As a consequence of this multitude of situations change happens quickly, everywhere, all the time and for all sorts of reasons. It is a natural, spontaneous and organic process, part and parcel of an evolving society.

But there are a number of features about universities that make them distinctive sites for change and those responsible for bringing about organisational change must orchestrate change by working both with the grain and across the grain. One significant characteristic for an organisation the size and complexity of a university, is the nature of the fundamental transaction which takes place involving students and their teachers. While students now pay significant amounts of money for their higher education, the transaction which takes place is not like purchasing a product or service, because it involves the customer (the learner) in a deep and effortful relationship with her subject, her peers, her teachers and their mediating artefacts, and her university. The relational side of the business of education lies at the heart of the motives that drive university teachers and support staff in their quest for improvement. Put another way, the motivation to improve performance for much of the workforce in higher education, is to improve their student's experiences and make a difference to their lives, which is the deep moral purpose of education (Fullan 1993:18). If the people who work in a university believe that they are making a more significant difference to students' lives by changing what they do, they are more likely to involve themselves in change.

Another significant difference to most other organisations is that universities are organised into disciplinary tribes and territories (Becher 1989). The cultural and intellectual dynamics of disciplines (Creswell and Roskens 1981; Becher 1989 and 1994) provide an important context for the way academic communities respond to change. Becher's assertion (1994:153) 'that the cultural aspects of disciplines and their cognitive aspects are inseparably intertwined' is borne out not just in behaviours relating to research, but in different pedagogic beliefs and practices (Braxton 1995; Hativa and Marincovich1995; Smelby 1996; Hativa 1997; Gibbs 2000; Neumann 2001). But the studies of Trowler (1998) and Knight and Trowler (2000) also show how important organizational contexts are in shaping thinking and behaviours. Trowler (1998) challenged some of the assertions made about disciplinary cultures being the key determinant in the way academics view a whole range of issues claiming that attitudes and values among academic staff were much more diverse and unpredictable than had hitherto been portrayed.

> People don't resist change. They resist being changed!
> *Peter Senge*

In addition to tribal complexity there is also the matter of professional autonomy in a university. Another distinctive feature of universities is that they permit and encourage significant levels of personal autonomy of large numbers of individuals who can therefore respond to change in ways that are consistent with their own beliefs, interests and prejudices.

> Institutions of higher education are characterized by extremely decentralized structures of authority, remarkably dispersed incentive systems, and relatively few restrictions on the way people choose to use their time. These prominent organizational features that render colleges and universities distinctive among social institutions certainly help the academy protect its freedom from unwanted political and external influences. But they simultaneously act to subvert change of *any* kind (Ewell 2004:2).

It is this organisational respect for autonomy in the academic workforce, and the extent to which leaders of change have to seek buy in to any change process, that renders universities interesting and challenging sites for any organisational change that is orchestrated from the top. This characteristic is a source of much of the 'wickidity' (Bore and Wright 2009) in the challenge of cultural change.

Drawing on the insights gained through studies of change in university departments, Trowler et al (2003) provide a practical guide for people involved in facilitating change. They suggest (ibid: 13) that change strategies might focus either on big problems and the development of solutions that are tried, evaluated and revised or on changing beliefs by setting out the case for a particular course of action or why a particular innovation is preferred to existing practices:

> There is a need for change agents to explain clearly repeatedly and in many ways why the change is beneficial. In that sense they need to focus on beliefs. Two significant limits to this focus are that we may need to affect networks of beliefs, going right back to root beliefs about learning, teaching and education; and changing beliefs is not sufficient to change practice because people need tools to support them in the practical business of change (Trowler et al 2003: 13-14)

The SDP provides an instructive case study in how a university tried to encourage change in both practice and beliefs. It appears to have tackled the wicked challenge of cultural change by framing and resourcing problem working within a set of concrete 'tamer' problems in the belief that activity around these themes would lead to changes in practice, behaviour and belief.

Why Change Fails or Succeeds in the Academy

In his reflective account of the lessons learned from educational reform in higher education Peter Ewell (2004) identifies a number of reasons why changing practices in higher education is difficult—noting that 'grant-makers are happy if only a third of the projects they fund are successful' (ibid: p2). Reasons for failure (ibid p2-6) include:

- *The double edged sword of distinctiveness*—proclaiming what is wrong with current ways of doing things can provide a powerful rhetorical launch pad for a new change initiative and this often entails developing a new and distinctive language. However, efforts to promote conceptual and linguistic distinctiveness can prevent the integration of innovative practices into the mainstream. The exception to this condition is when the compelling story for change and the rhetoric of distinctiveness resulting from change become institutionalised as was the case with the SDP.

- *The problem of extending experiments*—change efforts generally begin small as experiments. New ideas are turned into educational prototypes particularly if they are innovative and piloted before being fully implemented. This was the approach taken with the SDP. But what is beneficial to getting innovative change underway can be difficult to replicate and extend when individuals resist adoption of someone else's ideas rather than their own.

- *Special Funding*—change initiatives are almost always funded on a project basis using dedicated funds. These funds are often provided externally and are time limited. The transition from special funding (like the SDP) to core funding 'is one of the most difficult organisational manoeuvres a university can make.'

These challenges are all relevant to the SDP change initiative and how the University and individuals engaged with them is an important part of the narrative of this book. Ewell (2004: 6-8) identified a number of basic characteristics that engender collective and collaborative commitment to change initiatives in universities and colleges, and enable institutions 'to work *across the grain* of established academic cultures':

- *Creating permanent structures* [or enterprises] *for collaboration* for example by attempting to foster generic skills and capabilities that are common to all disciplines across the curriculum. In the case of the SDP for example a collaborative structure was framed around the idea of *employability*: enabling students to be more employable.

- *Co-creating substantive and meaningful products*—'the effectiveness of collaboration in undergraduate [change] initiatives depends equally on the extent to which effort is directed toward creating a tangible collective product'

- *Tangible benefits*—effective collaboration results in individual benefits for those who participate. Often the benefits derive from new productive relationships developed through working cooperatively with someone else on something that is meaningful and valued by all the participants.

- *Information as a lever for change*—effective collaboration depends on clear lines of communication and requires collaborators to have access to credible information about conditions and performance. Communication is a recurrent theme throughout the case studies in this book.

These ways of thinking about how change can successfully be accomplished across the cultural grain of departments are consistent with and complemented by the approaches recommended by Trowler et al (2003:17-18) for working within the cultural grain of academic departments. They argue that common sense, technical-rationale approaches to planning, communicating and implementing change, are appealing and necessary, but they need to be combined with approaches that are grounded in social practice theory suggesting that (ibid 18):

1   Any innovation will be received, understood and consequently implemented differently in different contexts (this is concerned with innovations and change that is imposed).

2   In HE the important contextual differences that affect the reception of and implementation of [educational] innovation relate to a) discipline and b) department

3   The history of particular departments, the identities of those within them and the way they work together are very important in understanding how innovations are put into practice

4   Successful change, like successful learning, is a constructive process—the change is integrated into the heads and hearts of those involved . . . the change is uniquely shaped during this process—acquiring ownership of change, the feeling that innovation is ours.

5   If there is congruence between an innovation and the context of its introduction at a particular time, then dissemination will be successful even if some pre-requisites are not in place. However, both the context and the innovation will be re-shaped in the process.

The SDP provides an example of an organisational structure and a set of strategies that were created to encourage collaboration and the invention of new practices both within and across the cultural grain of Schools, Faculties and Central Services.

Institutional Cultures

Institutional cultures, 'the way we do things around here' (Deal and Kennedy 1982) derive from many factors, eg traditions, styles of leadership and management, and structures and processes relating to governance and the delivery of services. On the basis of empirical work McNay (1995) and Dobson and McNay (1996) recognised four cultural conditions within UK universities. Building on Weick's (1976) concept of educational institutions as loosely coupled organizations, the dimensions of the model relate to the extent of tightness or looseness in the definition of policy to control practice and the degree of control over implementing policy. The four cultural conditions are termed: collegial academy; bureaucratic; corporation and enterprise. None of the conditions is exclusive. The styles of leadership and management (and therefore the environment for change) are different in each cultural context.

Collegial academies are organizations of consent in which the members of the institution have a right to be consulted and in which they can exercise considerable influence over proposals for change through their powers of veto. In such a cultural environment leadership and management are transactional activities and change is through personal persuasion and working through consensus and compromise.

In bureaucratic cultures the consent processes are formalized in committees—representative democracy—and procedural power becomes dominant. There may or may not be clear policy in any area but there are precedents against which to judge proposals for change and general principles which condition behaviour. Such cultures are good at saying no and rarely generate innovation from within. Leaders and managers need to command by rules and case law, the control of agendas, minutes and information flow.

In the corporation, the academics recapture the control that they may have lost in a plethora of committees that are replaced by more dynamic and flexible working groups and teams. Committees are slimmed down and dominated by managers. This is often a crisis mode of operating, with positional power and tight control of funding being used to promote conformity to corporate objectives. Key people scan the environment and position the institution in relation to perceived policy imperatives. Leaders are transformational, bringing new values and new visions which they evangelize with charismatic zeal.

The enterprise culture keeps awareness of the market to the fore. It relies on a clear mission statement with priorities and plans that link policy to practice (McNay, 1995). It relies on good market intelligence and good internal management information systems. Its enterprise is commercially focused and extrinsically motivated: values which do not attract most academics. The strength of this culture is that it may be good for innovation and bringing team members together from different cultural enclaves. But this may be ephemeral and novelty is valued more than sustaining quality.

Trowler and Knight (2001) criticise this view of university cultures for being oversimplified and unrealistic. In truth, 21st century universities have to incorporate all four of these cultural stereotypes into their way of being. Trowler and Knight (2001) adopted a complexity view of universities viewing them as 'protean and dynamic, not singular and static'. In their view every university possesses a unique and dynamic multi-cultural configuration which renders depiction difficult and simple depictions wildly erroneous. So values, attitudes, assumptions and taken for granted recurrent practices may be as different from department to department or building to building in one HEI as they are between one university and the next. They preferred to visualise academic organizations as networks of networks (Blackler et al 2000) or constellations of communities of practice (Wenger 1998) and argued that these fundamental social structures had to be recognised in bringing about organisational change. Because of these sorts of challenges there are no standard recipes for bringing about change in a university. Instead, the leaders of each institution, with their unique contextual understandings, must sense the pathway they need to encourage the people in their organisation to take, and act in ways that are more likely to take people in this direction.

Seel (2000, 2004) offers another view of organisational culture that is consistent with Trowler and Knight (2001).

> organisational culture is the emergent result of the continuing negotiations about values, meanings and proprieties between the members of the organisation and its external environment. In other words, culture is the *result* of all the daily conversations and negotiations between members of an organisation. They are continually agreeing (sometimes explicitly, usually tacitly) about the 'proper' way to do things and how to make meanings about the events of the world around them. If you want to change a culture you have to change the conversations—or at least a majority of them. And changing conversations is not the focus of most change programmes, which tend to concentrate on organisational structures or reward systems or other large scale interventions. (Seel 2004)

In Seel's view, to bring about lasting cultural change, an organisation has to change the paradigm with which the organisation sees itself, 'unless the paradigm at the heart of the culture is changed there will be no lasting change' (Seel 2000).

> A paradigm is a constellation of concepts, values, perceptions and practices shared by a community, which form a particular vision of reality that is the basis of the way a community organises itself. (Capra 1997:6).

The case studies in this book reveal the way in which the University tried to encourage this paradigm change through the strategic development programme.

The Complexity Challenge

Change, particularly large scale, transformational organisational change, can be a messy business (Jackson 2003). Context, scale, social interactions, culture, identity and tradition or historicity all influence the level of complexity and potential for messiness in any change situation. Open-ended poorly defined problems like strategic change require the vast majority of the people in the organisation to own the problem and be the agents of the solution (Heifetz and Linsky 2002). For system leaders and organisers this means creating the conditions and processes that will enhance the likelihood that people engage with strategic change and bring about change that is consistent with what is desired. Ultimately, the process is about stimulating the imaginations and inventiveness of people. Because of the multitude of factors involved, and because fundamentally changing organisations is about changing people, the study of organisations in the last decade has drawn heavily on complexity theory (Stacey et al 2000). Where large scale organisational change is concerned it is not possible to reach new horizons without grasping the essence of complexity theory.

> The trick is to learn to become a tad more comfortable with the awful mystery of complex systems, to do fewer things to aggravate what is already a centrifugal problem, resist controlling the uncontrollable, and to learn to use key complexity concepts to design and guide more powerful learning systems (Fullan 2003:21)

The Challenge of Leading

It is precisely because bringing about significant change in an organisation is difficult and complex, that good leadership is required to accomplish it.

> There is nothing more difficult to take in hand, more perilous to conduct, or more uncertain in its success, than to take the lead in the introduction of a new order of thing. Niccolo Machiavelli, *The Prince* (1532)

This is particularly true of the University environment with all of its cultural complexity.

The SDP grew out of the vision of a Vice-Chancellor who was newly in post. This vision became codified in a new strategic plan and the SDP became an important strategy for achieving this vision. The SDP was ambitious in its scale, scope and complexity and it is for this reason that it makes an interesting example of organisational change. But these characteristics also meant that it posed considerable challenge to lead and manage. The case studies and managerial commentary reveal how this was achieved.

George Bain, on the eve of his retirement as a Vice-Chancellor, made these useful observations about the role of a university leader in leading and managing change.

> Management is the ability to cope with complexity, to devise structures and systems that produce order and harmony. Leadership is the ability to cope with change, to establish a new direction, and to get institutions and individuals to move in that direction. A Vice-Chancellor's job involves both management and leadership, but the latter is more important than the former. The key function of a Vice-Chancellor is to lead the University: to harness the social forces within it, to shape and guide its values, to build a management team, and to inspire it and others working in the University to take initiatives around a shared vision and a strategy to implement it. In short, a Vice-Chancellor should be an enabler rather than a controller. The job is 'to set the target that beckons'—a stretch target that drives the organisation forward by forcing innovation through deliberately creating a misfit between its ambitions and its current resources—and, having set it, to motivate people to hit it (Bain 2007:13)

But leading a significant programme of organisational change involves more than a Vice-Chancellor creating a vision. The rich detail in the SDP story reveals that leading organisational change involves people at all levels each making a contribution that is woven together by the leaders, managers and facilitators of the change process.

The Challenge of Innovating

The SDP promoted change at all levels from small incremental changes to the creation of entirely new practices and business systems. In the formulation and presentation of the SDP to the Funding Council sponsor, the University emphasised the transformative nature of what it was trying to achieve and the need to create a culture within which creativity in the service of innovation would flourish:

> The nature of this programme is transformative in terms of the degree and breadth of change, but also predicated on high levels of connectivity between the different parts of the University in meeting these challenges. *Innovation and creativity are central to this programme* and we will seek to liberate the energy and ideas of staff and students in

realising our goals. *Strategic Development Fund Business Plan* (2009:7)

In a previous study of educational innovation in five UK universities, Hannan and Silver (2000) noted that systematised innovation—the purposeful and organized search for change to gain competitive advantage or deal with a problem was not as well developed in universities as it was in other sorts of organisations. The SDP was an attempt to engage the University in a systematic way with change some of which was seeking to be innovative.

Hannan and Silver (ibid) noted that traditionally, in HE environments, innovation was undertaken by individual enthusiasts and consequently it was subject to the difficulties identified by Ewell (2004). Their study revealed the complex interplay between individuals who were trying to be innovative and their institutional environment.

> Innovation [in teaching and learning] depends on a configuration of vital elements: how an institution's culture is interpreted by a range of constituents; the degree of conflict and consensus within it; the pattern of attitudes within which initiatives are received; the nature of and reasons for change and the ways in which it is managed; relationships between the centre and the periphery; and views of what needs to be sustained, adapted or abandoned in the historical moulding of an institution and its substructures. (Hannan and Silver, 2000: 95).

In universities innovation relating to teaching and learning is not normally conceived as original ground breaking change. Rather it is viewed as 'what people do that is new in their circumstances'.

> An innovation in one situation may be something already established elsewhere, but initiative takers and participants see it as innovation in their circumstances. Such changes may be new to a person, course, department, institution or higher education as a whole. (Hannan and Silver, 2000:10).

Because of this widespread perception, Hannan and Silver (2000:139) questioned whether the concept of innovation had any real meaning in higher education beyond 'what people do that is new in their circumstances'. The lesson from this book is that it is precisely because people have grown and developed through their own experiments in innovation that the University had a valuable asset to draw upon when it pursued a programme of strategic change that contained within it the desire to innovate. Although the SDP did not explicitly set out to sponsor innovation it did set out to create the conditions within which people felt empowered to bring forward their ideas and create new practices in the belief that some of these practices would be innovative and open up new opportunities for the University. The case studies reveal that when such conditions are created it is generally the people who are naturally inventive, who are entrepreneurial in their outlook and who are quick to embrace new ideas and practices, who take advantage of the new opportunities.

ABOUT THE BOOK

The book is in three parts. The first part sets out a context for strategic change at Southampton Solent University. It describes the reasons for embarking on strategic change, the ways in which the University was initially engaged in thinking about and exploring options for change, the process of securing the resources for change, the way in which the strategy for organisational change was conceived and the building of infrastructures to enable strategic change.

The second part of the book provides a number of case studies that reveal how change was and is still being accomplished by the individuals and small groups of people who make it happen. At the heart of the organisation's concept for change was the need to develop a culture in which people felt more empowered to enable the University to adapt and prosper in the ever changing and increasingly uncertain world. The case studies reveal something of how this was accomplished. They embrace change at the levels of systems, Faculty, School, Service, team and individuals and they provide personal insights into not only the nuts and bolts of making change happen, but also the feelings and personal impacts of becoming different. It is the voices of the innovators and people engaged in change that make this book special. The perspectives they capture and the feelings they evoke will resonate with anyone who has tried to bring about significant change in a university. 'Blood, sweat, tears' and perhaps a touch of joy and happiness might capture the essence of their individual journeys of being the person they want to be and becoming different in the process.

The third section of the book tries to draw out learning that has been gained through the experience of change and relate this to theories and research from the organisational change literature. Three evaluative perspectives are offered: 'the researcher's conceptual synthesis', 'the innovator and their environment' and a summary of the factors that seem to have been important in accomplishing strategic change through the SDP. These factors constitute a set of home grown principles that if applied might help the organisation to continue to move along its self-determined evolutionary pathway. The final chapter provides a reflective account by the leader of the SDP change process in which she identifies the most important learning points for the University.

This book is fundamentally about trying to make better sense of a long, complex, messy, change process through the stories of people who were immersed in the change process. As such it contributes to the retrospective sense making that seeks to draw more and deeper value and meaning from the experience. Over fifty people were interviewed during the course of the study and their uniquely personal perspectives have been woven into the overarching story of organisational change. This book is the story of their ingenuity and effort to bring about change that they and their university valued. Universities are inherently creative places and there is never a shortage of ideas but there is often an enormous inertia that inhibits ideas being turned into new and better practices.

> The three institutions I have [led] were not short of creativity—the ability to think up new things—but of innovation—the ability to do new things. They had lots of new ideas lying around unused, not because their merits were unrecognised, but because too few people were prepared to take the responsibility for converting them from words into actions. [Universities] need to create an environment in which more people are prepared to take on this sort of responsibility (Bain 2004:4).

The SDP, like so many other externally funded enhancement initiatives, provides people a reason and an opportunity to get involved in change and gave people the opportunity to be responsible and convert their ideas into action. The SDP successfully liberated individuals' creativity and provided resources and support to enable people to realise their ideas and ideals. Viewed this way the SDP was an 'innovation system' and this was its deeper value. This book is a tribute to all the people who not only used their imaginations but who also possessed the will and developed the capability to turn their ideas into practical reality. It is also a tribute to the leaders and managers who believed in, encouraged and facilitated this process.

CHAPTER 2

Starting Strategic Change

"However, they found that the most successful reorientations occurred in organizations whose managers foresaw the need for radical change and initiated it before crises occurred. It is not clear, unfortunately, how such managers get their foresight". Gersick on Tushman, Newman, and Romanelli (1986)

WHERE DO YOU BEGIN?

To appreciate beginnings we have to consider the history of the organisation and the point at which new conversations began to envisage a new future. When such conversations involve the leaders of the organisation, the conversations do more than describe imaginative ideas, the conversations *do* things—they begin to create the will to change. But change only happens in an organisation if such conversations involve the people in it.

This story about organisational change is about Southampton Solent University, a medium-sized university of about 17,000 students, located on the south coast of England. The University's origins can be traced back to a private School of Art founded in 1856, which eventually became the Southampton College of Art. Mergers with Southampton College of Technology, and later the College of Nautical Studies at Warsash, led to the establishment of the Southampton Institute of Higher Education in 1984. Southampton Institute became a university on July 12th 2005, and adopted its name in August that year. So as a university, Southampton Solent is very much a new arrival. It was proud of its heritage with strong traditions in vocational forms of education, particularly in business, technology, art and design, and maritime courses. Strong links with employers enabled students to gain valuable work relevant education which also strengthened their career prospects.

Its recent history demonstrated that the University was no stranger to change. Since 2005 the institution had grown rapidly in size and expanded and diversified its portfolio of courses. In order to become a university it had also submitted to a rigorous process of external peer review of its quality systems and procedures conducted by the Quality Assurance Agency for Higher Education.

When this story starts in late 2007, the University was still trying to forge its identity as a new university. It was still trying to understand how it was different from many other universities, and more importantly it was still developing its vision for the sort of university it wanted to become. As a university recruiting mainly from the 18-21 age group there were also concerns about the predicted 5% decline in 18 year olds between 2010-2020 in the south Hampshire region, it recognised that to fill this gap it would need to reach out to new types of learner and enter into a fundamentally different type of engagement with employers across all vocational areas. Thus in 2007 the time was ripe for re-examining, in a fundamental way the University as both a learning and a business enterprise and charting a pathway to a different future.

STARTING AT THE TOP

In August 2007 the University's first Vice-Chancellor, Professor Roger Brown, retired and Professor Van Gore, who had been Deputy Vice-Chancellor, took on the role of institutional leader. It is this point that marks the start of a new period of change within which the strategy that is described in this book was developed, implemented and is still being played out. A new Pro Vice-Chancellor (Academic), Professor Jane Longmore (subsequently Deputy Vice-Chancellor) was appointed in October 2007 and one of the first things she was asked to do was to co-ordinate the strategic planning process. The new Vice-Chancellor wanted the essence of the plan to be a one page presentation (Figure 2.1); this was developed by the senior management team during autumn 2007 and published early in 2008.

This was the first time that members of the University became aware of the University's new strategic direction and the simple presentation as a 'one pager' seems to have been well received.

> I remember the Strategic Plan being launched and it was quite a change from the normal form of strategic plan that we've had because they tended to be quite lengthy documents which . . . perhaps I'm being unfair here but were quite often difficult to get to the meat in what they were actually saying. Whereas this time for the first time, we had a strategic plan, which was actually presented in a very small leaflet with very clear mission statement, vision and quite succinct objectives. I remember being quite impressed by the leaflet, so much so . . . I had it

pinned to my wall for quite a long period of time. And it was very helpful because I think the fact it was clear and succinct, helped us as a Faculty looking at working on our Faculty plans and trying to make sure they aligned with the University Strategic Plan. *University staff member*

The power of organisational visioning is to create images of the future that others can relate to, interpret for themselves, and be empowered to enact. As we will see, the Strategic Development Programme was and is really many stories about this process.

Figure 2.1 Southampton Solent University Strategic Plan 2008-13

Vision

• A vibrant, inclusive and successful University that is well known for the excellence of its work with students and employers and the effective integration of theory and practice

• A stimulating student experience characterised by intellectual rigour, personal fulfilment and excellent career prospects

• Imaginative external partnerships which develop the University and make a significant contribution to social justice and economic competitiveness

Mission

The pursuit of inclusive and flexible forms of Higher Education that meet the needs of employers and prepare students to succeed in a fast-changing competitive world.

Objectives

1. Inclusive and flexible forms of Higher Education that meet market needs;

2. Imaginative working partnerships with Further Education and employers;

3. A significant contribution to social justice and economic competitiveness for Southampton and its region;

4. Knowledge creation and exchange that fuse academic rigour and professional practice;

5. Excellent student employability;

6. Entrepreneurship and diversified income streams;

7. Changed employment arrangements that support high performance;

8. Sustainable growth and investment in the estate.

Published January 2008, full plan approved by Board of Governors July 2008
Southampton Solent University Academic Handbook

Someone must take responsibility for making it happen

Responsibility for leading a bid to the HEFCE Strategic Development Fund was also given to the new Pro Vice-Chancellor (Academic) when she took up her post in October 2007.

> I was asked to lead the Strategic Development Fund bid three days after arriving at the University. Looking at our emerging strategic plan I realised that we had three 'delivery' strands—employability, flexible delivery and new forms of progression . . . . , but what else do you need to make sure that real change happens? If it was going to be deep change and long lasting, we should have other elements, such as an organisational development strand. We should have a quality assurance strand and we would need new business systems, which was to be a huge strand. We would then be changing every aspect, this would touch every part of the institution and in terms of fundamental change we would go through a process that would accelerate what we wanted to do . . . *Pro Vice-Chancellor (Academic)*

In October and November ideas were assembled to form the basis for a bid. The senior management team was keen to submit the SDF bid as early as possible and invited HEFCE Officers to a meeting in December to present the University's case. The University was required to undertake a detailed scoping study and options appraisal to create a strong business case for SDF funding.

Figure 2.2 Executive Summary of Proposal for Options Appraisal Funding

---

Southampton Solent University Institutional Transformation

Southampton Solent University wishes to pursue strategic transformation to build capacity and re-orient the institution towards a hybrid model for delivery of further and higher education qualifications based around flexible learning modes. This entails a programme of urgent and radical change that will ensure a sustainable future for the University based on a demand-led approach focused on meeting the needs of employers and work-based learners. This programme of rapid change will:

- build on the University's considerable existing capacity for flexibility and responsiveness;
- unlock the full potential of the University and its partners to deliver new forms of learning to new and existing constituencies;
- require the development of new financial models, including options for co-funding methodologies;
- stimulate the development of new forms of pedagogy;

- require a new quality assurance framework;
- require significant changes to the University's infrastructure of systems and services.

Initial development funding is requested for an extensive options appraisal that will ensure that the change programme is rigorously evidence-based. It is intended that this options appraisal will be the first phase of the Solent Transformation programme, identifying and evidencing the detailed developments necessary to realise our ambitions and beginning the process of change. The outcomes of phase one will provide the basis for a fully worked business case to fund phase two, the full implementation of the Solent Transformation programme, which will be submitted in July 2008.

January 2008

This scoping exercise was to be undertaken over six months and its purpose was to explore options, conduct market research, create a comprehensive bid document explaining what work would be undertaken and develop a strong business case for consideration by HEFCE's Strategic Development Funding Panel. The executive summary of this proposal (Figure 2.2) makes it clear that the University saw this process as the first stage of a significant programme of strategic change which might offer new models of change for the wider HE sector.

THE OPTIONS APPRAISAL PROCESS

In mid-March 2008 a small coordinating team was formed under the leadership of the Pro Vice-Chancellor (Academic).

> We got together a team of people. Each person was loosely allocated to a strand, so each of those strands had someone within the University who was going to do the thinking and the chewing over and reflecting back to us the ideas as they started to evolve. The early meetings were quite disturbing, I think, for some of the attendees because it was very different, lots of ideas circulating and we'd move around the six strands. We'd start to draft sections . . . . but what began to emerge, was that this was not going to be a conventional project.
>
> The little co-ordinating group . . . were great in that they appreciated that this was an ideas factory and they were generous with their ideas. I think . . . if you asked them privately, I think they thought this wasn't going to go anywhere, that the institution was unlikely to get the funding. But here was the new PVC who was very enthusiastic about this process and it was interesting and something they'd never done before, having that kind of

discussion and visualising an institution and how it might be very different. So there was a fun factor in it and we were quite disciplined about the amount of time we spent on the meetings so people didn't feel these were formless, time wasting affairs. It was very focused, we'd come together, we'd talk about it. [The Chair] would then have the almost impossible task of trying to turn this into some kind of summary. *Team member 1*

A detailed planning document (milestones, actions, key dates, people, anticipated outcomes and completion date) was constructed, with a timeline from April to July within which the scoping exercise would be completed. Six strands of activity were identified (Table 2.1). Each strand was led by a member of the project team who was responsible for organising and coordinating activities including the appointment of external consultants to undertake some of the work.

Table 2.1 The six strands of activity within the options appraisal

1 Flexible curriculum
2 Employer engagement
3 Progression and partnerships
4 Systems infrastructure and processes
5 Quality assurance
6 Staff and organisational development

The Project Team met every two weeks between mid-March and September 2008 to work on the Options Appraisal and build the bid for Strategic Development Funding. Like many transient project teams brought together to fulfill a particular need, the team had to learn to be a team. There was a lot of pressure to gather and process a lot of information quickly and to manage the political fallout from their work.

It was a tight time scale and there were lots of other things going on at the time as well. It was exciting, I was really excited to be involved in the process and for me it was something completely different, I'd never been involved in anything like that before. In terms of was it organised, it was organised in that we did have regular meetings so it was well managed from that point of view. But we were progressing many things at the same time. There were tensions and there were things that perhaps moved in directions that were different to originally anticipated. So it was a bit of a challenge to manage the complexity of what

> was trying to be done . . . . In terms of issues, there's a certain amount of politics that I think you get in any large complex organisation which created some challenges. And initially, there was the whole thing of the team working together. *Team member 3*

Structuring the process around six strands had its advantage from the point of view of managing a complex learning process but it also created difficulties as so many elements connected across the strands.

> I didn't think it was going to work from day one as six separate boxes and it very rapidly became clear that doing it with strand 'owners' was going to lock it into an unhelpful structure. We needed much more fluidity and much more opportunity for things to advance and recede and for some things to connect and some things to disconnect at various moments. And there wasn't going to be a particularly clearly mapped progression for each of the strands, you know, on day one this will move to this and then on day twenty it'll be here, and so on. Because inter-relationship between them was going to be crucial and would be moving all the time. *Team member 1*

There was little spare capacity in the University to gather and process the information required to complete the analysis so external consultants were contracted to support the work.

> the University recognised that it did not have the expertise it needed in house to take this forward . . . . there were external consultants brought in to nearly every strand. *Team member 2*

In spite of the tight schedule and undertaking the work at a busy time of the academic year, a wealth of knowledge was collected, synthesised and evaluated in a way that could directly feed into decision making and the bid for strategic development funding.

Each strand leader produced a report to a common format and each report considered at least three options: maintaining the status quo, a programme of limited change and a more radical 'transformation' option. All six reports rejected the status quo option. Limited or incremental change was seen as beneficial, but without additional investment to develop new capacity, too slow to address the challenges faced by the University in the period of the strategic plan. Strand teams agreed that there was a compelling case for co-ordinated action to implement the necessary cultural and organisational change to support more rapid change around the agendas addressed in the appraisal.

Organisational conversations

During the Options Appraisal there were three discursive events which gave a wider cross-section of staff and employers the opportunity to take stock of the current situation, offer perspectives on needs and generate ideas that could feed into the scoping exercise. The events were visualised as a series of ever-widening circles of involvement across and beyond the University.

May exploratory discussion

The objective of the first discursive event was to involve the project team and some key members of staff e.g. Heads of School and Heads of Services to explore together the challenge and opportunity of imagining and creating a new type of educational institution. The event was facilitated by two external consultants and activities focused on developing 'future profiles' of the type of learner and learner experiences that the University might aspire to support, and how the University would need to change in order to support such learners and these sorts of experience.

The twenty five participants explored in an open-ended way the strategic 'problem/opportunity' expressed by the question: *How can we develop a distinctive and successful institution that provides and supports further and higher education learning for a diverse market of individual learners, employers and other enterprises?* The problem was explored first through their questions and then, using creative thinking techniques, potential solutions were imagined.

Different groups of participants then focused on: 1) learners: *What sorts of learners are currently well represented and under-represented in the University? Where are potential new learners? What new sorts of organizational partners might contain new learners? What new sorts of learning enterprise might be developed to support new types of learner?* or 2) flexible, accessible, demand-led curriculum models/learning experiences. *What flexible curriculum/delivery models do we already have that might be extended? What are the possibilities for greater flexibility/ accessibility?*

The final stage of the process involved individuals identifying one new type of potential learner in a context that is not typical for the University; then creating an imaginary profile of that person and their life and the setting in which they live and work.

Apart from some very interesting insights into new sorts of non-traditional learner, a number of general themes and challenges emerged through discussion.

> I seem to recall that it did expose the challenges faced, and some real gaps in understanding of the world the University inhabited. The enthusiasts were there to learn but others were much more sceptical. *Team member 2*

The creative thinking techniques used at this event produced a long-lasting impact: one Head of School confirmed that, two years after the May event, she used them in her School's Away Day—in order to engage her staff in thinking in an open, imaginative way about how they might make use of SDF Funding.

Employers' Forum

The second discursive event involved seventeen employers who participated in discussions that were framed around three questions:

Q1 *Relationships*: what are the key considerations for employers in any cooperative relationship with the University aimed at developing further interactions for education, training, learning and development?

Q2 *Needs*: What is the particular short and longer term education needs of your organisations and businesses?

Q3 *Content and delivery:* What types of education, training and team-based development for your staff would be valued by your organisation? What forms of delivery would have to be used in order to make these forms of education and training opportunities useful to your organisational business?

The Forum raised a number of issues but also provided much useful advice on how the University could improve its ability to meet employer needs, and develop relationships that would be mutually beneficial.

July Strategic Forum

This day and a half event involved over sixty staff, including senior and middle managers, teaching and administrative staff. Its purpose was to examine various options for change and the practical challenge of creating a new type of educational institution: one that made full use of flexible forms of delivery and was more responsive and entrepreneurial in its engagement with new employer-led markets. Prior to the event a number of Faculty and Central Service teams were created to develop perspectives to inform and stimulate discussion. In addition, each Faculty had, with the aid of an external consultant, reviewed its current provision, created a curriculum map and produced a self-appraisal of where the Faculty was in terms of its use of flexible delivery and engagement with imagined new markets.

There were two parts to the day and a half event. The first part, conducted as a World Cafe, aimed initially to raise awareness of current practices across the institution. Each Faculty and Central Service had its own table with pre-prepared poster. Participants moved around the different tables to be exposed to what was happening across the institution. At the end of the process each faculty/central service team re-convened and identified three concrete ideas inspired by other Faculties that could be adapted to their own faculty; three collaborative projects that they would like to develop with other faculties and three collaborative projects that they would like to develop with central services.

Day two involved cross-institutional groups considering a range of case study scenarios based on approaches being used in other universities to engage with the central issues of employer engagement, flexible learning and progression from FE to HE, being tackled in the options appraisal. Groups were invited to pick a case study scenario and imagine that the University was going to adopt it. The group then had to create a compelling case for why the University should adopt it and consider in detail the implications of adoption. Possible solutions were devised to meet the challenges that were identified. To make the teams focus on concrete rather than hypothetical ideas, each team had to create an action plan showing the steps that would need to be taken to implement the case study over five years and then pitch its plan to the whole group. The use of an electronic voting system during the presentation session allowed the whole group to reveal how feasible/desirable they thought the scenario was.

The event served the purpose of a sounding board and the SDF Bid team was able to identify a number of useful perspectives from the discussion. The chance to meet and network with people from other Faculties and Services was widely appreciated and it was felt that any strategic change process needed to incorporate the opportunity for on-going cross-university social interaction and discussion. Although anxious about 'big change' that the event was signalling, staff were pleased that they had been invited to contribute to the formative discussion and they were also pleased with the high visibility and involvement of senior managers, especially the Vice-Chancellor, in the process.

The use of the voting system had proved to be useful in making visible what people felt or believed. From the results it was felt that there was a core of people (perhaps around 7%) who will never be convinced of the value of change. There was also a large category of Don't Knows (perhaps 25%)

who would need to be won over. But the majority of people taking part in the forum were more or less favourably disposed to the sorts of changes that had been discussed.

There were perhaps three important outcomes from the event: the first was it enabled the senior managers to feel that they had engaged in an effective public debate, with a cross section of staff, about the sorts of changes that would need to be made in the coming years. Secondly, it had exposed many staff to ideas they had not previously encountered, and through the discursive process it had enabled them to share their views and perspectives and hear what others had to say. In other words it gave them the chance to think about their future in a relatively unconstrained way. Thirdly, the Vice-Chancellor was so impressed with the ideas that emerged that he proposed a fund be established to support a number of the ideas that were presented at the forum.

HEFCE's Strategic Development Fund was intended to facilitate projects that were high risk but had the potential for high rewards. If the innovations being proposed were of value for the sector as a whole, the Funding Council was prepared to make a higher investment and accept more of the risk in return for wide dissemination of practice from the project. Confident that the proposal would have wider relevance for the sector, the team completed the initial writing and submission of the bid in early September 2008. There followed a protracted negotiation and re-drafting over the next five months until the final bid was submitted in February 2009 and agreed by the Funding Council in April 2009.

The total amount of funding was £7.8m over three years, including the Full Economic Cost element. This amount of HEFCE funding dispersed within the institution was therefore just over £1.3m a year, with a similar amount contributed by the University for the development of the business systems strand.

Figure 2.3 Starting strategic change. Summary of some of significant events and the three Review, Planning and Decision making processes: 1) University Strategic Planning 2) Options Appraisal 3) Bid for HEFCE Strategic Development Fund. Arrows indicate direction of flow and influence.

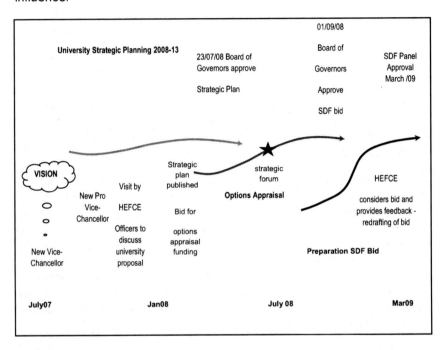

DISCUSSION

What is the importance of the process that has been described? From this account it can be seen that the start of the University's strategic change process involved nearly a year of preparation and incorporated three connected processes (Figure 2.3).

The new Vice-Chancellor and Senior Management team offered a vision which was crystallised in a concise mission and vision statement and which became the principal tool for engaging the institution in the development of a new five year strategic plan (2008-13). Discussions of this plan began to engage the University in thinking and talking about change.

The options appraisal provided the opportunity and space to think imaginatively and expansively about the intended changes and created the discursive processes to enable the ideas and visions to be shared and further ideas to be added. It enabled perspectives, resistances and barriers to be appreciated and encouraged development of a new vocabulary for discussing change.

As these discourses unfolded, they were important in that they began to create an organisational reality, the discourse was not just describing things, it was initiating the beginning of "doing" things; it was providing the guidelines for future actions as shall be seen as we move forward and as such was an important factor in the achievements of the Programme. Observing how the "talk" produced "action" is the substance of much of the book.

An interesting explanatory model and example of how discursive activity begins to bring about strategic change is given by Hardy, Palmer & Phillips—"Discourse as a Strategic Resource" Human Relations Vol.53 (9) 1227-1248.

CHAPTER 3

Moving Forward: a different approach to organisational change

This Chapter seeks to look at two areas, firstly our view of how strategic thinking about the Programme became enacted in decisions and actions and secondly the methodology that informed the SDP perspective and the way the Programme was taken forward. It presents an alternative to the traditional rationalist view of strategy deployment and change. It uses different but not unique approaches and offers the opportunity to reflect on how, when and where this approach might be used to deliver appropriate outcomes.

How does talking about a new strategy translate into action? How do we believe this happened for Solent? What did this mean for the delivery of the Programme?

We began with a belief that we needed to think differently about change within universities, informed by two interesting perspectives from writers concerned with organisational change:

> When planning for significant institutional change it is helpful to think of higher education institutions as large, complex societies which continually change (adapt/ invent) in spontaneous and unpredictable ways through the everyday conversations, relationships and interactions of people. New patterns of behaviour (new practices) tend to emerge through social interaction rather than through the grand designs of planners and architects (Seel 2004).

> It is not enough simply to "make a decision" or even to make a decision and announce it. A decision takes its meaning from the social practice and discourse within which it is located . . . a decision must not be communicated but recommunicated through text and speech, until it becomes embodied in action. At the same time it must also be continually refined and adapted through dialogue so as

> *to meet the specific and ever changing needs of different*
> *actors and different circumstances. (Hendry 2000)*

From Strategy to Action

The traditional models of strategic decision making espouse that following analysis, a rational process is undertaken to commit the organisation to proceed in a specific direction, the way in which this is done may be iterative but decisions are "made" and become the main context for action—intentional decisions. In contrast, the action perspective—Mintzberg and Waters (1990) argues that decisions within the organisation at strategic level are emergent and come about through evolution of commitment, which is gradual, complex and mostly un-observable; it is the action, committing resource that is fundamental and may just as likely come before as after decisions, which are viewed as acts not intentions. The third perspective conceptualises strategic and organisational decisions as emergent but also as part of a process of retrospective sense-making and legitimation—the interpretative perspective.

From a practitioner viewpoint each perspective is insightful but does not fully explain the elements of interpretation, choice and action that appear to be woven into the development of the Solent strategy and SDP. The traditional perspective does not appear to offer a window on how decisions and actions are related; the implied rational and linear relationships are empirically doubtful and certainly "interesting" within the culture of an HE. However, the action and interpretative approaches also fail to capture the experience in that intentional decision making can be and was part of the strategic process at Solent. The strategic decision embodied by the Strategic Plan 2008-13 was a statement of intent and agreement, was decisive in committing the University to a particular course of action and played a critical role in framing the possibilities (SDF bid and Options Appraisal) and mobilising and facilitating action and responsibilities for it (Strategic Development Programme).

However what was an intrinsic part of all these developments whatever perspective is taken, was the amount of conversations and communications that took place with the wider community (Options Appraisal, May Exploratory Discussion, July Strategic Forum.) It is therefore not too great a step to conceptualise that for the practitioner it is these organisational conversations and communications that could be thought to bind the perspectives together. If from our own observations and reflections we can accept that these played a fundamental part in the strategic process then the interesting factor is the mechanisms that turned them into actions; how do these conversations and communications get translated into actions?

Reflecting on the experience at Solent we can see how a whole series of discursive activities resonated with staff at Solent and began to move us forward towards turning these into actions.

If we trace back to the initiation of the new strategy we can see from the narrative in Chapter 2 that the University had a new Vice-Chancellor, was still trying to forge its identity as a new university and trying to understand how it was and could be different from many other universities. It recognised that as a university recruiting mainly 18-21 year-olds, a potentially shifting demographic would require it to reach out to new types of learner. The time was therefore ripe for re-examining, in a fundamental way the University as both a learning and business enterprise and charting a pathway to a different future.

The new Vice-Chancellor initiated discussions with his senior management team concerning a new strategy, the essence of which would be a one page presentation developed by the senior management team during autumn 2007 and published early in 2008. In this way his discussions were beginning to manage the meaning around the intentions of the senior management team for the University.

What this clear and succinct document did was to create images of a future to which staff could relate, and interpret for themselves.

> . . . And it was very helpful because I think the fact it was clear and succinct, ...

The language, narrative and values had meaning for staff; they could see a context for the University and an idea of what it was and was not going to be; for example the predominant ethos amongst staff for widening participation was strongly echoed in the Strategic Plan and resonated with what they thought the University should be.

However these were still words, although even at this stage they had begun to show signs that they might move to the "action" phase

> . . . and then as a Faculty we were looking at working on our Faculty plans and trying to make sure they aligned with the University strategic plan.

By putting together a bid for the SDF, this "intent" began to develop more specific narratives, the SDF bid became in itself a symbol:

> Southampton Solent University wishes to pursue strategic transformation to build capacity and re-orient the institution towards a hybrid model for delivery of further and higher education qualifications based around flexible

learning modes. This entails a programme of urgent and radical change that will ensure a sustainable future for the University based on a demand-led approach focused on meeting the needs of employers and work-based learners.

The small Options Appraisal team began to formulate what these narratives might look like but these needed to reach a wider audience and be regarded as meaningful to this wider circle if there was to be any chance of any action occurring.

The 'wider circle' took the form of the three discursive events—May Exploratory Discussion, Employers Forum and July Strategic Forum. This gave the participants an opportunity to explore if these concepts, employer engagement, flexible delivery and new forms of progression had meaning for them and resonated with how they saw the context within which the University would need to operate. Because these events were being run by the PVC and attended by senior management, it meant that they were taken seriously; the feedback from the Vice-Chancellor regarding the quality of innovative thought after the July Forum further reinforced their importance and it was becoming evident that conditions were being created where certain types of changes were going to be encouraged that centred on the bid.

The announcement of the success of the bid—the symbol—and the arrival of the funding signalled the start of activity; Faculties were "asked" how the funds should be utilised, what were their plans and projects, what did they want to try out? New staff were recruited and new initiatives linked to the main narratives were "authorised" by Management Board. The Innovation Fund projects (Chapter 6) offered individuals and small groups the chance for funding, which they took up—the talk had been shifted into action.

What can be taken from this? As a model it provides a practitioner a view on a process through which conversation and communication around strategy can be a resource which enables the strategy to be translated into action. It shows how the broader discussion around the impact of external factors such as being a new university and shifts in the student demographic, generated "conversations" and dialogue around the strategies to address these challenges. The senior managers and academics involved in these discussions were recognised by others in the University as having the credibility and authority to warrant their paying attention and what they were talking about was sufficiently familiar and understood as to possess a strong rationale for moving on from some of the current thinking around academic provision and produce new and different offers and concepts for learners. Much of this book is focussed on what and how they delivered and why they were motivated to turn the conversation into activity.

These foundations were a strong influence on how the Programme was moved forward and the next section looks at how the Programme was managed and interacted with University business and the methodology which underpinned it.

Managing SDP

It has often been said that managing change where academics are concerned is like herding cats (Garrett and Davies 2010) and the use of traditional project management methodology to manage innovation in the academic environment has the potential to create cultural and procedural dissonance (Kenny 2002). Bates (2000) compared a university to a "Post-Fordist" organisation—a term used to describe an organisation where teams of largely self—governing experts are loosely held together by a common goal or purpose, only in universities there are at least two common purposes formed around teaching and research.

Although not explicit, the approach of the Vice-Chancellor and more directly the PVC (Academic), who had leadership of the Programme, set the tone in utilising a non-traditional method of change. This was recognised by the Vice-Chancellor in his early "advice" to the Programme Director that he "did not want a PRINCE 2 type programme"; highly structured planned change of this type was, in his view, not going to work.

Then how do you keep an institutional wide programme moving forward, deliver on its quantitative outputs and outcomes and maintain an appropriate level of governance for what was public funding? How can you move away from a very traditional and planned approach that builds excellent motorways but appears not to be a reliable methodology for beginning to change culture and ways of working, especially within the culture of HE? What could other Organisational Development approaches offer?

The traditional Organisational Development approach recognises much of the complexity of our organisations and the need for an iterative change process but is nonetheless based on a presumption that a cycle based on careful analysis and planning will deliver a predictable and logical outcome.

The Programme Director had wide ranging experience of this traditional approach in commercial organisations and had observed and been part of when this had worked and when the predictable and logical outcomes failed to materialize.

In view of the "no PRINCE 2" advice and the Programme Director's experience it therefore seemed that the Programme needed to utilize a methodology that would build on the approach that was already evident in the development of the bid and would resonate with the work to date. This implicitly acknowledged that these changes were not and could not be controlled in a top down way, the SDP Team needed to sponsor and create conditions in which change of the sort envisaged in the bid was more likely to happen than not, with groups and individuals being enabled to interpret the vision and create the changes they believed were right.

Against this background it therefore appeared opportune but not without risk to adopt a methodology rooted in the Complex Adaptive Systems approach. It is a great tribute to the senior management team that they went along with this approach and probably symbolic of an underlying attitude to change and development that they were prepared to work without a formal highly detailed plan.

> It is the willingness of the Senior Management . . . to work with an emergent process that makes this different. I think the mental construct of many senior managers when you want to bring about strategic change, is for a very formal structured OD approach, oh this is what we're going to do, these are the objectives, we have to do this, this and this by then. *SDP Programme Director*

However whilst the Complex Adaptive Systems can from the outside look *ad hoc* and intuitive it needs a framework and in this case the Programme Director based this on the approach of Olson & Eoyang "Facilitating Organization Change: Lessons from Complexity Science", 2002.

The Approach

A useful starting point to understand the approach, especially the differences between those shaped by traditional and by complex adaptive systems, is referenced by JISC in their Infonet resource on change management. This provides a helpful table contrasting the traditional and complex adaptive systems approach

Table 3.1

Traditional	Complex Adaptive System
Few variables determine outcomes	Innumerable variables determine outcome
The whole is equal to the sum of the parts (reductionist)	The whole is different from the sum of the parts (holistic)
Direction is determined by design and the power of a few leaders	Direction is determined by emergence and the participation of many people

Causality is linear: every effect can be traced to a specific cause	Causality is mutual: Every cause is also an effect, and every effect is also a cause.
Relationships are directional	Relationships are empowering
All systems are essentially the same	Each system is unique
Efficiency and reliability are measures of value	Responsiveness to the environment is the measure of value
Decisions are based on facts and data	Decisions are based on tensions and patterns
Leaders are experts and authorities	Leaders are facilitators and supporters

In taking this different approach what did this mean for the way the programme was undertaken from the perspective of the central team?

Under Complex Adaptive Systems Olson & Eoyang (2002) see leaders as having essentially three jobs:-

> i) to influence the environment to shape the speed and patterns of change, by setting an overall agenda—in this case, the six themes of the bid—, not giving instruction on what to do but setting general requirements for the outcomes, distributing control and leaving how to proceed to those undertaking the changes, generating a sense of urgency, stretching boundaries via the small innovation projects to encourage learning and adding new staff or new roles and responsibilities (with the last being perhaps the most challenging), to keep the rate of change at a level which could just about be accommodated and not engender major disruption in the "business as usual" of recruiting and teaching the undergraduate cohort;

> ii) to focus resource on important differences that will form the new and emerging patterns by encouraging different viewpoints and new approaches, to raise difficult questions or issues, to encourage diversity, by bringing into groups individuals with different experiences and drawing in potentially disruptive ideas from the external environment. Inevitably these will bring with them a degree of conflict, but without this "symptom" occurring, not much growth or learning is taking place;

> iii) to foster co-evolution by developing linkages between individuals and groups by identifying and helping make

linkages of ideas and individuals, encouraging information flow and encouraging feedback, the "how am I doing?", "how are we doing?" questions.

The latter part of this chapter provides illustration of how these "jobs" were enacted during the programme, how formal structures and reporting are as much part of the change as emergence and unpredictability and as usual in the CAS approach, how the "jobs" themselves have no neat boundaries; they fold into one another, blur at the edges and sometimes deliver across all three elements simultaneously.

As a publicly funded programme, it was important that the team set up appropriate governance that was auditable and gave reassurance to Governors and HEFCE that the programme was being managed, whilst ensuring that these mechanisms complemented the CAS approach and did not create dissonance.

The shape of the team, the leadership, effective governance and oversight and the mechanisms for funding and reporting that were required, were a fundamental part of setting up the programme and were also most important in signaling that this was going to be different from "expected" but not so different as to cause any issues with the University meeting public governance standards.

The SDP was lead throughout the whole process by the Pro Vice—Chancellor (Academic), who provided both continuity and close connection with the operations and strategic development of the University and line managed various and changing Faculties and Services during the programme. The day to day management and development of the programme was devolved to a Programme Director, who was part of the Senior Management Team and sat on Management Board. The Programme Manager and Co-ordinator completed the small dedicated central team.

As in traditional methodology but important from an information flow perspective was the requirement for a Programme Steering Committee (whose purpose in HE is to ensure proper and effective accountability when large public funding is received,) The decision was taken to make this the existing 'Management Board', who were the senior collective managerial decision making body of the University.

> We didn't want a heavy steering group structure, We didn't want to spend a lot of time and money on creating a great bureaucracy. We recognised that if we lodged it with Management Board we were putting out a powerful message that every Dean and Director was represented on Management Board. Management Board became

> in effect the project steering board, and that located it firmly in one of the University's own existing structures so there was no creation of any great collection of new committees or working groups or anything else, it was all intra-Management Board. *PVC Academic*

Further the PVC (Academic) viewed SDP not as a discrete project but as part of an integrated portfolio. The strength of this was that it kept information flowing and enabled connections to be made that might not otherwise have been made. As an "accelerant" to the Strategic Plan it had to be internalised and part of the University to be successful.

Initially the bid had identified a headcount of twenty-two staff, however both the Programme Leader and Director had arrived at the view that SDP needed to be predominantly about the people in the institution undertaking the activities, not an imported team that would leave when the funding finished.

> the bid had identified twenty-two people would be contributing to the SDP programme but [the SDP Director] was quite clear from an early stage that she didn't want a huge central team. We'd talked a bit about what had happened at [another university] and one of the issues there was that the change process had been quite centralised and this had led to the feeling that the rest of the University was having something 'done' to it and we didn't want to go for that model. So the central SDP team was kept to three people." *PVC Academic*

The decision was therefore made that additional roles either resided in the faculty or service or the headcount allowed in the bid was utilised to release staff to develop and deliver their projects, the monies being used to provide backfill/temporary resourcing. This action further reinforced that this was the University accelerating its Strategic Plan with its own staff.

The role of developing the mechanisms of governance and reporting resided with the central team. This consisted of installing appropriate reporting and monitoring mechanisms (formal and informal), reporting to Management Board and HEFCE, budgetary oversight, communications, website, evidencing outputs, interacting with Audit and with the external evaluators.

> The Programme Director reported to every meeting of Management Board at two-monthly intervals during the academic year. So it meant there was a real focal point for reporting, but also for people to question . . . .

there was this constant flow of information to Management Board which was a good discipline for us and part of the normal workings of the University, so it didn't feel as though SDP was happening somewhere else. *PVC Academic*

This reporting cycle, albeit light touch for Faculty/Service and individuals, played a significant part in enabling the SDP team to keep the Programme subtly on track without enforcing "targets" and milestones.

Once the Faculty projects had been approved, Management Board had taken the approach that although they were interested in requirements for outcomes, decisions about how to proceed would be left to the Faculties; a mode of working that was maintained both for individual and larger projects throughout the SDP.

However being time bound with respect to resource, (no carry over was to be permitted after agreed funding date ended) injected a sense of urgency into the process. Initially this occasioned a little surprise, delivering to a tight deadline and spending the budget within the deadline was not wholly part of the wider University culture but the SDP team was adamant that recipients adhered to the few funding specifications, which were:-

i)   Proposals must support achievement of SDP Outputs & Outcomes.
ii) You set the timeline and budget for achievement not the SDP Team.
iii) Money will be re-allocated not retained if unspent within the timeline.
iv) You need to complete reports for Management Board.
v)   We would like you to succeed but it does not matter if you do not achieve all you intended but we need to learn from the experience.
vi) Talk to us if you are experiencing difficulties and blockages.

The reporting documents enabled the SDP team to keep in contact with the projects both in terms of achievements and as a mechanism for developing information flow through informal contact and discussion. Collectively the team could set these against the progress towards the Outputs & Outcomes that needed to be delivered to HEFCE; this was a major enabler to understand the rate of progress.

Asking the "what's missing" questions generated discussion internally within the team about how we could help to move pieces forward. With the role of SDP leader integrated into the PVC (Academic) role it provided a major linkage to other thinking and activity in the University.

> There are so many linkages across the University: you've got to be looking for opportunities all the time, where are the open doors, and allow for emerging opportunities that had never been anticipated. . . . this role is a very privileged position in being able to see so much of what is going on across the University, to talk to other senior colleagues and get insights into where things are shifting for them as well. One of the key parts of my role was to see those connections, between what the University was doing and what was happening within SDP so that if there was mutual advantage there we didn't miss the moment. Throughout the project I've tried not to miss the moment, and that's impossible to write into a project bid or a timeline. But it's been absolutely key because opportunities come up and sometimes you just have to take them at that moment and see those connections and do it. Many of the things that emerged from SDP would not have happened any other way. So perhaps that's been the most important contribution I've been able to make to ensure that the vision that we had for SDP could be realised, the constant searching for the opportunities, linking up, connecting things . . . . I'm just weaving all the time, just pulling threads across and weaving them together. *PVC Academic*

The reporting process also encouraged feedback; answering the "*How am I doing? How are we doing?*" question. This was a very broad programme, which to varying extent over the three years, touched all the Faculties and Services; their Deans and Directors needed to appreciate the wider picture of where their activities were sitting relative to the rest of the institution. The SDP team collectively also needed to understand this and the whole University context in which they were operating: this led to the establishment of what became known as the SDP 'Information Exchange' with the PVC (Academic). It fulfilled a number of purposes but underneath the Information Exchange sat the 'how am I doing?', 'how are we doing?', 'what's missing?' questions as well as the opportunity for the team to come together with the Programme Leader and talk about what help they needed for themselves and other university staff.

> We had a network of people who were working for us on SDP, so they were out across the University We had people in the partnerships team, we had people in the employer engagement specialist's role, and people who

were embedded in services or in faculties, people in the Information Services team, or the ICT team who've come together at this information exchange, it was literally that, an opportunity to update everybody and to get a sense of what was going on in these pockets around the University. These people were vital for us in the communication channels across the University to make sure that we kept nourishing all the faculty linkages, the service linkages, that people felt they were in the loop without us having to do vast amounts of sending around constant communications. Although there was also a set of SDP web pages and an update of what was going on on the project, but it's very hard to keep that absolutely live on a project moving as fast as this. So those people were hugely important in terms of just making sure we all kept abreast of what was going on. *PVC (Academic)*

It was important to give them a feeling that although they were working in a very distributed way, that they had a sense of belonging to this programme, so I saw my role in part to create that sense that there was a heart to this programme and there was a mind, and an identity, and that there was thinking that was going on all the time to support what they were doing to help to guide it and to see some of the connections and facilitate some of that. *SDP Programme Director*

It also allowed for guidance and exchange about the rate of change that could be accommodated. There were some areas of intense frustration for the team, who would have clearly preferred to "facilitate" a change in a way of working or process, but too much emergent change in too many places was a high risk and required leadership judgment on what to ignore and when.

Because the team roles in this type of change require one to act as a participant rather than a bystander, the team members often encouraged, sought interest and helped developed ideas—part of the linking and information flow tasks. For example, a project focused on social and student enterprise and employability developed from a corridor conversation between the Programme Manager and the Director of the Business School; both coming from slightly different interests, they worked together on a successful bid "Accelerating Enterprise". As a member of the Programme Team this was not in the script for a "traditional" change role focused on facilitating organizational process and staying at arms—length, this was becoming a stakeholder in the organization. It surfaced that we had the highest survival rate of student entrepreneurs from a previous round of funding, so here we had a team member supporting a Director in finding and exploring what was making us distinctive.

A further role for the team was to facilitate focusing of resources on areas where new practices were being or needed to be created. This was probably the least comfortable aspect of the role in that it deliberately created a necessary degree of conflict or discomfort to produce growth and learning. Sometimes the discomfort was internal as a result of undertaking new things, where University systems and staff were being stretched and participants frustrated, the case studies in later chapters give expression to this, at other times it was more deliberate as SDP allowed and encouraged recruitment of staff from outside the HE sector. We needed to be careful to ensure a cultural fit without introducing too much dissonance, in which case the individual was "blocked" in their work, but they brought with them different ways of working. We deliberately tried to recruit good quality, experienced people, often as contractors, who questioned "why" we worked in that way and could contribute their experience through subtle development of internal staff they were working with, not least because their expertise made them highly credible if not comfortable working partners.

There were three categories of these externals: individual short term contractors, who supplemented both capability and capacity; organisations who delivered specialist expertise and development (Chapter 12) for rapid change in capability and process; and individuals who brought particular knowledge of the external environment and current innovations to "disrupt" thinking.

We have already referred to the third team role of fostering co-evolution by developing linkages and encouraging information flow. If an activity analysis of the team had been undertaken, this role was the one where most time was expended and which was critical in allowing the programme to develop. In terms of mass communication of what was being achieved, it was also the most problematic.

The SDP Team fulfilled this remit in a number of important ways including: building trusting relationships with staff, sensing the needs and interests of the University community and how they aligned to the needs and interests of SDP, promoting the programme and raising awareness of the opportunities it provided through events that they organised. It also involved finding people who had ideas that they wanted to turn into new practices and encouraging and mentoring colleagues so that they were able to secure the resources to undertake this work. Above all the team had to put their energy, enthusiasm and creativity into the process of engaging the University so that the intended outcomes could be achieved. This was a complex and interconnected remit which meant participating proactively rather than reactively in the change process.

The ways in which the wider SDP team put this into practice were varied from mentoring and helping people, to acting as broker, overcoming institutional blocks, organising events and communicating what was happening.

> So my role is to provide advice and facilitation really to help them get a proposal through [Management Board] and help the University get the most out of the SDP funding. . . . . we have had a few iterations on some, "This is how you need to write it, if you want this to work." I think we're more facilitators and encouragers. *SDP Programme Director*

> I have worked here a long time and I knew that the culture of the organization was such that people resisted the management edict, in common with most HE institutions. But there were people who were very enthusiastic about helping students develop their employability skills within faculties and services to some extent. And because the SDP worked by fostering faculty projects and identifying champions and so on I could work with those people and others that I knew to encourage, advise, support and in some cases mentor people trying to develop new things and gradually grow these sorts of activity in areas where it wasn't already there. *Employer Engagement Specialist*

> . . . . so what I ended up doing was finding useful and engaged people to do what they could and then celebrate that success. The Design School project flowed from some of that activity. . . . So we ended up with a lot of innovation from projects coming out of that faculty because there were a lot of good ideas and people wanting to do the work. and it was worth encouraging because then there was a sense that the initial project wasn't a complete failure and there was something to celebrate . . . *SDP Programme Manager*

> As soon as I hear about a blockage I work with whoever that person is to try to resolve it. Because we are now at the end of the SDP programme I am much more careful to do it within faculty structures and processes because I am a time limited resource now. So rather than directly intervene I'm identifying where, in the organization post-SDP, should people be taking these challenges on and solving them. *Employer Engagement Specialist*

In the Solent Exchange events (a yearly all hands event) we made sure that there was evidence of a narrative for the whole institution that people could see at regular points through the project. We positioned the three Solent Exchange events at the beginning of the academic year so people were both looking back on what we'd achieved over the past year and what we were going onto in the year ahead, and that's always been the focus. Again we stressed the idea of including people, the value is in conversation, trying to draw more and more people in. I had a vision for Solent Exchange as an opportunity to keep widening the circle of involvement in SDP; it has always been directed at getting as much of the University as possible involved, it was purposely ambitious in that sense. *PVC Academic*

The event also enabled the University to publicly acknowledge the contribution of the individuals and teams undertaking their projects and to provide others with the opportunity to network with their colleagues.

The hook line for the second Solent Exchange—"the value is in the conversation" epitomised the underlying mechanisms that were seeking to drive the Programme forward and echoes the first part of this narrative about how strategic intent changes into action. The un-measurable but most interesting and fascinating aspect of the Programme from the team's perspective was how the conversations within the University changed over the three years. What individuals said and what they did reinforced the ground rules that kept the change on track and, as Seel (2004) observed, "New patterns of behaviour (new practices) tend to emerge through social interaction rather than through the grand designs of planners and architects". The narrative continues in the day to day conversations of staff and if they are unaware of any connection to SDP that is an achievement in itself. This was about the ongoing life of the University and not about a Programme that came and went.

Finally leading and managing using this methodology is not comfortable— the supposed certainties of planning tools and spreadsheets are absent, you have to have patience, be very watchful, join the dots, support relationship building and build them yourselves, remember you are not outside but inside the process—if you have ideas about achieving the objectives, if it's not working get in and find out why by talking (not reporting), if certain outputs are not being met, nudge, enthuse, help kick start activity. The speed of developments when they come can also be a bit scary, you have to comfortable about relinquishing control, but in the words of the racing driver Mario Andretti "If everything seems under control, you're just not going fast enough."

I think the biggest challenge of devising and implementing the new business systems has been the scale and complexity of what we have done and the speed of change. There have been times when all of it seemed to be very, very complex and it's been very hard to move all of these things along. Sometimes it's felt like pushing water uphill. However, in retrospect so much has been achieved in three years. For example, if you just take one of the things we did, the speed with which we researched, procured, installed and implemented the whole system of swipe card readers across the University, given the resources we had, was quite staggering, less than a year, probably about eight months in the end. That was a huge undertaking, but it was really necessary because when you start a project like this you have a ticking time bomb. *(Dean Learning and Information Services).*

CHAPTER 4

The Strategic Development Programme—what happened next?

INTRODUCTION

Chapter 2 described how Southampton Solent University's Strategic Development Programme (SDP) came about. It described how the change was started, drawn up through a deliberate process of information seeking, idea generation, discussion and benchmarking. This chapter outlines how the SDP was enacted—the story of SDP—the tangible and quantitative outcomes and the cultural and organisational change that came about with these.

The themes (Strands) that formed the basis of the Strategic Development Fund bid and subsequent programme were represented to the University as a series of concentric circles (Figure 4.1) with the outer circle containing the six key areas for development and the inner circle representing the fundamental change in culture that was anticipated as an outcome from the process. The measurable outputs were represented to HEFCE as a series of quantitative deliverables, "Outputs and Outcomes" to be monitored by HEFCE on an annual basis.

While these Strands and the Outputs and Outcomes provided a convenient way of assisting in building understanding and communication, the reality was that they were intimately connected and separation was merely a construct. However they provided the linking themes for both conversation and action that was needed to start the Programme and start people "doing".

Fig 4.1 Key elements of the Strategic Development Programme

☐ Funded jointly by SDF & Southampton Solent University
■ Funded by Southampton Solent University

Like any good story, a *beginning, middle and end* were useful for the telling; for the University the *beginning* of the funding period was indeed significantly focused on engagement, with the *middle* a period of intense activity where many experiments were undertaken (see Case Studies, Chapter 5-12) and infrastructure put in place and an *end,* focused on sustainability—embedding the changes into the business as usual. However, with six interrelated strands, in reality it would have been difficult to predict exactly what was taking place when.

For example sustainability came in at the beginning, middle and end—experiments did not become funded without a sustainability plan (what happens when this activity is no longer funded?), the QA framework (infrastructure) entered into the Academic Handbook very early on. Possibly the best way to understand the overall pattern of development was of two years focused on achieving the objectives set out in the bid, with the final year of the programme transitioning as seamlessly as possible to business as usual combined with ensuring staff at a wide level had the capability and confidence to continue to move the organisation forward.

But where is this leading us? We have Strands but actually they are so interconnected that they only serve a purpose as a construct. We have a story with a beginning, middle and end but "pieces" of engagement, infrastructure, staff capability development and sustainability all happening at the same time. One could either conclude it was an unplanned "muddle" or rather mirrored the complexity of organisational life.

The reality was that its method of prosecution was no accident. Purposefully it was never to be a story of linear change governed by a Master Plan but there was a methodology sitting behind it. In that respect it was not conceptually always easy to explain to senior managers how the Programme was going forward, they could observe and in fact were part of what was happening but there were no templates to fall back on, no detailed project plan. It was as later described "Following the Yellow Brick Road," no map but a journey with a tin man, a lion and a scarecrow, i.e. those who wanted to engage with changing the University. It therefore says much about the senior team and the prevailing culture that the leadership was willing to "let go". Possibly this was also born out of the knowledge that the use of formal "project management methodology to manage innovation in the academic environment has the potential to create cultural and procedural dissonance." (Kenny 2002).

> I remember the Vice Chancellor at my interview saying "we don't want a PRINCE 2 project". For me this was potentially an exceptional opportunity, could I, would I have the opportunity to really move away from a traditional approach and use a different method, could we make it work? I think the PVC knew how she wanted the Programme run, it didn't need labels, and we never explicitly discussed "the how" in terms of methodology until quite a way through the Programme. *SDP Programme Director*

The Beginning—Year 1

Once the bid was awarded the Pro Vice-Chancellor (Academic) continued to head the Programme, a role in which she remained for the duration of the funding, which was a key factor in providing the continuity of leadership and approach.

The SDP-bid identified the need for a dedicated team to manage the SDP so the appointment of a Programme Director and team was an important step early in the life of the programme. However with funding starting shortly after the bid was accepted and the need to move forward with utilising the funding, an interim Director took on the role.

After a meeting of the University Management Board it was decided to start the Programme with projects initiated and devised by the Faculties; an important factor in engaging the Faculties and signalling the start of action. The original bid had visualised that SDP-funding would be distributed through an Innovation Challenge Fund, accessed by Faculty-based change agents, but on further reflection senior managers decided that this approach might not fully engage Faculties.

> We looked at the budget and realised that a considerable amount was vested in the Innovation Challenge Fund because we'd originally had the innovation system with 'change agents' who would have access to this fund. There was a strong view that if we did that, the Faculties would feel marginalised. So we went into a Faculty bidding process instead, and had a much smaller innovation fund. We ended up with a much smaller fund for small projects and with the faculties taking a considerable amount of the funding.

> It was really important in the first few months of the SDP to get the Faculties involved and to give them a sense that we were foregrounding the whole project with activity that they determined. There was quite a long gap between when the bid went in and when we actually started so re-engaging the Faculties was really important, giving them the opportunity to be involved was utterly vital at that point.
> *PVC Academic*

The guidelines for these projects were to focus on achieving the Outputs & Outcomes surrounding employer engagement to enable identification of employer responsive provision and move forward with the development of provision for non-standard UCAS entry learners in employment, part-time, credit accumulating or work based mode.

Varied approaches were taken by the Faculties in addressing their outcomes.

The Faculty of Business, Sport and Enterprise adopted a capacity building strategy within their SDP project embarking on a training programme to develop staff capability to undertake training and needs analysis in external companies. This was a way of engaging companies, finding out what their needs and interests were so that the Faculty was in a better position to know how to meet those needs.

> We wanted to develop our capacity to deliver training skills and needs analysis in companies. So we went to the Faculty and invited staff 'Who would like to become involved with this?' and we got eighteen staff who wanted to be trained up in training skills and needs analysis . . . . Then we commissioned a company to work with us to

train us in training skills and needs analysis and we were then trained up in a workshop . . . . Through the market research we had found six companies that wanted to work us, to have training skills and analysis done for free by our lecturers with the consultants. So there was one consultant with three lecturers that went out to a company. They went out twice. We worked with a fairly prescriptive model to identify their learning needs. The idea was that this would then generate and kick-start external activity. But the main thing was getting our staff out into companies, which was what they wanted to do. *Dean Faculty of Business, Sport and Enterprise*

The Faculty of Technology's project mainly formed around market research with a view to developing new short credit bearing courses Professional Development Units (PDUs). Existing close connection with employers initiated joint development work surrounding digital enterprise, focused on e-learning. Information was gathered and later used as the foundation for more concrete development such as the PDUs in Fashion (Chapter 5).

The Faculty of Media, Arts and Society focused on engaging staff across the Faculty through starting the thinking on different types of learners and development of a wide range of Professional Development Units (PDUs). Although the strategy was very successful in engaging many staff in the process and raising their awareness of PDU design and there were a number of valuable relational spin-offs, the infrastructure for supporting staff to market these was not immediately available and raised valuable questions about how and to whom we would market if this type of course was not driven by specific external partners. The PDUs and Masters degree developed in partnership with City Art Gallery was at one end of the spectrum, Creative writing, at the other, which potentially had a mass appeal or needed "selling" to the leisure industry—an unfamiliar marketing requirement that the University was not resourced for. The Faculty's other focus was on creating tighter ties with employers through providing students with real life briefs from employers and exploring co-location—locating teaching activities for students within a commercial organisation.

The Warsash Maritime Academy (subsequently part of the Faculty of Technology) pursued a very specific brief using their funding to develop the MSc Shipping Operations and its associated Professional Development Programme in collaboration with the shipping industry. This was targeted at a particular learner market of shipping personnel wishing to return to a shore based job. It was conceptualised as blended learning design with block learning on shore being mixed with e-learning on board ship. (Chapter 7).

An evident requirement from each of the projects was an immediate need for "support" for e-learning, both the technical delivery and pedagogy and a set of Quality Assurance standards and procedures to apply to short credit bearing units.

[For the reader from outside UK higher education, every UK university has the responsibility for maintaining the quality of the education it provides and the standards of the qualifications it offers. Universities are their own awarding bodies and they continually evaluate their systems and the performance of their courses to ensure that they are fit for the intended purpose.

UK Universities take these responsibilities very seriously. They use a common set of tools, the 'Code of Practice', developed by the Quality Assurance Agency for Higher Education in collaboration with university staff, to underpin their work to maintain quality and standards. Their systems are also periodically subject to peer review and reports of these audits are published. A higher education institution cannot become a university until it has demonstrated through peer review that its systems for assuring the quality and standards of its educational work are robust and effective. Thus HE exhibits many of the characteristics of a regulated industry in the way in which it functions.]

In anticipation Academic Services had begun to work on appropriate QA frameworks for what became known as Professional Development Units & Awards and by late September 2009, drafts and consultation with Faculties were already well underway. This process was not only to provide the appropriate QA framework but to help explode the myth that QA obstructed and delayed what academics wanted to do.

It was during this period July-September 2009, that the initial members of the SDP Central Team (Programme Director, Manager and Co-ordinator) were recruited and thus "inherited" a programme of work to "manage". By October 2009 some Faculties were beginning to signal the need for greater support in delivering on-line learning. There was a perception by the Programme team that the University (with a number of e-learning projects,) needed some way of bringing together to both identify the extent of the activity and ensure that more formal cross institutional learning would take place. This was already in the mind of the Dean of Learning & Information Services and in response a proposal to form a central Flexible Development Team (FDT) located in Learning Information Services but under the auspices of an Advisory Group was approved by Management Board. The FDT was set up not only to provide a technical and advisory service but also set about delivering a version of the existing student environment, (MyCourse) suitable for the professional learner, modelled on what the team regarded as best of breed.

I was fortunate enough to look at the bids that the Faculties had put in and they were kind of the same but different. So they were talking about e-learning and new forms of e-learning and things like that, and what I'd said was, because we're very collegiate in this university, what wouldn't be helpful to the University is if the Faculties went off in three different directions and we end up with something that doesn't work for everyone. Because we've got a great deal of e-learning expertise in the department already, we had the idea that we could support the development of a central capacity and then other people could work with us. So it wasn't meant to get in the way or negate anything that they were doing, it was just to say we've got some pretty good ideas about how we could make the e-learning part of it really good. We already had learning technologists and e-support officers so we added some new people—a curriculum developer, media specialist and a co-ordinator and then brought the technologists in as well, so we formed a team with a nucleus that could grow or contract, depending on the size of the project. And always we were able to go to the wider group and say, "Ok, we're doing this, what do you think?" and get input.

One of our first activities as a team was to start developing a set of standards, what we originally called the Gold Standard, in the sense that institutionally we were setting our bar high and trying to achieve high quality. We now call it the Solent Online Learning Standard which came out of two activities. One was an informal survey of the existing provision for distance and online learning from other higher education institutions in the UK and overseas. Places like the Open University obviously, and then Stamford and MIT, a lot of places have got open educational resources now as well and looking at the manner in which they deliver their content and what we felt was effective and what was less so. Also looking at some of the private providers as well, places like Adobe TV and Lynda.com and again, people are doing quite high quality online training or online education. From that survey we distilled components that we felt different providers were demonstrating. But we also noticed that nobody had the whole package as far as we were concerned, so we were consolidating a set of standards that we felt if we could

work towards so we would be creating the whole package.
Manager e-Learning Centre

The FDT toured the Faculties to explain what they could offer in the way of support. The Faculties engaged in different ways with the FDT: Warsash Maritime Academy and Faculty of Business, Sport and Enterprise quickly took up the opportunity to work with the team while the Faculty of Creative Industries and Society (later FCIS) and the Faculty of Technology were less involved at the start.

> We were looking for the Faculties to engage with us because . . . . we went round and talked about what we were doing, talked about the funding that we had, talked about the concepts and said we've got some great stuff going on here. Here is Shipping Operations as a bit of a beacon of how it could be done and some people took us up on our offer and some didn't and it's just interesting culturally it was Business School and Maritime who went for it.

> Pretty quickly we started to work with course teams. Warsash came on board with the MSc Shipping Operations because they'd wanted to do that for several years, have a fully distance course. So we hit the ground running with them really quickly. Also the MA Business Studies had already been in existence for a year before it was a blended course and that was ripe for coming into that firmament of courses we could help with.

> I think where culturally it's been more difficult to work with course teams in Faculties . . . . is, maybe because . . . they were thinking about something different, we didn't invent it and that's me being really honest. It's not our concept so we're not sure about that. So they still don't engage with us really . . . . Faculty X got off to a bit of a false start where they started off engaging with us but went off at a tangent and then felt restricted by what we were doing and wanted to reshape what we did and reinvent it almost. And then that stalled and it didn't materialise into a solid course, so that was disappointing, so we had a couple of failures which is not surprising in this line of work. *Manager e-Learning Centre*

Further activity on flexible/e-learning took the form of helping to build a wider base of staff capacity via offering a Post Graduate Certificate in

Blended Learning and involvement in two Higher Education Academy funded e-learning related projects.

The Employer Engagement Agenda

Within the bid, both working with employers to provide educational provision and improve the employability of our students were major components. To help move this agenda forward two positions—the Employer Engagement Specialist and a Head of Employer Led Learning—were recruited from within the University. An important factor in the recruitment was that both had a considerable amount of credibility and experience in the University; as they had applied rather than been seconded, it signalled to other staff their commitment and belief in the Programme.

Their roles developed to support the embedding of employability within the curriculum, help build capability and capacity of staff to work with employers and support new departures in employer provision via building collaborations, accrediting employer provision and introducing kite-marking.

The Employer Engagement Specialist initially carried out an audit of real world experience and employability embedded within the curriculum, which took varying forms, some courses involved placements, others live briefs from employers, some encouraged students to take optional work related units. However activity across courses was very uneven. Her role was to engage with Faculties and Course teams to raise awareness and encourage them to both look at building this into the curriculum and actually record what they were doing. Much excellent work was simply going unrecorded.

It was also in the autumn that conversations between the Programme Manager and the Head of the Business School sparked a decision to put forward a bid to develop student enterprise (Accelerating Enterprise) via a mentoring and support programme for students wishing to develop a business idea. This was enhanced by development of two academic Units, which enabled students to firstly "imagine" and develop a business idea and then move in the second unit to work up the idea into a business plan. Around 50 staff came forward who expressed an interest in this initiative and received initial mentoring to support students. Simulation games, entry to student enterprise competitions and talks by entrepreneurs drove the communications and student engagement.

The success of this project generated a rise in the visibility of the employability agenda and SDP targets and was swiftly followed by academics forming an employability network, an employability conference and a raft of activities outwith the SDP.

My work involved supporting curriculum development in relation to employability initiatives and work experience which we defined as live briefs, placements or work-based learning. So that might be formal staff development stuff or just talking to people about what was possible, what counted as work experience. People were greatly relieved when we started talking about live briefs fulfilling the work experience target because they knew that in their areas they wouldn't be able to get placements for their students. I also set up an employability forum across the whole university so people could be informed and the employability forum could test things out and try to get a handle on what direction to go in. *SDP Employer Engagement Specialist*

Some widely different approaches were initiated, the School of Fashion & Design pioneered a whole School-approach to achieving SDP objectives (Chapter 5) whilst the Faculty of Creative Industries and Society developed and implemented 'Solent Creatives'—an "agency" which allowed employers to connect with students in the creative industry sector to take on real live briefs, on which staff were able to mentor students (Chapter 10).

In terms of sustainability, employability in the curriculum quickly became embedded in the academic framework and a permanent team was established—Employability & Enterprise, who as part of their roles are continuing this work.

In July 2011 the decision that all students should have work experience got mainstreamed by including in our academic framework the requirement for every course to have real world experience equal to 20 credits at every level. So initially it was working with individuals through the SDP, it gets mainstreamed and because it is now policy the Associate Deans Enhancement are now involved in ensuring implementation. *SDP Employer Engagement Specialist*

Another strand to working with employers and developing a flexible curriculum was the development of the academic framework to accompany this.

The SDP drive for more flexible curricula responsive to employer needs were going to pose new challenges for the institution's existing quality assurance systems that had been designed to support more traditional higher education curricula. As noted with respect to the PDUs the development of new quality procedures to enable SDP objectives to be realised was therefore important and the creation of the Professional Development Awards Framework was an early priority.

> We didn't have a framework for small packages of learning at the time, so the Dean of Academic Services, worked with colleagues in Academic Services to design the Professional Development Award Framework. This had to be taken through all the University's committees to create a framework into which we could slot Professional Development Units. *PVC Academic*

> The biggest quality toolkit that SDP has used is the Professional Development Award Framework. It came out of the meeting at Chilworth in September 2009 at the very beginning of the SDP. It's really our Employer Engagement Framework. It's flexible, it's based on credit accumulation, it's based on small chunks of learning so if you want to develop a programme with an employer, it gives you tremendous freedom to tailor what they need without the restrictions that you've got on more traditional awards. For example, under the Professional Development Framework you don't have a programme specification, because when you're starting the journey as a professional learner, you may not know where you want to be in five year's time. You may have a big picture, but you've got no units, so you start off and you can do the units and get your credit accumulation and then you can move towards a Professional Development Award. So it's a very different philosophy to traditional programme design. *Dean Academic Services*

The creation of the Professional Development Award framework right at the start of the Strategic Development Programme acted as a catalyst for many Faculties to engage with creating new Professional Development Units (PDUs) and begin to think differently about different types of learner.

> once we had the framework it resulted in quite an interesting period where a lot of Professional Development Units were developed, probably too many and there was a great rush of enthusiasm . . . There were all kinds of ideas that people came up with. And I suppose in some senses they modelled them on the conventional adult education approach, we can do all these bits, and we can get the people in and different kinds of learners will come. And then there was a slow but important realisation, that actually the Professional Development Units that were

going to work best were the ones where the demand came from outside. So we executed a real shift in institutional culture, away from a belief that we design things for the outside world and then we wait to see if people come, to starting by finding out whether there was a demand before designing the PDU. In fact the best situation was when someone came to us and asked for a PDU. For example, Hampshire County Council wanted a PDU in the Social Work area, and . . . they wanted a PDU, and I think our first PDU that recruited students was in that area. *Dean Academic Services*

Alongside the developments in the Academic Framework we also needed to build organisational capacity and capability by focusing on delivery of tangible "knowledge" around the employer engagement agenda such as pricing and costing, PDU development, working with employers, co-funding, and develop wider networks through joining external "employer" related Communities of Practice.

At this point we brought in an external provider to deliver this training for us and ensured interested staff had access to the EBTA (Employer Based Training Accreditation) network, which provided links with employers looking to partner with HEIs and associated opportunities for access to cross institutional learning around a range of employer engagement issues.

Partnership & Progression

Part of engaging with employers is of course about building partnerships and Partnership & Progression was also a strand that ran strongly thorough the Programme.

This reflected the ethos of the University to widen participation on the broadest front and ensure that we built with local colleges and their learners, better two way knowledge of our curriculum and progression routes into HE especially with those from non-traditional backgrounds. The team of two recruited to undertake this had a number of outcomes on which to focus; to build partnership accords and a set of action plans with local colleges, to develop new progression routes and to strengthen the alignment of curriculum so that learners and college staff could see routes for acquisition of higher level qualifications in their chosen areas of study and work related learning. This encouraged the Partnerships Team to become more proactive in seeking out opportunities within the University to work collaboratively with partner colleges and to work more imaginatively and creatively with the Faculties.

The Partnerships Team helped university staff prepare plans, encouraged University Schools to look more strategically at recruitment, and advised them on which curriculum areas would align to the interests of colleges as well as providing logistical support to put programmes together to market the programmes to feeder colleges. The team acted as a bridge between the University and the Colleges but was proactive in identifying new ways in which connections and relationships could be expanded.

For example, the School of Design, in collaboration with the Partnerships Team and a business partner (IKEA) created a design competition for college students and through this a set of on-going working relationships with college teachers of design (Chapter 4).

> Since SDP started we've tried to be more proactive in our partnerships within Schools, we attended Faculty team meetings and met senior managers within all Faculties where we introduced ourselves, talked a little bit about our role, what our responsibilities were, what types of activities we could do, and how we could support the Schools. We started developing those relationships quite early and we managed to create some really great relationship with some Schools. *Member of Solent Partnerships Team*

Developing new progression routes for apprentices to higher education featured highly, with the team taking the opportunity to promote progression opportunities at Solent, with early discussions with relevant FE and employer training associations about progression from Advanced to Higher Apprenticeship. We delivered two academic Units PDUs designed to enable apprentices to transition to the learning requirements of higher education and as a result, Construction and Engineering working with the Business School began to link these bridging units to their courses and market an integrated offering particularly to (but not exclusively) apprenticeship students from engineering who wished to access HE.

The Middle—Year 2

The second year of the Programme from early on had been anticipated as the peak of funded activity—all the SDP team members, most of whom were embedded within the University Faculties and Services, were in place, knowledge about the Programme was spreading and Faculties & Services were already formulating plans for second year projects and further funding. FBSE—Change Support Academy, FCIS—Year 2 Follow On, WMA—MSc suite, FTECH—Projects from Faculty Schools, LIS continuation of Flexible Delivery Team, Accelerating Enterprise 2 and the SuperYacht Academy, (Chapter xx) which had to wait for full Faculty support, but eventually came to fruition outside the SDP.

However we also wanted to bring forward small proposals (max £15,000) from individuals and small groups from any level or area within the University. This was not just about assisting the delivery of the more explicit parts of the bid but was part of the cultural change that was sitting behind the Programme. It was a chance for the individual to come forward and was badged the "Innovation Fund" (Chapter xx). We wanted to encourage and reassure staff that it was acceptable to come forward with ideas that contained an element of necessary risk and failure was not a reason for blame, as long as they could exhibit learning through the process.

In fact such was the commitment of the fifteen that came forward, that overall they achieved their aims and experienced a degree of personal learning that they had probably not anticipated. They ranged from developing PDUs for Football Administrators to Instant Messaging Enquiry services for Library Services to non—traditional learners and came from Senior Lecturer to Clerical grade staff.

Considerable progress was also being made in developing programmes that met the needs of employers and as these emerged we tried to ensure that the infrastructure and organisational development kept pace to support them.

During the second year of SDP the development of Solent On-Line (SOL) as an e-learning platform together with its pedagogic underpinning resulted in recruitment of the first distance learners to the MSc Shipping Operations programme, entirely supported through the on-line environment. External recognition of the value of the on-line environment was also achieved with a number of public service organisations exploring options and then contracting with the University.

A significant development in the approach to engaging with employers was the building of a strategic partnership with the University Hospital Southampton Foundation Trust and the recruitment of the first learners for the FdSc in Health & Social care as a co-delivery provision between the University and the Hospital. (Chapter 8) This partnership went on to encompass other academic provision, real life briefs for fine art students, volunteering and a raft of other initiatives that are signalling new development areas for the University.

For the University the special aspect was the way in which the engagement was delivered, not through a central or Faculty led business development team but through embedding a member of the Hospital Trust one day a week at the University; they began to understand us and see opportunities, we likewise had a window into their organisation; a very cost effective solution for both parties.

The concept of co-delivery, collaborative provision, accreditation of third party provision and kite-marking were all features of that second year of working with employers, but these presented new challenges and opportunities for staff development.

One of the challenges, in the area of quality systems, was convincing staff that the systems were flexible and responsive enough to meet the needs and demands of new clients and learners. In particular, it was not unusual for academic staff to complain that the process of validating a new course is too slow for external clients like employers. So the speed of response in such situations was one of the things that the University had to try to change. This was not so much systems related as the administrative processes and practices that had built up round them.

> actually I don't think the systems are the problem, it's the way that we manage and resource our practices. For example people were saying it takes too long to validate a course. We proved that if you actually changed the way that you worked, you did things in parallel and you got yourself organised and you put the necessary resources in, you could go from initial idea to validation in six weeks, and that was a full-blown course!
>
> . . . there's nothing in our current systems that say you've got to do things linearly and slowly. So one of the things that we have encouraged Faculties to do is to try to do things in parallel. . . . So we haven't radically changed any of that, but we are trying to say don't do it linearly, try and do as many processes as you want, you know, at one time, and it'll speed things up. *Dean Academic Services*

Doing new things—accrediting third party provision, kite marking also needed academics to develop new organisational capability, so where university staff had no prior experience external consultants were used to help them quickly gain the expertise and confidence to develop entirely new areas of practice.

> We've been working with the Institute of Internal Communication. They wanted to have their Foundation Diploma of Proficiency to be scrutinised by a university and to see whether it could be awarded HE credit . . . . We've looked at the programme in detail and tried to work out actually how much credit it could potentially be awarded

> at higher education but also what level within our HE Framework it actually fits. Having made those decisions it went to an external verifier to give an independent opinion on whether our judgement was right.
>
> She wrote a report and agreed with us. We've very much had to create the process because this is the first time the University has been through this. We now have new QA guidelines for the future. I had never done anything like this before but I was helped by an external consultant employed through the SDP Team. She acted like a mentor giving feedback to me at the end of a meeting with a client in terms of the way I had handled things; she was really very supportive . . . I think it is about building confidence and I think [the external consultant] had a lot to do with that in terms of the feedback she's given me. *Academic staff member FCIS.*

Improving the administrative processes and practices was also part of the development for enhancing the student experience for all students, but the important aspect for the Programme, in respect of sustainability, was the need to begin to develop the capability of staff to drive continuous improvement themselves and to initiate change, when circumstances required.

Thus in the summer of 2011 we decided to offer an external programme to each of the Faculties to support administrators in taking a pro-active and engaged role in developing and improving all aspects of service standards for students, both traditional and non—traditional.

The programme activities (developed and delivered by the external consultants) are described in Chapter 12 but provided the opportunity for teams of administrators to work on the real challenges of their role with advice and support from external experts. Once again we found another group of people at a mostly junior level within the organisation, full of ideas and who grew in self—confidence during the process, delivering the output from their challenges to Vice Chancellor's Group, senior managers and the Higher Education Funding Council at their bid monitoring visit.

These activities continued throughout the 3rd Year as we further pursued the development of staff capability to keep moving the University forward post SDP.

The End?

> Shifting the focus to sustainability for those activities that we wish to continue will be crucial to the last year of the

programme. The University, supported by the SDP team will therefore be working through what further action needs to be undertaken to embed these activities into the institutional mainstream. The current strategic agenda, which aligns with much of the focus of the White Paper, remains in place with the knowledge that the SDP aims of developing flexibility and adaptability are becoming subtly embedded in the culture of the University. *HEFCE Annual Monitoring Visit August 3rd 2011:1*

We recognised that real sustainability would only occur if we not only embedded new developments but also nurtured new capabilities and extended the confidence of staff more widely. So this period was not focused on generating further new initiatives but on continuing to deliver on and learn from our new capabilities and build on what we had gained. Learning from our experiences and increasing our capabilities was a significant feature of the one "strand" we have not discussed, yet which sat as enabler to many of our developments and was an area in which the University developed profoundly during the three years.

The Business Systems strand underpinned the whole SDP programme. It was probably something that marks it out as a being different from other programmes that the University might have funded because it was centred on the infrastructure needed for the University to work differently and better. *SDP Project Manager*

Although Business Systems were not part of the HEFCE bid funding, nonetheless the University had committed to undertake significant systems development to underpin SDP activities.

We realised that we couldn't transform the institution unless we were able to transform the systems that underpinned it. And in those early days of the development of thinking around SDP, that was about a more flexible agenda, working with different sorts of students and stakeholders, working with businesses and with employers, with students who may not be in the traditional mould, who would therefore need to be able to engage with the University in a different way. So I think there was an underpinning thought that our systems had been designed for other purposes and they needed to change. They were too rigid and inflexible; they weren't going to allow us to be able to work with students in a way that we needed to work in the future. At the same time our staff admin. systems, our HR systems, were inflexible, and they were not going to allow

> us to be able to work in flexible ways with staff in the way that a transformed university might need us to work . . . we needed systems that were more resilient, more reliable, more flexible, and improved our ability to engage with, monitor and support students and their learning more effectively. *Dean Learning and Information Systems*

Having made the commitment the University had to build new capacity in its business applications team.

> We needed to make sure that we had the capacity to be able to manage the development of entirely new business systems. That meant boosting capacity within the Business Applications team within the University. We seconded one of the managers from ICT to an SDP-funded Technical Development Manager post and put additional funding in to the team to make sure we had some additional capacity. We also appointed a Business Analyst to work alongside the Technical Development Manager in the development of business systems. So those were two very significant roles for the business system development for SDP. *Dean Learning and Information Systems*

The Business Systems strand differed from the other strands in its methodology, as a more conventional form of project management was felt to be appropriate for a major infrastructural programme. A coordinating team was established to manage the ambitious programme of work, make sure the multiple developments stayed on track and ensure that there was a good level of connectivity and integration.

> So in the early days of SDP we established a coordinating team comprising myself, SDP Director, Head of ICT, Business Systems Technical Manager and the Business Analyst, to look at what the overall requirements of business systems development were. We met weekly in order to monitor the work that was being done on business systems against the requirements of SDP. With such a hugely demanding programme, even spread over three years, we knew that we would not be able to deliver all the aspects of business systems unless we had a very clear project monitoring process. And in fact right up to today we have a weekly meeting. We also brought in to the group from time to time others such as the Dean of Academic Services and key members of Academic Services who have continued to report to us around the development of Quercus (Student Information System),

and the HR Manager overseeing the development of the HR/Payroll. And the purpose behind this, particularly for the SDP Director and me, was so we could monitor exactly what developments were going on and whether or not we were on track, and whether or not we needed a different intervention, or make decisions about the direction of travel on some of these systems. *Dean Learning and Information Systems*

To give some insight into the breadth of the changes progressed over the three years a synopsis of the projects provides some indication of the achievements but this hardly does justice to the amount of change both in IT itself and the engagement with users that was required.

We did a lot of the work around the development of new business processes. For example, if you introduce an attendance monitoring system, you can put the system in; you can put the wiring in. We spent the best part of the first year of SDP focusing on simple things like getting cables run around every part of the campus, it was a massive programme, in order to be able to get the readers in, in order to create the system for new swipe cards and get them distributed to students. And people could say what's that got to do with business systems? But it was a very necessary element in then moving to the next stage, which was how do you then implement a system where a student swipes as they go in to a classroom and something intelligent happens with the information? And actually that's the important thing that involves Faculty admin teams and the Academic Services team . . . it's about using information wisely *Dean Learning and Information Services*

A central underpinning to the SDP work was the need for extensive change to the student information system, **Quercus Plus** to transform it from the course centric nature of this type of software to a more student-centric and flexible system, able to manage commercial and partner courses running across all faculties with multiple entry points during the year, different modes of study and block payment arrangements. As part of this project we also moved the Warsash Maritime Academy to using Quercus Plus, meaning there is now a single and flexible Student Information System for the University.

The use of Quercus Plus was also further extended to enhance **Student Relationship Management.** We replaced our current central booking system with online prospectus requests and open day booking and introduced the 'Communication through the Application process', which allows Admissions Tutors to make decisions electronically about applications and embed auditable workflow into the process.

Potential change to our student profile, and particularly the need for a **Solent Virtual Campus,** required technical modifications to the systems—the unseen requirements of change. This led to the redesign of the identity management and provisioning systems to allow for students studying more flexibly and requiring continued access to services after graduation. Our existing approach had been to provision students for all services at pre-enrolment status and terminate their access after graduation. This modification opened up the requirements of a "virtual campus" from a technical point of view and initiated some radical thinking around Identity and Access management, which has a much wider application and greater implications than merely an extended VLE.

New software was deployed to deliver a fully integrated **HR/payroll system** (ResourceLink) to handle both permanent and associate staff, with manager and employee self-service—My Details, My Pay, My Attendance and My Team were deployed in Year 2, followed in April 2012 by an e-recruitment module. Staff returns, equal pay, equality and diversity audits were all enabled and the future phase of development—the deployment of the performance management module to ensure that appraisal data is logged—is now in planning to ensure we have better systems to support talent and career development in the future.

The new **Student Attendance Monitoring** infrastructure was implemented during September 2010 with the installation of 325 networked readers in teaching rooms at both campuses to be used in conjunction with a new smart campus card. The academic year 2010/11 then focussed on bedding in the infrastructure and agreeing policies and procedures. In the 2011/12 academic year, the next step was the identification of students who were not attending and the tracking of communications with those students. An internal development, known as AMTrack, was developed in close liaison with all three faculties to enable us to achieve this.

Attendance Monitoring was the initial piece in the jigsaw of looking at student interaction with the University. For learners and the University, spotting individuals who are struggling with their studies and life in higher education is extremely important in supporting and retaining these students, whether pastorally or with their studies. Interestingly during the programme our thinking changed radically from purely picking up the electronic heartbeats of student engagement—attendance, library usage, log on to MyCourse—to looking at a much wider range of qualitative interactions with learners, which involved academic, faculty and service staff. In turn this has had interesting implications for systems development requiring linked components of Business Intelligence, Case management/Student Relationship Management, Workflow and Communications management, which will be fundamental to our future enterprise architecture and has been at the heart of the transformation in the way in which Business Systems are conceptualised and managed.

During SDP the University moved away from point solutions to software needs and began to look at building blocks to provide a range of "solutions" based on more robust and effective architecture. Implementation of project governance and prioritisation, training in PRINCE 2 principles and effective change management were all initiated with a significant amount of staff development, some of which came from working with short term contract staff, selected because of their Blue Chip private sector experience and ways of working.

> I think one of the things that having a focus on business systems within SDP has done is highlighted to the University that our systems aren't optional, I think there is now an understanding that our business systems and our IT systems overall are absolutely essential to the success of the University and to its total operation, and I don't think there was that appreciation three years ago. *Faculty Dean*

> We didn't have any kind of programme management office with specialist skills and resources available for managing key programmes and projects within the University. Prior to SDP there was no consistent use of formal project management methodology. Some people were using different approaches to others and it was very ad hoc. . . . .

> An indication of the sort of cultural change that has happened through SDP is that over the next few months there will be a review looking at not only the ICT department but also how the University delivers its IT services generally. Because I've worked in the IT department for many years, I've noticed that the role of the ICT section is changing. I think there is better recognition that it needs to be much more closely aligned to business requirements rather than providing a set of distinct services, it needs to effectively align itself with the business so that it can help the University achieve its strategic objectives. I feel in the past we've been rather reactive to what the University has been asking for. I think if the IT department is to thrive in the future it needs to be more proactive in creating an infrastructure and set of services which can help the University achieve its objectives. So understanding

the business drivers is much more important than just delivering a distinct set of services. *Technical Development Manager*

So how does the University continue to build on its "story" and sustain the momentum that has been generated? Five key areas have emerged from the SDP that we continue to focus on today:

- Investment in organisational development.
- Further embedding of employability into the curriculum
- Strengthening partnerships and alliances
- Innovative curriculum developments in areas defined by employer needs
- New systems and ways of working

However, the main question is will we continue to change?

Across the University there is now a more urgent realisation that we do have to respond to change. It's important for us to keep adapting and changing as skilfully as we have over the past three years. Our staff have been the core strength of this programme. Working together as one organisation will be the key to sustaining the benefits achieved by SDP. *PVC Academic.*

Whilst this chapter has provided an overview of how the Programme progressed, the case studies in chapters 5-12 examine in more detail how this was achieved in terms of managing and leading the Programme with a different methodology to those often deployed in large and complex programmes. The case studies also provide the most obvious evidence of the capacity of our staff, to turn into action, to innovate and to sustain the momentum generated by the programme.

CHAPTER 5

A School-Based Approach to Strategic Change

INTRODUCTION

This chapter considers how change was accomplished through the Strategic Development Programme in one of the University's Schools. It focuses on the question, *What happened when the School of Design responded to the challenges and opportunities provided by the University's Strategic Development Programme?* Nine members of the School voluntarily participated in the interview-based study, together with three other members of the University who worked collaboratively with members of the School. Their stories form the basis of this account of how change was accomplished.

Background

Prior to August 2011 the School of Design (SoD) embraced the disciplines of Design and Fashion and was located in the Faculty of Technology (FTEC). In August 2011 the School was divided into the School of Design which remained in FTEC and the School of Fashion which moved to the Faculty of Creative Industries (FCIS). In 2009 the School participated in FTEC's initial engagement with SDP as part of the WALL project *(Workplace Activity-Led Learning)* undertaken between October 2009-April 2010. This project aimed to develop professionally relevant bite-sized units in three main areas—Business Information Technology (the digital enterprise); the Built Environment and Fashion and Design and the first stage was to conduct market research in these areas.

The results of this project informed a bid by the School of Design during the second year of SDP funding. In June 2010 the School submitted a bid for funding for a 12 month strategic development project which they called 'An Agile Portfolio for the Next Generation Learner'. It aimed to engage with all strands in the University's SDP strategy. The bid was approved in July and work began in September 2010.

The School of Design's SDP proposal identified four key areas in the 'portfolio of activities' namely:

1. Demand-Led Learning Portfolio

- Development of 12 Professional Development Units (PDU's)

2. Co-funded approach to Course Delivery and Development

- Co-Funded ASN's (Additional Student Numbers co-funded with employers)

3. Innovation and Enterprise

- Design for Enterprise Village
- Flexible Delivery Students First
- Succeed Beyond Solent Initiative

4. Partnerships

- Employer for Schools Partnerships
- FE Collaboration and Progression agreements
- Industry Partner Affiliation Network

A summary of the specific areas identified for development, together with actions and activities imagined at the time the proposal was prepared (June 2010) is shown in Table 5.1. The proposal aimed to deliver:

a) 20[1] co-funded additional student numbers and contribute to the Faculty targets of 120 by 2012
b) improved opportunities for student work experience, and by extension student employability to 100% of students
c) improved employer relationships and engagement, specifically partnership with three employers to co-fund courses[2]
d) diversify income streams for the University
e) a sustainable framework for a flexible curriculum through the development of twelve PDU's and alternative forms of learning
f) 'off the shelf' e-learning material for 6 award bearing units (20 credits+).
g) three 'Employer for Schools Partnerships' events for the local regions

---

1   HEFCE acknowledged that this target was no longer relevant in the new funding environment for higher education from September 2012. It was replaced by the goal of co-delivery (employers helping to deliver a course).

2   Ibid.

h) two Partnership accords to enable improved progression and partnership with key FE feeder colleges[3]

i) an Industry Partner Affiliation Network (two per course or programme area).

---

3 The Partnerships and Progression Office manages formal agreements with colleges. 6 partnership accords which have been signed with 6 colleges. This is a partnership between the whole college and the whole of the University and so targets within the accords span a variety of subject groups. All of these colleges have Art & Design departments hence the Design school partnership target has been delivered as part of this work

Table 5.1 School of Design Proposal for SDP Funding

Demand-Led Learning Portfolio

i. To build on the two employer-focused market and needs analysis reports that were undertaken in October 2009 through to April 2010 (as part of the WALL Project).

ii. To identify a number of key areas for development as bite size learning opportunities targeted towards demand-led employee education, industry training needs and professional development planning.

iii. To specifically target both Design and Fashion/Lifestyle related industries in the Southern UK regions (although a national/international market is also anticipated).

iv. To develop a number of bite size award bearing credit/units as exemplars in structure, content and delivery utilizing blended/e-delivery in order to cascade the practice to the wider subject areas within the school, faculty and wider university community (in collaboration with the School of Computing and Communications and aligned to the WALL project, FTECH).

v. To provide on-line/e-learning taught provision with a 100% 'off the shelf' approach to delivery recognizing learners may wish to learn at more suitable 'off peak' times. 12 PDU's will be developed initially, importantly providing an exemplar framework to sustain momentum and future innovation in on-line delivery across the school, faculty and wider university community.

Co-funded approach to Course Delivery and Development

i. To identify and build key relationships with targeted employers to implement a co-funded approach to course delivery and development (Co-Funded ASN's).

ii. To increase, develop and formalize imaginative partnership working with current and new employers who have expressed an interest in working with SSU with both under graduate and postgraduate provision which fall within the HEFCE co-funded ASN requirements.

iii. To pursue interest from 5 employers (to date) who have expressed an interest in further developing and formalizing links with the School of Design and SSU. 3 companies are considered large employers. Target 20 co-funded-ASN's.

Innovation & Enterprise—Succeed Beyond Solent

As an enhancement activity an opportunity exists to extend the rationale of the Succeed

Beyond Solent initiative:

i. To capture the breadth of employer engagement activities that the student experiences during and as part of their studies. To devise an 'experiential based' certificated award for the purposes of contributing to the individual student CV profile and Professional Development Planning.

ii. To capture/record the Work Experience, live project work, Industrial set competitions, guest speakers, consultancy, sponsorship, industry visits etc where courses have employer focused activity associated with unit delivery or course delivery within the school of Design.

iii. A further opportunity exists for analysis/data collection and a 'black book' approach to relationship building to fully utilize companies/ industry professionals that willingly and regularly provide opportunities for our learners.

Design for Enterprise Village

i. The development of a collegiate range of garments (SSU branded) will be designed, manufactured, merchandised, promoted and marketed by the student body and as part of their learning activities.

ii. The seasonal range of SSU branded garments will be sold through a pop up retail/e-tail environment.

iii. Opportunity exists for both course, faculty and cross faculty/service collaboration.

Flexible Delivery Students First

i. To research and develop flexible, non-traditional methods of delivery encompassing teaching, learning and evidence based peer and self-assessment for both the new (next generation) and traditional learner types. To develop 'off the shelf' e-learning material for 6 award bearing units (20 credits +) in collaboration with the Services of LIS.

ii. To address and identify new learner constituencies and expand/ strengthen employer engagement and experiences through flexible delivery and work based learning opportunities (WBL). 4 units will be developed/identified.

Partnership—Employer for Schools Partnerships

i. Facilitator of 'Employer for Schools Partnerships'. This activity will play a central role in bringing industry and schools together to develop imaginative partnerships and enhanced employer focused experiences for schools (11—18 year groups). A team of academics will facilitate opportunities for partnership working, competitions, schools visits and key central liaison duties. Target will be a minimum of three 'Employer for Schools Partnerships' in the local regions.

FE Collaboration and Progression agreements

ii. To take a lead role in securing at least 2 Partnership accord FE Collaboration/Progression agreements.

Industry Partner Affiliation Network

iii. To increase the number of course specific aligned industry affiliations, associations and sponsorships. The prime driver will be to increase and build brand awareness (image) and position the SSU brand image by association whilst formalizing an Industry Partner Affiliation Network **distinctly** aligned to curriculum areas. Target will be a minimum of two per course or programme area.

The proposal showed how the resources that were being bid for would be used to create the capacity necessary to deliver the ambitious objectives identified in Table 5.1.The Head of School was confident that the risk implications of the proposal were low.

> This is low risk, as it builds on existing initiatives, curricular strengths and employer relationships within the School of Design. The key risk is not to see some of the potential realised, so adequate resourcing in terms of project management and releasing of staff is key to ensuring implementation. *SoD SDP Funding Proposal*

Meta story

The meta story provides a broad descriptive framework of 'what happened'. It creates the landscape within which the details of change are enacted. The meta story begins with the School's involvement in its Faculty's (FTEC) SDP project (known as the WALL Project—*Workplace Activity-Led Learning*) between October 2009—April 2010. Two external consultants with knowledge of the fashion industry were commissioned by the School to undertake market research aimed at identifying opportunities/markets for on—line Professional Development Units. This work subsequently informed the School's own SDP proposal which was prepared by the Head of School in June 2010. The bid was approved by the University's Management Board in early July and £102,000 was provided to support the development work. Over the next academic year (September 2010—June 2011) members of the School of Design, together with staff from some of the University's support services engaged in development work to turn ideas into new practices. Although some of the participants received some remission from their teaching and administrative responsibilities, the development work was accomplished simultaneously alongside normal teaching duties.

The main achievements brought about through the change process are summarised below. In the period between September 2010-June 2011 members of the School:

- Designed and produced 12 Professional Development Units (PDU's) delivered entirely on-line
- Designed, organised the manufacturing, marketing and retailing of Solent's own Collegiate Range of garments as part of a major live industry-relevant project involving over 200 students
- Designed, developed and implemented, with the help of the e—development team, a new level 1 module for 150 students. Student engagement involved a blended learning approach which utilised on—line discussion forums. The approach is now being rolled out to other programmes.
- Through an Employer Affiliates programme developed good relationships with a range of employers who are willing to endorse and support the School's programmes
- Developed strong relationships with IBM and MRA which has resulted in employees of these organisations making significant contributions to the curriculum improving the industrial relevance of the courses and benefitting student employability
- In collaboration with the Partnership Office and IKEA, organised a competition for 16-19 design students in partner colleges. A similar competition is now being offered with B&Q. These strategies have resulted in deeper relationships with college tutors and encouraged more college students to consider applying to the University in these disciplines.
- Developed and piloted a *Real World Certificate* to provide recognition for any employment-relevant experience gained by students. A new member of staff now developing the framework to support deeper levels of student engagement in reflective learning.

These achievements were only the first step in the change process and the changes were being implemented, refined, adapted or extended without the help of SDP funding in the 2011-12 academic year. In the following sections we consider the how these innovations were accomplished.

STORIES OF CHANGE

Starting

The SDP Team had sent out numerous communications to the wider University about SDP and the Senior Managers had been informed about the SDP project through the University Management Board. The University might therefore expect the messages about intentions and opportunities to be cascaded through the institution—through the Faculty—School and Central Services organisational and communication structures. But the detail of what actually happens is often more complex than is imagined. In the case of the School of Design there was a Faculty context to consider.

> it was at a heads meeting when I realized that the WALL project wasn't delivering on what it needed to deliver. I sat there listening to what other people were doing and I think I heard that FCIS were developing lots of professional development units . . . Listening to what other people were talking about I just thought, we need to be doing this, and that was important, that day. I can picture myself in that meeting thinking I feel like . . . we need to do something about it. And that, to me, was the day when I decided we would do something about it.

From this story it might be inferred that the decision by the HoS to commit her school to a strategy for change and create and submit a proposal for SDP funding was as much an emotional as a rational decision. The decision to act was triggered by feelings of dissatisfaction with the Faculty's response to SDP and a sense that an opportunity was being missed: an opportunity that was highlighted by what other Faculties appeared to be achieving.

Two contextual factors are omitted from this story. The first relates to the personal qualities and characteristics of the key actor—the Head of School. Without the organisational leader choosing to be involved, strategic change within a School or Department will not happen. The HoS describes herself as a *'middle character'* in the SoD's strategic development process and a crucial part of the role of this middle character was to set things in motion and sustain the momentum.

> as much as I moan about how busy I am all the time, if I'm not busy, I make myself busy. I suppose I'm not at

> ease when I've only got one thing to do. I feel that I'm not achieving. That's the person I am. I'm always looking forward . . . . I'm not ambitious but I am an achiever and that's crucial to this and I haven't done it for any brownie points. I have done it because I like to achieve and I want my School to achieve and for my staff to feel they're part of that achievement as well . . . I wanted to ensure my school would jump above the parapet, if you like, because I knew we were doing lots of good stuff but it just wasn't getting out there in the way that I wanted.

The second contextual factor is that most of the ideas that were included in the School's SDP proposal did not magically 'appear overnight': they had been the subject of professional conversation within the School. What the HoS did was bring these ideas together and blend them into a narrative that linked areas for intended development to the University's strategic objectives. Indeed, half a day had been devoted to the SDP at the June 2010 School of Design Away Day.

> We did an Away Day in late May and half a day was devoted to SDP . . . . the smaller team that I had on board at that point presented their ideas on where they were wanting to take it and then we invited people to write on post-its their contribution and their ideas and what they could bring to bear. And so, yes, that was a moment where everybody came on board . . . This was the first time as a School we talked about all the areas, and of course everyone understood all the areas because it was very much discussed in our kind of language.

> It's always about trying to get people on board and to get buy-in and to get their ideas. I'm saying, look at all this great stuff we can do. We [have the opportunity] to get some money, let's have your input because everyone then feels a part of it . . . And then also everyone understood what everyone else was going to be doing too, and that's important.

What is being signalled here is the importance, in a practice community, of creating opportunities for people to come together to generate, consider and evaluate ideas that will then be utilised by the community. In doing so they are co-creating their future and understanding how each contributes to the whole enterprise.

Design for change

Preparing a successful bid was an important part of the change process. An alternative way of looking at the bid was that it provided the blueprint for strategic change encapsulating a coherent vision and a narrative about that vision that linked it to the University's strategic intentions. As such it created an important 'artefact' to facilitate and mediate thinking, discussion and action. An artefact that once approved by the Management Board was circulated to all members of staff.

Preparing the bid

> Once I'd got to know what the requirements were for SDP and to put this in perspective I had a meeting with [a member of the SDP team] on the Thursday afternoon . . . . As I was talking about the ideas she said, 'Do you want to put in a small bid?' Over the weekend I thought, 'Okay, but no maybe I won't. I haven't got time, I'm busy.' Then Tuesday morning came and she rang me and said, 'Do you want me to help you?' . . . so I said 'can you help me?'.

> By Tuesday afternoon I'd written everything I could . . . . at that point I just had this list of all these projects and they obviously needed to go into this [format], so she took some of my stuff and put it into an appropriate layout. I really didn't know what I was writing because this is very much internal understanding, isn't it? . . . . I was very grateful for her help because I wouldn't have had the confidence, so she just lifted some of my text out and said, right, put that in there, and then I seem to remember she wrote the background because I didn't have that knowledge at the time. So, yes, it was great that she helped put some of this in and gave me the confidence. By Wednesday the draft was finished.

> My approach was a portfolio of activity. It wasn't going to be one project. It was going to be a number of projects that I thought we could deliver on . . . . I don't set about doing things I don't think we can deliver on. I'm an ideas person but I like to be realistic in the environment that I live. The project had its challenges without a doubt and tested the University systems and processes to the end . . . What was really important to me was working out a costing model, sort of putting names to tasks. *Head of School*

Informing Faculty managers

The SoD proposal departed from the way the Faculty of Technology had begun the SDP project which was as a single Faculty-wide project so before the bid could be submitted the HoS had to inform her Faculty Management Board and try to get their support.

> I presented the main ideas to the Faculty management team to seek approval. I tried to do that before it went in . . . there was lots going on because . . . the Dean at the time wasn't well. An Acting Dean came in . . . . I suppose at that time I didn't feel I had the support of Faculty, the other FMT members were probably a bit shocked by it because they hadn't seen it but I wanted to do the right thing and make sure I put it through FMT first so at least there was some sort of acknowledgement or approval before it was submitted.

Celebrating success

Good managers know that it is important to keep their staff informed and celebrate success. Winning funding in a competitive process is a significant achievement and the HoS used the opportunity to send an email to all members of the School to inform them about the SDP project, to celebrate success and to invite people to get involved.

> I got the approval in early July . . . the minute I got approval, I sent an e—mail to the whole School to say, look, brilliant stuff, we've just been awarded this. It's a great confidence boost for the school and now we've got to set about looking at how we can achieve it. I then started meeting individual members of staff to make sure there was some sort of clarity about what part they could play in this, and then it was about building teams so I talked to my academic leaders as well as other staff to put the right people together with the right sets of skills.

What we learn from the personal account of how a School came to be involved in the University's strategic development programme, is that it was not a simple linear process of a leader acquiring information, seeing an opportunity and creating a bid. We witness an evolving situation in which a leader is exposed to different sources of information and is able to compare approaches being used in other Faculties. The School's involvement in the SDP was dependent on the key actor becoming on the one hand increasingly 'disturbed', and on the other hand becoming increasingly 'inspired'.

Even then, because of the demands of the day job and the time and effort required to formulate a bid (the bureaucratic device to enable SoD to become involved) the School may have missed the opportunity. It required a 'nudge' and an offer of 'practical help' from another key player (a member of the University's SDP Team) in order to take that initial step. It's also clear from the account that the only person who could create the bid lacked the knowledge and confidence to put the bid together in the way that was required and that this barrier to participation was overcome by working collaboratively with a member of the SDP Team. The subtext to all this was a Faculty that was not actively engaging in the opportunity provided by SDP.

IMPLEMENTATION

Engaging people in a change process is the hardest part of any change project, because everyone is already busy doing other things. The HoS was the key actor in engaging people, checking that they understood what was expected and communicating a sense of urgency so that their contribution to the SDP work did not get overlooked in their day to day work. This was a challenge because the start of the strategic change project coincided with the start of the new academic year.

> Any time we try and do any formal project, we have to get it [up and running] before we start teaching because otherwise everyone just gets drowned in the day job. So I just [met] with all the key players that would get this going. I also wrote the advert to get the project manager in post. Those were my two key priorities at the start . . . . So within that first week I discussed each project with everybody, looked at how we could make it happen and tried to align it as much as possible to what we were currently doing or could be doing. So we had a team in place probably within the first couple of weeks. A team that I knew I could rely on to deliver what we said we would deliver.

> So I spent probably those first few weeks circling the two or three floors that we lived on, just checking in, how people were doing, did they fully understand what they were doing? Did the academic leaders understand how to lead their project? and I don't mean that in a patronizing way but it's attention to detail that makes these things happen. And so I was always just sort of checking in, chatting to them, all very informal but just making sure that everyone fully understood what was required.

In this account we witness sensitivity to the local culture of participation which required face to face conversation to discuss ideas, focus attention and convey expectations and a sense of urgency and purpose.

Project Management

One of the features of a university that makes it distinctive as an organisational change environment, is that it is full of people who don't like being told what to do. Academics, have significant autonomy over what they do and how they do it. This view of academics and how best to involve them in the change process was echoed by the HoS.

> Designers don't like [being told what to do] . . . if I just issued everybody with a work plan . . . . people would switch off. You've got to keep it exciting and interesting and visual and the ownership is clearly with the people that are driving it forward. It's about facilitating their belief that it's their project. You get people to buy into an idea that they then start to believe in it as if it's their own . . . you feed the idea and they believe it's theirs and that's the important thing.

This is the beginning of the process of engaging academics in change but then there is the job of sustaining continued engagement. It has often been said that managing academics is like herding cats (Garrett and Davies 2010) and as stated previously the use of project management methodology to manage innovation in the academic environment has the potential to create cultural and procedural dissonance (Kenny 2002). Bates (2000 pointed to a clear tension between the classic project management approach used in business environments and the traditional way in which professional staff at a university work. In an attempt to overcome this problem, he advocated a looser approach to project management: 'a much looser project management approach that specifies responsibilities and completion dates but does not attempt to quantify every activity on a micro level' (Bates 2000:73). The cultural aspect of the independence of academics and the nature of their work, in which they have a range of teaching and other responsibilities, makes traditional project management practices problematic for educational development projects in which they may be involved. So how was project management approached in the School's SDP project?

There are a number of indications that project management was conducted in a way that was sympathetic to the way Bates (ibid) considered it had to be conducted in a university setting. The HoS emphasised the importance of appointing a Project Delivery Manager (PDM) and her contribution to the overall success of the SDP project.

In the bid I put in for a project manager and that was the best thing I ever did. There is still a day job to do so to have a project manager chasing people, making sure we were hitting deadlines, liaising with external bodies if we needed was fantastic. It was a significant reason for the success of the project. When the project manager came on board, it was an immense relief because she was somebody that organized, followed through and didn't take no or, I'm too busy, for an answer. She just kept going and going to keep the project on track.

During interviews several participants mentioned the helpful involvement of the PDM who described the role in these terms.

> It was my job to make everything happen from an operational side, and also keep people motivated and reminding them that we had deadlines to meet and so forth . . . it was my job to make sure all the projects were delivered and so I tried to take a lead.

> I had to be very adaptable and because I was dealing with creative people who can be temperamental. I think [the role] needed people skills and also good organisational skills because these people had to constantly be reminded of their deadlines and that they had to think and act much more urgently, rather than taking their time over things because we only had a short period of time to make sure that everything was delivered. I felt as if I was constantly on their backs reminding them constantly.

Good and continuous communication with the leaders of individual projects, and the development of good working relationships, was key to effective project management. Here we see the role of PDM in helping to clarify and communicate what was expected and the direct and regular face to face contact with people to ensure that the SDP work was given the attention it needed.

> When I started on the project I got the impression that the people who were involved in the project, didn't really know what was expected of them. Where I was located was quite helpful. I was on the third floor which gave me access to most of those people. We had regular meetings . . . . almost on a daily basis for some periods because we had to keep on communicating and making sure that things got

done. And then we also had group meetings . . . to make people aware of what was going on.

Bates (2000) emphasises the need for a looser concept of project management than is normally used in business environments. The PDM had considerable experience of project management in business environments and it is clear that she realised that a looser approach was needed, with frequent contact and the development of good relationships. She therefore adapted her approach to meet this requirement.

> We had a grid and we itemised what needed to be actioned. I started off the project in the way that I would normally approach a project, which is very systematically and giving people deadlines, etc. But very quickly I learnt that this environment was not like a traditional business environment and that I had to adapt my approach. First of all there was no motivator for these people to do this extra work in addition to their lecturing. So that was one of the challenges I had. How do I motivate people to get things done? So we started off with a bit of a planning matrix and then I had to change my approach so it was more to do with me actually physically going to see them and sometimes standing over them and saying have you done this? How can we achieve this? I know it's very difficult, I know it's extra work for you but you've agreed to do this, we need to see it to completion and everyone's in the same boat.

One of the characteristics of an innovator is that they are full of ideas and there is a tendency to keep starting new things. So another role for the PDM was to try to keep people focused on the key objectives in the School's SDP action plan.

> So constantly reminding people what the actual objective was because there were some people trying to stray away and come up with different ideas that didn't relate to what we needed to achieve. I think that happened quite a lot, you know pulling people in and making sure that we kept things first of all simple and not stray too far away from the objectives.

Through direct contact with the people involved in change the PDM was able to empathise with colleagues who were very busy and move beyond this to providing individuals with practical help to keep their project moving forward.

I tried to lift people out of situations where they felt really overwhelmed with their workload. There were several lecturers who did have a lot of work to prepare and they had to do this on top. And so this is where I started getting involved with doing some of the tasks as well to help alleviate some of the pressure. On the collegiate range for example I sourced the suppliers. I helped also with trying to meet their deadlines with designers. I realised that the person who was involved was having trouble managing the workload, so I changed the focus a little bit and got students involved and I launched them as live projects so the students were writing a marketing plan instead of the Project Leader. We also got some students to devise marketing material as well and I got involved with those students, briefing them and making sure that they were meeting deadlines, etc.

People engaged in significant change often experience anxiety and stress as they work in situations with problems and challenges that are unfamiliar. The PDM recognised this and was able to assist colleagues.

I was directly involved in mediating the anxieties related to some projects. In particular, when project leaders needed the assistance of their team and they did not feel comfortable asking colleagues to get involved with extra duties. Also, there was the pressure of senior managers having information on which lecturers were involved in the different projects. A few of the project leaders were keen "not have egg on their face" (a phrase used on many occasions) through their projects failing. I was asked to make decisions for them. . . . . Talking through issues and offering help definitely reduced anxiety . . . However, it is fair to say, the short time given to deliver the projects in conjunction with their lecturing duties caused a fair amount of anxiety throughout the project and it was only reduced significantly after the projects came to an end!

The PDM also helped in the preparation of regular monitoring reports for the University Management Board.

Every time there was a Management Board report, I wrote out where I thought we were with each project and then sent it to the teams to put in their deliverables. That was key because it made sure that everybody realized there were targets and we did have deadlines and deliverables to meet and progress had to be formally reported through

> the University structure. So that was quite important and it was my way of getting peace of mind that we were going to deliver and we were on track. So as much as everyone gets annoyed at writing reports . . . . it was very useful to make everyone aware of what their objectives were for next time and also to make them aware of the achievements of all the projects.

There were sometimes occasions when a member of a team did not pull their weight and action had to be taken to ensure that progress is made.

> Most of the projects ticked along. We had little issues which were resolved very quickly and most of it was to do with just being motivated and saying we've just got to do this . . . . I think in hindsight it would have been better if someone else had led that project. In the end I did a lot of the work.

This scenario shows how difficult it can be in a development process to manage such situations, especially when participants' involvement is essentially through their goodwill. But the story also illustrates how in an effective team other members of the team take responsibility for the shortcomings of colleagues to enable objectives to be realised.

CREATING NEW PRACTICES

Good leadership and effective and sensitive project management are essential ingredients for accomplishing significant change within a School but change is only accomplished if creative practitioners adapt their practice or invent new practice. Where change is concerned, the devil is in the detail, detail that is documented in the personal stories of activity and achievement told by each contributor to the change process. These stories reveal the emotional and physical effort required to change, the capabilities and creativity of individuals and the challenges they encounter and try to overcome. They also reveal the new partnerships and relationships that were developed in order to accomplish change. From the accounts in this section it is clear that people involved in the School's SDP project engaged in a wide range of activities to bring about change including:

- *Planning and designing:* creating plans (both in the head and on paper) *and* designing new processes for learning
- *Relationship building:* developing new and productive relationships with other people in the School, the wider University or outside the University

- *Managing:* themselves and their own work, coordinating others, commissioning others, writing contracts and managing performance
- *Engaging in productive inquiry:* finding out what they needed to know in order to do the things they needed to do.
- *Communicating:* through conversations, emails, skype, with people inside and outside the institution in ways that were appropriate to achieve objectives involved pitching/selling ideas, questioning, negotiating, arguing, persuading, participating in meetings, liaising with the project manager.
- *Experimenting and adapting existing practice or inventing new practice,* adapting the curriculum, developing and implementing new teaching practices, building new knowledge and developing the skills to change practice
- *Collaborating:* Working productively and creatively with other people
- *Evaluating and accounting:* evaluating new practices/gaining feedback from participants/organising focus groups, providing reports of progress to Project Manager

Here are some personal accounts of how members of the School accomplished change.

New blended learning experiences

One innovation involved significant changes to the curriculum to improve the learning experiences of students who are already studying at the University through the use of a blended learning approach. The project was led by an enthusiastic early adopter who designed, developed and implemented, with the help of the University's e-development team, a new level 1 module for 150 students. Student engagement involved a blended learning approach which utilised on-line discussion forums—the first use in the School.

> I began to teach a unit which had a cohort of 150 students for a weekly lecture and a series of seminars. It occurred to me was that if we brought blended learning into this unit it would encourage learning outside the classroom environment. I set up a forum for the whole cohort . . . in seven groups. I have to say it was a lot of work but it was worth it.
>
> Each week I would give the students the theme of the forum and I'd introduce it in the lecture and we'd discuss it in the seminars. But at no time did I interfere with the forum

or take part in it. It was their platform for discussion. It was their place outside of the classroom for discussion . . . and it was amazing. Absolutely amazing. The way that I got them to contribute and kind of guarantee that they would contribute is that part of the learning outcomes allowed for it to be part of the marked assessment. So if they didn't contribute it was detrimental to them, to their final marks. I set them a subject every week and off they went and they posted pictures, they posted links to websites.

It was my first year teaching this subject—I had to learn an awful lot . . . . all this information that students were posting on a daily basis I was learning from . . . . just by monitoring exactly what it was that they were using to feed their work I could identify the places [and things] that they weren't covering. So I was able then in the seminars and the lecture to concentrate on the areas I knew they weren't working with as well. I used the final forum to gain 'feedback' on their experience and I got absolutely tons and tons of feedback.

This year I decided that, because it was quite a valuable experience, I wanted to step it up a bit. So I've put it back into a level 1 first semester unit to try to get them to use these systems right from their first day at the University.

This unit is 13 weeks long so I've been able to give the students two weeks per theme and then what I do is close the forum. I leave it viewable but they can't post. So they can see it to write up their reports—they have to write one report every two weeks—and then a conclusion. And I encourage them in the lectures and seminars— "How's your forum going?" Some people would say, "Well everybody's posted at the last minute so it's not very useful for us. We can't get feedback." So I'm constantly encouraging them and this time around some of the groups have been saying things like, "Come on, let's be the best forum group again for this theme. We got 36 posts last time round. Let's make it 50." And they're actually now competing with each other. They can't see what the other groups have posted but they can see the number of posts. So it's brilliant. They're really, really enthusiastic.

They have to write every two weeks one report on the key issues that were discussed, their own contribution and a bit of reflective evaluation. In their final report they have to write how they felt about the experience of the forums, how useful it was to them, how it tied in with the seminars. And because it's part of the marked assessment. I've got 160 feedback reports on their experience without having to ask them to sit down and fill a form in. And it's great. Really good.

Real world curriculum

Drawing on his commercial experience working for UCLA, which designs and markets a collegiate range of garments, a teacher attempted to transfer the practices of garment design and production in the commercial world to the academic curriculum in the Collegiate Range project. In year 1 over 200 students from a range of courses were involved in the project which resulted in the design and production of a branded range of student clothes manufactured by a Turkish company. In Y2 the clothes are being marketed and sold through a series of pop up shops by students. It is hoped that profit made during the retailing phase will be re-invested in a second complete cycle of activity thus creating a sustainable enterprise-based curriculum.

> It was basically fitting a commercial framework into an academic framework . . . . the frameworks are very different . . . . it is like putting a square into a circle.

> So where did I start? I flew to Paris. It was important that I looked at the manufacturing side, the production side, of the process. So I went to Paris to Premier Vision which happens in September and February every year. It is an industry show that looks at fabrics and looks at manufacturing. Also to meet the manufacturers that would produce. The difficulty was the minimums, the amount of clothing that we needed. The factories that I usually use produce high minimums. What we were looking for was very low minimums and a very specific quantity because of the budget.

> We needed to ensure that the design students, that they could produce an industry standard technical pack to specifications that would be understood by an external factory. . . . We also needed to make sure that we came in on budget, came in on costs. So that also meant the eventual manufacturer that we got on board, Trend Moda, had to be put in the system. These things take so much time. So they had to make sure . . . they had to go through ethical and sustainable and sort of all these sort of policies

that the University has as well. We had to think about intellectual property as well and think about who owns the property. We had to think about copyright and things like that. All these things had to happen for me then to produce to get the designs.

We had to make sure that the knowledge was there for the students . . . . because the students designed all the collections. They needed to know about fabrication. These are first years that are just starting their second year so it was their first project. They probably have not thought about industry that much, so they had to know about fabrication, colour, specs and wash. They needed to know a little bit about intellectual property. They couldn't just take images and steal them. They need to know about fits and size etc. and design and design development process.

So all of that had to be done and then produce six technical packs to industry standard which they all did reasonably well. Then the graphics students produced the graphics which would be placed on garments and used as badges and prints etc. Then we would as a team we looked at all of them and had focus groups [to evaluate the designs]. Those are essentially the key things that needed to happen, and to varying degrees of success they did.

There are a lot of staff that I needed to oversee because it is spread across different units . . . .

A lot of meetings . . . . to make sure everybody was on board. We used to send out a critical path to say this needs to be done, this unit is going to finish then, we need the work to be marked so we can have the graphics approved. Production is always a nightmare, even in industry. So the production side and the managing of the production in Turkey and making sure that the samples that came back was, for myself, quite time consuming.

The students would underpin everything that was done for the development project, but there needed to be people at the top saying 'Okay that is good enough from that standard.' . . . But the students were involved in nearly every process . . . . It was a big enterprise—over two hundred, three hundred.

New opportunities for professional learners

One project focused on developing a suite of Professional Development Units (PDU's) for people working in the Fashion industry. Here the innovator describes the experience of working with external fashion consultants to develop the units.

> I used the research that we had done [in 2009] and discussed, with the Head of School and the other school management, the outcomes of this research and how we might begin to develop short courses. I had to find external people to help with writing content . . . . I worked with Terry at the e-Development Centre . . . to develop an effective way of delivering taught modules online . . . Basically I wrote most of the unit descriptors and then provided them to the external consultant. I found these people by utilizing my own contacts and appealing to people's better nature because I think the payment that they received wasn't equivalent to the freelance pay they would normally receive. But I worked very closely with them . . . a lot of email communication took place with them sending me materials and me checking it and going back to them with feedback. It was really resource heavy and time consuming for me . . . I was doing a considerable amount of reading through materials and feeding back during my own time in the evenings and weekends. Without that, it would not have happened. But I felt very, very strongly at the time that these have legs. These are winners. These courses, there is a market for them and if we can market them in the right way I always felt they would be successful. I believed in the framework that I developed and that it was an effective, clear and understandable way to go through a short course for anyone who is working.
>
> Once I had actually got past that initial stage of how do I put these first drafts of the units together, things began to roll. One of the most difficult issues was managing the externals because some of them didn't have a lot of experience of teaching . . . . it was very difficult to find people that could actually do this with me. I chose them based on their expertise, of the areas that I wanted the content developed around. So I was having to coach them in learning and teaching as we were going as well as try to help them understand how their material was going to be used online

> It was a huge learning curve for me and because at certain times I was quite vocal about the fact that I wasn't getting answers and I was quite persistent and tenacious about sorting things out and getting through this project.

New relationships with external partners

Building on an existing informal relationship with an industrial partner whose staff gave guest lectures from time to time, an enthusiastic teacher developed a strong link with IBM. Following a successful pitch involving the innovator, HoS and Dean, IBM decided to engage more formally with the University (one of only three Universities working with IBM). The innovator created a co-delivery model in which staff of IBM, and another Company, MRA, each deliver 50% of a module on a Masters Course. This was followed by IBM staff also contributing to one of the undergraduate programmes.

> It started with people I know coming in as guest speakers and then gradually the relationship became stronger and they became more involved . . . we worked on the unit descriptors but they became involved in influencing the projects that the students were doing to make them more relevant to their industry . . . . So that is where we started to develop the model . . . .

> I went for meetings with both of those companies following on from the casual contributions as guest speakers. I spoke to the Head of School about the potential for development of the relationships and we went to have meetings with both of the companies. They both agreed to formally support the courses and we are working towards a formal MOU [Memorandum of Understanding].

> What now happens is that within the time tabled sessions of teaching for the units roughly half of the teaching takes place by these external members from IBM and from MRA. I continue to be the unit leader, the academic involved in the delivery of the units to ensure that the academic requirements are met. But there is no doubt that the contribution from the companies and the way that they provide their expertise allows the students access to information that they wouldn't otherwise have, including visiting their premises and using research information that they have. My role is to keep the relationship going. To make sure there is efficient communication between

us and the companies to ensure that, they always know what is going on, when they should be here, and what is expected of them when they are here.

The story illustrates the importance of developing productive and meaningful working relationships but why would a company like IBM want to cooperate in this way? What advantage is it to the company?

IBM were really impressed with the level of communication and the efficiency with which they had been dealt with . . . they trusted us to work with them in an efficient way and for the relationship to be two-way . . . . they trusted that we would be as helpful as we could if they assisted us. They have their own directives about making sure graduates and students coming out of higher education have the relevant industry skills that they need. They saw the project that they are involved with as feeding very well into their [business interests] because it focused on retail innovation and technology in fashion retail—they work with lots of big fashion retail businesses.

New relationships with colleges and schools

Building on existing relationships developed through the Employer Affiliates programme and working closely and collaboratively with a member of the University's Partnership Office, a competition was organised called the IKEA Hack for 16-19 year old design students in partner colleges. The competition ran over an academic year and was judged to be successful by students, college tutors and the sponsoring employer as well as University staff. In Y2 a new partner is involved and the competition process has been refined based on the experience gained in the first cycle.

the University had been developing partnerships with a number of local feeder schools and colleges . . . One of the initiatives we set up was something we called the Design Award. We found a local sponsor—IKEA and created a competition to design an IKEA Hack, where you take one or two existing products and then you hack them together to create something new.

With the help of the University's Partnership Office, the IKEA Hack competition was advertised to local colleges which offered courses in A level Design. This included six colleges that the School was already developing a close relationship with and three other colleges.

We put an invite out to the colleges. We weren't quite sure how many students we were going to have and we had about 140 students from the different schools and colleges which gave us a bit of a logistic problem in terms of being an art or design studio they tend to be geared up for 30, 40 people. We had to run these sessions three times and then we had two master classes so that was actually six sessions I had to run. That was probably one issue that I had in terms of finding the additional time to run these. But I think the value of doing those and what we do is we get feedback sheets from the students so the partnership team got that information back to me fairly quickly on the first one so I was able to tweak some of the things that we did to just make it more appropriate. We had lots of interaction, lots of good stuff they could take away and then use not only on this project but we were giving them skills they could actually use within their own curriculum which was the important thing.

So for instance, one of the master class sessions was on idea generating techniques—what are some of the problems that we come across when we're trying to think of ideas, how to overcome those barriers, how to influence others and we did some work on intellectual property. But importantly when you start with a blank sheet of paper how do you get a range of ideas down there and then how do you take them forward? So we did a number of some creative thinking techniques and some we've been developing ourselves here.

So we gave those as tools to the students which they could then use within the project and use later on in life. So that was received very well. We also then did a second master class which was all about advance manufacturing techniques because with IKEA it all about the flat pack technology. We also got the students to book in with IKEA to have a session there on both marketing and manufacturing and also to see how some of these units are stripped down and put together. . . . We also delivered these as master classes—one on advance manufacturing, so although they perhaps weren't using all the advance manufacturing we were showing them we were trying to inspire them in terms of what is available.

Working with the SDP-funded University partnership team the School was able to send student ambassadors to the participating colleges to help mentor the students who were involved in the competition

> Our HE second and third years paired up . . . and went into each of the colleges on a regular basis to work with the tutors and do some mentoring and feedback tutorial sessions with the students giving them guidance on the project either in terms of their methodology or in terms of what they were producing. It just helped drive the project forward and gave it the level of engagement that it needed to get a good result. What we were aiming to do is by the time we got through to April—and this was a year-long project I forgot to mention. So we started in October and we purposely left it quite a long duration so that tutors were able to allow students to fit this in around the curriculum somewhere. Some would embed it within the curriculum and some would do it in their own time outside of the curriculum. I'll come back to that later.

> But the climax of this is we would have a presentation awards evening in late April . . . We had entries from each of the colleges—they'd already had a pre-selection in conjunction with our mentors and their tutors they'd pre-selected some of the work which would then represent their school or college in an exhibition. With the partnership team we booked out the conference facilities rooms, there's a couple of suites and we put up an exhibition of work. In the evening we then invited the students that had been involved, their teachers and the students' parents to the award ceremony and representatives from IKEA. We had a judging panel which was our staff, IKEA and the partnership team and we awarded prizes which were pre-agreed again with IKEA. . . . There were drinks and canapés so it was really like an opening of a new gallery show or something. It worked very effectively.

> To complete the cycle with the three winning designs we worked with IKEA to source those products and then we gave those winners a further opportunity to come to the University and work in our workshops with our technicians to actually build the product that they'd designed . . . . And we set up a display in IKEA in their new community engagement area and we exhibited the work there with an explanation of the project, how it works, how we're engaging with colleges.

So for us we suddenly discovered this is actually quite a good marketing tool. Previously we'd gone to all of the individual colleges in key weeks of the year when the students are looking to complete their UCAS application forms and that's very time consuming. But what we were actually finding is that because we'd been developing this relationship over the year with the tutors, the tutors are now recommending that their students actually check us out, have a look to see what we have on offer here. And there is one college in particular who I know produce students who essentially will get an A in their A Level programme. They traditionally had sent them to other universities and now they're telling those students to come and look at us and this year for the first time we've actually got applicants coming in from there which helps us in terms of getting a good mix of students from different backgrounds again.

Recognising real world experience and achievement

A Real World Certificate was developed and piloted to enable students to gain recognition for the experiences students gained when working with employer designed projects, part-time jobs and any other employment or career relevant experiences. A second stage of development, supporting deeper levels of student engagement in reflective learning, was rolled out across the School in Y2. The Careers Service recognised the value of the Certificate and it is now being offered to all students studying at the University by the Employability and Enterprise Team.

The Real World Certificate has a link on 'MyCourse'. The idea is that the student, having completed a live project or had any employer engagement could enrol on the Certificate [to gain university recognition] it was no extra work for them and it wasn't complicated in any way. We worked extensively with the learning technology team to make this happen. Students go onto MyCourse, they enrol on the Real World Certificate and then they go through a series of questions about what they've done and what the engagement was, because it might have been work placement, it might have been a live project or it might have been a site visit or whatever. So they just choose what it is. And we want them to actually think about the experience, so we put reflection in there, so what do you think you gained? . . . The idea is that they can print them or they can have an electronic version of it which they can then put in their e portfolio through Mahara . . . .

CHALLENGES

It would be surprising indeed if the extensive and rapid development work that was undertaken within the School was completed without any difficulty. Challenges to accomplishing change were identified by participants in three main areas namely: 1) time and timing, 2) sufficiency of resources for some projects where the amount of resource was underestimated or could not be estimated in advance, 3) slow responses of some institutional systems and procedures to accommodate or exploit the innovation or provide information to people engaged in innovation

Time & timing

This challenge relates to both the amount of time available to busy academics with teaching responsibilities to accomplish change within the University's SDP annual cycle of activity (July to July), and to the particular demands of some projects which had critical deadlines to be met within short timelines. The latter was compounded by what some participants believed were slow responses of some institutional systems as challenges emerged in the course of executing the project. Some examples of specific issues are described below.

> We need to get better at planning for these things because . . . . you don't know whether the bid's live or not until quite late on and then all of a sudden, you've only got a year to deliver and we all know in academics' terms, a year is not very long to make things happen . . . we could plan the year before with what we know we need to do for the following year, we would be in a better position whereas actually, it's always backtracking on the hoof a little bit because the minute term starts teaching takes over. Actually the financial deadline for the next year is June which means you're going to do your final report in May and you must have delivered by April. You know what I mean? It's very, very tight so really, it's just a six-month window to do all these things.

> Time, it was a massive constraint. I don't think it is always realized how much time it takes to actually complete something or when you have to give the time . . . . Trend Moda will be on Skype at home on a Saturday. What about . . . can we approve this? Send this picture. We are going to get these samples today. Can you do that? Can you do this? Can you send this back? The immediacy of stuff had to be done because of the critical path.

> I could never have anticipated how much time I would have put into this. When we were discussing how much time we felt we needed as allowance to do this, you know, six hours a week it sounded fairly reasonable at the time. But having now gone through the process it has absolutely not been enough time.

Matching resources to tasks

One of the problems with innovating is that it is very difficult to calculate the amount of time needed before a project has begun and sometimes impossible to anticipate where the problems are going to occur, especially as some may be beyond the control of the innovator. Furthermore, once resources have been allocated it is usually not possible to gain more resource if the estimate has proved to be inadequate.

> I think rather than time, more resources would have been helpful because . . . . each of these projects, didn't realise how big the project was, so ideally each of those projects should have had an extra person giving their assistance and that would have been very helpful to all of them.

> I was getting I think six hours a week in which to do this. But to be developing twelve short courses that are to be accredited . . . all at once with externals helping for some of them and not for others, six hours doesn't reflect in any way, shape or form the amount of time that I put into these. I was doing a considerable amount of reading through materials and feeding back during my own time in the evenings and weekends. Without that, it would not have happened.

> I guess the biggest surprise was that there wasn't the amount of support that I thought there would be and how much longer all of this took. I asked the question [could I have more support?] and the response was, if I could find someone to replace me in my other responsibilities then okay. But I was struggling to find people just to work with me on the project, let alone replace me in my normal work . . . There is no one to replace you.

Lack of agility of institutional systems and procedures

Innovation at the chalk face always poses challenges for institutional systems which have been established to support more standardised practices. Systems and procedures often cannot adapt at the same speed as the innovation is taking place and to the innovators this can be a source of frustration. Sometimes it wasn't that systems and procedures were absent, more that communication between an innovator and the people responsible for the system faltered. Some examples of these situations are described below.

> 1: we set about a collegiate range, developing a branded collegiate range . . .—then we started talking to manufacturers and you get into university financial regs. To get somewhere near competitive to what we could afford we found a company in Turkey. Now, of course you get into contracting this was over £20k, three bids. How do you get different companies to actually then put in their costing in line with the University, they want payment up front. The University doesn't pay for things up front, only on delivery, enormous amounts of problems with that. But we did it by the skin of our teeth. On, I think, virtually the last week before the financial year ended, we managed to get them delivered and then paid for and the company went with it but the company aren't used to being paid after the delivery; they're used to being paid before. So actually, the kind of agility of the University to work with external forces is really difficult.

> 2: We developed eleven Professional Development Units getting them through our quality and assessment regs was very difficult because they had to be turned around very quickly. It wasn't that you could just put them through a validation event, that would take a year. These had to be put through within weeks and we . . . . and the people that helped get that through still found it difficult. They weren't actually approved through the quality process until probably April/May time, so that was a long haul with a lot of frustration.

> 3: we've had inquiries come in to do these PDUs but getting people enrolled and paid, paid up to do them through the website is now a source of frustration . . . when they get to the website, it needs to say, enrol here, make it very simple because these are short thirteen-week courses. No one's going to want to do much more than fill out a form and pay their money. So it's about logging on, paying their money and then having an enrolment process that can adapt and get them through the system.

4: We did what we called a Real World certificate which was when the student went on work experience or had any live industrial engagement. What I wanted them to do was log the details on Mycourse and then they get a certificate. We'd also then get a database of where they've worked, what experience they've gained; we'd also get then percentages of work experience, students, and lots of good stuff going on. It was like asking for the moon to get that to happen, and it still hasn't happened. When staff face these brick walls they tend to start giving up because you're against a bigger force. The good news is we found a work around.

5: [it was] a constant battle because I always felt as though I was having to push other departments and other areas of the University to give me answers to questions that I had. It felt as though the answers didn't exist at that point in time, but I needed them. I needed to know answers to certain questions and I needed some kind of framework for me to be working within and none existed. Eventually I got a hold of the guidelines for developing professional development units from our quality department, I was actually quite aggrieved at the time that they existed and I hadn't been alerted to the fact that that existed before I felt I had just floundered around and come up with my own template and I looked really uninformed to my externals as well.

Value and benefits of being involved in the SDP

From the interviews, it is clear that the SDP provided:

- a stimulus for decision making, resource allocation and action
- a tool with which to engage the institution in considering new types of learner, new forms of learning and relationships
- a framework within which developmental activities were undertaken
- an accountability framework within which activity and outcomes had to be justified and accounted for additional resources to enable new activity to be undertaken.

But in what ways did it help and enable individuals and teams to bring about change? Here are some the ways that participants recognised.

It gave people confidence to do new things

> it has given the School and the staff within it a confidence to move forward and make change knowing that actually it was fully supported by the University

It enabled deeper more productive relationships to develop

> [For example with] B&Q we might have managed to get the students a day going to their Head Office. Whereas the relationship going through the SDP process has now turned that into a Memorandum of Understanding with clear aims and objectives for both sides. I think the formality of it that the SDP has allowed has been vital to give them an identity [within the University].

It resulted in new capacity and expertise to undertake the work necessary to bring about change

> The SDP funded my work . . . So the SDP created the resource which was me and the filmmaker and *Jenny* who helped co-ordinate some of the activities between the different participants.

It enabled feasibility studies to be conducted in relation to the use of technology to support learning and enable the costs to be evaluated

> It's allowed us to establish whether it's feasible for us as an institution to start moving towards online distance provision and [to understand] the resourcing that's required in order to do that effectively. We've established that effective development and delivery of online courses . . . does need to be highly resourced and we're now just moving to the point institutionally of recognising that if we want to continue to provide distance learning in this way, we need to have members of our team as part of the core business of the University.

It reduced the risk and anxiety associated with trying to do things that might not be successful

> . . . in terms of anxiety levels our buffer was the strategic development funding. We've had failures. We've had projects that have gone nowhere and we've had to put a lot of work into them, so those were risks but they would've been much higher risks if it was being funded

centrally because in a sense, we would've been much more answerable to having results.

It encouraged experimentation and helped people think and act on a scale to provide real world experiences for students

It allowed you to think on a different scale, because sometimes the scale in academia is just within the unit . . . . this actually made it larger, bigger and real across several units . . . . That is what made it quite special . . . students are learning and it is real and you are getting assessed on something that is real as well . . . to actually do it within the course is quite unique.

It conferred status and authority to help overcome some of the organisational barriers to change

. . . . the good thing about the SDP, it gave the project the clout to make it happen. That was quite important because if this was just a project that I was pushing through on a school budget, it wouldn't have happened. All those barriers would have just kept up but the barriers came down because everybody knew it was an SDP project.

It has enabled people to become much more in tune with and sympathetic to university thinking about the future direction for the organisation

as an experience, I think it's been enriching and it would be good for other people to have experienced it in the way that I have. But in this . . . privileged position because I've [been able to develop deeper] understandings of the bigger picture, and feed that down to staff in a way that's completely the right fit . . . I think we're in a fantastic position now to move with the University in all the changes its making so I feel quite confident that we understand where [the University is] going.

It enabled participants' to be creative: to actualise themselves

But perhaps the hidden value of SDP is in the way it released and enabled ordinary (actually extra ordinary) people to be creative. To realise some of their creativity and to actualise themselves through their inventions of new educational practices and all the intricate detail of how such creations are brought into existence within a busy and challenging organisational setting.

I think when you are developing any aspect of the curriculum you are being 'creative', you have the feeling that you have the opportunity to 'shape' what is available for students to learn and you are 'creating' that learning experience. I personally find that a creative process. It isn't entirely without edges though, there are boundaries and quality considerations to work within but still, there is room within the set frameworks to 'create' the richness of content and the teaching and learning strategies that encourage an inspirational learning process

This is a most uplifting message with which to conclude this chapter. The idea that people are able to actualise themselves through their work and in this process they help the University to realise its vision of itself.

CHAPTER 6

Using an Innovation Fund to Accomplish Strategic Change

INTRODUCTION

Organisations use many strategies to stimulate activity that is more likely to lead to innovative change but perhaps the most popular is an Innovation Fund whereby a sum of money is set aside explicitly for the purpose of funding project-based activity. Members of the organisation are invited to bid for funding to resource a project that meets certain criteria. The assumptions in this approach are:

1) that there are people or groups of people in the organisation that have ideas that if they are given the time and resources could turn these ideas into useful innovation
2) that additional resources will encourage individuals or groups of people to undertake such work in addition to their existing commitments
3) that the outcomes from such funding will create useful innovation that will either make the organisation more efficient (reducing costs), effective (making better use of existing resources) or profitable (generating additional revenue), or the process of innovating will expand know how to enable other innovation to be accomplished at some future date.

This chapter describes one of the strategies used to stimulate change and innovation within the University's Strategic Development Programme, namely the Innovation Fund. Participants involved in 12 of the fourteen projects were interviewed and their stories transcribed and evaluated for clues as to how they accomplished the changes they were seeking to make.

Innovation fund

The purpose of the SDP Innovation Fund was to encourage individuals or groups to bid for funding (up to £15,000) to develop new practice in three key areas to support the targets set within the Outputs and Outcomes document of the Strategic Development Programme Plan, namely:

- *Developing Business Responsive Programmes*—working with employers to develop programmes to fit their needs, work based learning.
- *Delivery to and support of different types of learner* e.g. part-time, mature students
- *Progression from FE to HE*—e.g. curriculum enrichment and alignment with schools and colleges.

About £100,000 was set aside for the initiative and bidding was open to any member of staff from Faculties or Central Services. The opportunity was intended to encourage 'ordinary' members of staff to bring their ideas forward and to get more people involved in the strategic change process.

> I think for me it was about, trying to get the University to react flexibly, quickly and do what it said it was going to do on time as well as getting some, hopefully, useful outputs for the individuals concerned and help achieve some of the SDP outputs and outcomes. (Director SDP Project Team).

However, to ensure alignment with existing or planned activities, project proposers were asked to discuss their ideas with their managers and it was expected that submissions would be signed off by their Faculty Dean or Head of Service.

Bidding process

University staff were made aware of the Innovation Fund via email and the SDP website in March 2010 with a proposal submission deadline of May 31st 2010.

> We put out the bid on the web, people are quite used to doing that because they have the teaching/learning fund bidding and waited for things to come forward, which they did from all areas, both service areas and academic areas and pretty wide ranging.

The SDP Project Team wanted to minimise the bureaucracy involved in bidding. A simple template was provided for what in most cases amounted to a two page document. Project bids were expected to include the following information:

1. Overall purpose and description of the idea and intended work

2. Explanation of how the project would contribute to achieving progress in the key areas, including expected outputs; how the project integrated with or supported the Faculty or Service Plan; the benefits in terms of staff development
3. Timescale and key milestones to enable evaluation of progress
4. Resources—costs—academic/non-academic   staffing together with non-pay from within the Faculty or Service and any additional support from other services.

Bid documents were reviewed by the SDP Project Team who also decided on the allocation of funding.

> It was a very simple process for them, they had to say what it was for, how it fitted in with the outputs and outcomes and the resources that they were going to use on it, how much it was going to cost and a planned timeline—when they were going to start and finish. It was a very lightweight process and as long as their Dean agreed and the Heads of School knew about it and it met those objectives, they got the money. So it was a very quick process and we were the decision makers (Programme Director).

An assumption was made that if the Dean (and relevant Head of School) or Head of Service, had seen the proposal that the project broadly fitted with Faculty or Service strategic plans.

> It wasn't so much about obtaining the Dean's permission as exchanging information about what was going on within their faculty . . . . we put that safeguard in just to make sure the Dean and the Head of School actually knew what was going on and approved of it . . . We didn't get any of them sent back by the Dean. But they liked the comfort of knowing what was going on in their faculty (Programme Director).

Bids were often provided in draft form and the SDP Project Team worked with some of the bidders to improve the bid.

> Some people came in for advice. Others we helped them move their ideas in a slightly different direction. We were quite concerned about sustainability, so the question was, okay, so when you've done this now what are you going to do next because you won't get funding for it again so what is the sustainable position?
>
> Some of the proposals were a bit difficult to untangle what they were trying to do. But if they had the Dean's

support and we could talk to them we thought they might be worthwhile . . . we were quite flexible, because what we were trying to do was to draw people in, first of all to engage them in the process. We were also trying to get them to say what they were going to spend and go and do what they said they were going to do in a very rapid time scale. These projects were only for 12 months—the funding was removed if they didn't deliver.

At the end of the bidding process there were 15 bids involving nineteen members of staff. There were sufficient funds to cover all the bids and all except one was funded.

Progress was monitored by the SDP team. Near the end of each quarter a member of the SDP Team would speak to the project leader to check on progress and write a short summary of the conversation.

[It was a] lightweight reporting process, our project coordinator would phone them up every three months before management board and say, "so what are you doing, what have you done, tell me about?" and would write it up so it was reporting light, but we would also then monitor their financial spend. If nothing was happening we would phone them up and say, so you don't seem to have spent any money, you said you were going to spend X, Y and Z what are you doing, do you need any help and support to move this through?

Project leaders completed a summary report at the end of the project. A standard template was provided but there was quite a lot of variation in reporting formats.

INNOVATION PROJECTS

A list of funded innovation projects is given Table 6.1 and short summaries of each project are provided in Appendix 1. Projects covered a diverse range of themes including the provision of information, research to aid decisions about course provision, development of new professional courses, development of new technology aimed at providing better access to existing services, gaining accreditation to run courses by other providers, creating new more engaging and work-relevant student experiences, relationship and partnership building.

Proposals had to identify the particular SDP strategic themes they were addressing. Of the fourteen projects that were funded twelve addressed the theme of business responsive programmes, four aimed to help support different types of non-traditional learner, and one (possibly two) helped to support the HE-FE progression agenda. The Innovation Fund appears to have attracted most interest from staff who wanted to improve the business responsiveness of curricula and employability of students.

Who were the innovators?

The people who bid for and/or who delivered projects included middle managers (sometimes as a leader rather than doer but sometimes as a doer), academics (including a Reader, Senior Lecturer, Lecturers and Associate Lecturers), and people involved in delivering central services like library staff. More males than females made successful bids (10 male and 3 female). There were 5 bids from FTEC (now MARTEC), 5 from FBSE (including a joint bid), 2 from FCIS (now FCIS) and 3 from LIS (including 2 library service bids and 1 joint bid with FBSE). The characteristics of the people who got involved are revealed in their stories but one general characteristic is that they are people who liked to get involved in doing new things.

Table 6.1 Innovation projects funded through the Strategic Development Programme

Project	Faculty or Service	Strategic theme Business Responsive Programmes Delivery/support different types of learner Progression from FE to HE
1 Information for non-traditional learners	FTEC but x-inst.	Delivery/support different types of learner Progression from FE to HE
2 Built environment course	FTEC	Business Responsive Programmes
3 Acoustics Accreditation	FTEC	Business Responsive Programmes
4 Southampton Emergency Medicine Education project	FTEC	Business Responsive Programmes
5 BiB collaboration for employability and international exchange	FTEC	Business Responsive Programmes
6 Active Ageing	FBSE	Business Responsive Programmes
7 PDU's for football administrators	FBSE	Business Responsive Programmes (PDUs) Delivery/support different types of learner
8 Mahara Lite—Application development	LIS & FBSE	Business Responsive Programmes Delivery/support different types of learner *Inclusive and flexible forms of HE that meet market needs* Progression from FE to HE

9 Instant messaging enquiry service	LIS—library	Delivery/support different types of learner
10 Referencing reading lists	LIS—library	Delivery/support different types of learner
11 Partnerships working	FBSE	Business Responsive Programmes *enhancing students employability*
12 Sport for social change	FBSE	Business Responsive Programmes
13 Pop up exhibitions for fine arts	FBSE	Business Responsive Programmes *enhancing students employability*
14 Antigone—collaborative interactive storytelling	FCIS	Business Responsive Programmes

How were resources used?

Table 6.2 shows twenty two different uses of SDP funding but the main uses were 1) to buy out staff time from teaching, service delivery or management in order to participate in innovation or 2) to employ staff on temporary contracts.

Table 6.2 Use of SDP funding

Use of Funding	1	2	3	4	5	6	7	8	9	10	11	12	13	14
Buy out staff time		√			√	√	√	√	√		√	√	√	√
New (temporary) appointment	√		√	√	√							√	√	
External consultant								√		√				√
Technical support													√	
Administrative support		√												
Guest lecturers (stipend/travel)													√	
Intern/RA						√								
Job shop students		√												√
Customer services													√	
Training staff			√											
Travel—external visits/ visitor expenses		√			√		√		√	√			√	√
Participation in external conferences		√												
Staff development day					√									
Marketing products/services							√		√	√			√	

Purchase of licensed product								√					
Equipment													√
Rewards for students								√	√				
Hosting symposia												√	
Workshops	√												
Student project film in partnership with employers										√			
Rent space—city centre shop for exhibition												√	
Equipment hire												√	

Innovation curve

If we think of innovation as a process from conception to the realisation of a new product, practice or experience then different projects engaged with different parts of this continuum. Figure 6.1 represents the innovation process as a series of steps from the initial idea to the conversion of the idea into products, services and experiences. Eight of the funded projects reached the point where they have been realised. One project was only concerned with research to inform a decision to progress. Three projects are at the design and build stage and have potential to move along the curve to implementation.

Figure 6.1 Distribution of projects according to the stage they had reached on the innovation curve in May 2012

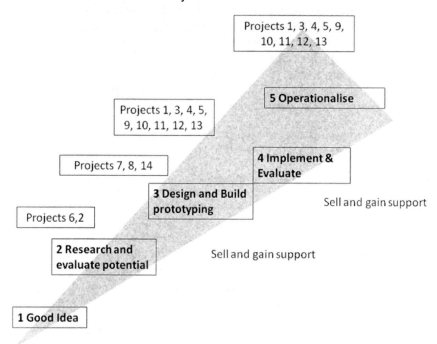

ACCOMPLISHING INNOVATION

We can see and experience the results of change in the form of new practices, experiences, designs, courses, technologies etc but we cannot appreciate the thought, effort and emotion that has gone into their creation. There are two ways of gaining insights into the ways in which such changes are accomplished. The first is to analyse documents that explain how change is intended to be brought about: the second to talk to the people who made change happen. Both of these techniques are employed in the next section. Twelve of the people involved in the fourteen innovation projects were interviewed using a semi-structured process. Their interviews were recorded and transcribed and their stories are used to build a narrative of change. Names have been changed to preserve anonymity.

At the outset, it should be said that people recognise that it isn't easy to bring about significant change in a university.

> *Edward:* because I've worked in the game for a long time . . . I just know how difficult it is to implement change. . . . . from a pragmatic, practical point of view, I know how difficult it

is to effect change in higher education. I've seen that from the point of view of a course leader for instance and as an academic leader in terms of trying to promote change in teaching and learning . . . . and there are no doubt all sorts of reasons for that. Resistance to change and time and all the rest of it and also you've got to—particularly within academia, you've got to produce some evidence of the beneficial effects—or some compelling rationale for change and some evidence for why one should change.

If bringing about change in a university is so tough, why do people get involved in trying to do it?

Why do people get involved in innovation?

A range of reasons and motives were given for why people got involved in SDP innovation. Some people just like to get involved in change. Many of the participants in the innovation project had a history of involvement in change they see it as a way of achieving what they personally value as well as contributing something that will be valuable to others—especially students. Getting involved is a way of being who they want to be—of creating meaning and purpose in their professional life.

> *Edward:* because I'm always trying to do things that are relevant to and meet the needs of the faculty and the University, but at the same time of course if they can meet my needs, then everybody wins. While it's always a temptation to kind of put together a project that meets your own personal needs, I'm always looking to make sure that everybody's needs are met and generally I guess if you're going to get funding, then really you've got to make sure that you address the needs of the funders.

> *Sophie:* It was something that sparked my imagination. I'm always keen on thinking about ways in which new technology can be used to improve the experience for students and more specifically, improve the experience of using our library . . . . if it means we can get more people involved in using libraries if we're offering different ways of accessing it and making better use of the information, that's something I'm interested in doing.

Some participants with management positions used SDP to secure additional resources to achieve what they personally valued. The time for development in some service roles is very limited and/or episodic. SDP afforded a more sustained opportunity for doing something different.

> *Henry*: Obviously there was a funding resource but what that offered was ring fenced, concentrated effort on one particular area . . . . the summer tended to be the time that new things happened or things were upgraded. I looked at it sometimes and thought, well, I've been here 10 years but I've only actually had 10 opportunities to do something.

But it's not just about a funding source: there is always a deeper story.

> *Henry:* I think I fall into the category of being the champion of it. I wanted to do a research project to start with, or get some research, because I could see a need. People had said, "Is this available? Is there a mobile version of this?" So when we'd introduced an e-portfolio which was very much desktop computing based, a few people said, "Is there a mobile version of this" And the answer at that time was, "No, there isn't. You can use the desktop version on your mobile but it's not very nice and not very easy to use. There isn't a dedicated mobile version, there isn't an app."

Some participants were prompted by a senior colleague to consider the opportunity and then supported by their colleague in bidding and implementing the project.

> *Emma:* This whole project actually started with an email from [a colleague] saying, 'Oh this looks interesting, shall we have a look?' And we were like, 'Oh yeah, why not?'

For others, involvement in SDP innovation was part of a personal mission to encourage development of a new curriculum area that they valued, and to use the SDP opportunity to make a stronger case to give greater attention to the area they were seeking to promote.

Joseph: this new area was going to be a challenge because there is no mechanism in the Faculty to support this. So I was working long hours because I had to prove the case. I had to make them start seeing that there was a niche area here which could be developed and this was a way of proving a case in a sense. It was about . . . [me saying] we need to do this. I was going to do it. I mean I worked extra hard to create the MA without the SDP. I think for me the SDP became an incentive, to help me prove the case.

In a few cases innovators indicated that they were trying to solve a specific and definable problem.

> *Emma:* From my perspective reading lists are always a really, really sticky problem because the students want

> them and the academics don't always provide them in a way the students want or don't give them to the library. They are time restricted as well and the librarians want them for buying the stock. It is always a sort of a messy area. We've had the reading list system for a very long time. It's not very good. In my subjects reading lists are quite important . . . they use a lot of journal articles. It was a case of we set up a project to try and find an alternative because it wasn't meeting our needs

In other cases innovators were exploring the potential of a situation or opportunity and their passion for innovation was aligned in a more general way to the needs and interests of their School and the University (it was a good thing to do) rather than attempting to solve a specific problem or achieve something with immediate value.

> *James:* . . . it was . . . personal from the point of view . . . [that] the impetus for developing it came from myself and a colleague. We were both interested in developing this area. In a . . . broader context the sort of technical, aesthetic and production processes that were involved is something that we . . . wanted to bring into the curriculum within the School . . . . it was signed off by the Dean . . . as a kind of good thing to do for the School and . . . . when the bid was written, it was very much written . . . with the recognition of its value to a School rather than it being a kind of isolated research project. I mean it was really located in students, teaching and learning, research into teaching and those kind of things.

> *Henry:* It's looking at the wider landscape and what students were doing and more and more coming in with their own devices and so on. So, I thought maybe there is something about this. So then I did really push on and champion it and get the funding to do research and say, "Right, am I just mad or is there a real need or is this a pet project or what have you?" So hence wanting to do a research project first and happy to stop at that point almost. It may sound like wasted resource or money to research something and say, "Actually, no, we won't do that." But that's still cheaper than going on and just doing the project and then discovering at the end that nobody wants it. I do think things need to be backed up with valid research.

Another reason people got involved in innovation was to satisfy a deep intrinsic need. Using Maslow's (Maslow 1940) classification of needs, it would be grounded in the desire for self-actualisation.

> *Edward:* The bottom line motivation actually is to do something different and interesting and developmental, above and beyond the normal stuff that we do. I know there is the teaching and the admin, you know some of that is great of course, but it's nice to have a bit of spice in one's academic life. Others take a different view of course, they'll just settle for whatever.

Taken together we can see that the desire to be involved originates in a multiplicity of personal motivations, reasons and contexts, and in most cases an intermingling or coming together of personal and organisational reasons and values. But what shines through all the personal stories of innovation is the passion of individuals to turn their ideas into something useful and valuable. To extend educational opportunities and improve the learning experiences of students, to make education more relevant to particular business/industry sectors and to enhance the overall reputation of the University and their area within the University.

> *Robert:* So for me the project ticked both the corporate and personal boxes. It was something really important for us to do to help us further embed the ourselves within the industry at a time when we'd just launched the research centre. But that all comes back to me anyway, wanting to build from my own personal perspective, wanting to build the brand of the centre because it opens up doors for us in other ways. It opens up access to sample populations which academics and other universities might not normally gain access to. It further raises the profile of the institution so that it makes it easier for us to place our students at clubs, and it further embeds us within an industry which has typically been referred to as a closed shop. But because of our approach we're very much on the inside of that closed shop and we can have conversations with people and bring people into the University who otherwise wouldn't perhaps go to other places. And what we were doing was embedded within all of that, so there was no sense that the two were mutually exclusive, they were very much connected.

Where do ideas for innovation originate?

> *Between stimulus and response there is a space and in that space is our freedom to chose, and in that choice lies our freedom and happiness . . . . Stephen Covey*

Ideas that lead to change/innovation are born in the space between stimulus and response but what causes the ideas that get turned into new practices, services or things to be born?

In some cases the idea for an innovation project stemmed from what was already being done. Often it was rooted in a dissatisfaction with current practice and a desire to improve. The overwhelming driver was to improve the learning and learning experience of students.

> *Sophie:* I was interested in the concept of having instant messaging available at Solent and I'd seen it in action at other university libraries and saw what an extra benefit it offered to the students. So I took this to [my manager] and discussed whether there would be a possibility of doing something like this. [He] recommended that I bid for SDP funding

> *William:* (talking about the idea for pop up art exhibitions)— what we used to do was to look at two things in the course, one was basic requirements such as how you really approach a statement about art work, how you then negotiate the art world, and then how you try and get exhibitions of your work. So those three areas were the sort of areas we were looking at and we did that for two or three years. Then when SDP came along we thought that we could do much more . . . Because what we would do is we would go to say somewhere like Southampton City Art Gallery when they're in the middle of doing an exhibition so the students would see that there's an immense amount of work goes on behind the scenes, and some of them would even work for them for a while, you know, not internships but just go and work for them. We saw the opportunity of having two elements to it, theory and practice, and also the opportunity of running one into the other. . . . . We saw this opportunity of talking to the students about exhibitions and exhibition making, how they put up works and how they decide what works are going to be on show . . . and then going on to actually putting that work on in a public space.

Ideas were also inspired through discovering what other universities were doing.

> *Sophie:* I went to a meeting at the tail end of 2008 in Winchester, it was actually a meeting on Asperger's awareness so it shows the benefit of attending professional development, even if it doesn't appear to be directly relevant. I got talking to somebody from Bournemouth University, they talked a lot about how this was a new thing that they'd introduced and how it's proven popular. So I came back and had a go at playing around with how I might introduce it here.

Another source of stimulation was where there was an opportunity to improve the students' experience of using a institutional system. For example, in the case of the Mahara-lite project the idea to drive innovation came about through trying to enhance support for the learning of students who were working at sea. Such students have limited access to the internet therefore cannot access their on-line institutional-hosted e-portfolios (called Mahara). The idea was to create a simplified ('lite') version of the e-portfolio which students could use to store evidence of learning on computers or mobile devices while they were at sea, and then upload their evidence and artefacts of learning as soon as they could connect to the internet.

> *Henry:* we have quite a lot of maritime students . . . they are working at sea for three months or six weeks, whatever with very limited internet connections. But at the same time they are obliged to come back with a portfolio of signed off sheets . . . There's a loss of communication between the tutor back on land and the student out at sea somewhere on their placement.
>
> So one thought was, can they get their competency signed off online and can they provide evidence through that? Where most people will have some sort of mobile device or access to a computer on a limited basis out at sea, they can still record their reflections. They might be in a meeting, they might have done some training, they might have done something, taken a photograph of something, jotted a few notes down. But they can put the basics of their evidence together on their mobile device. When they next get to a port with some sort of internet connection, wifi cafe or even back at Solent, they can press the synchronise button and push it all back up to our servers.

> So although they're still disconnected from us, they're not entirely disconnected. It also means they can do that at the point of learning, at the point of reflection, go back to their cabins or whatever, make some notes, put them up online, when they've next got a connection it's synched up, the tutor can look at that. It means that they don't have to rush into an internet cafe and buy an hour's time and type like mad. They can just gather this evidence as they go.

In other cases, the problem, challenge or opportunity was not so concrete or clear. In this case ideas for innovation were motivated by the need to find things out in order to clarify the problem or opportunity before it could be addressed in more concrete terms. This was the case in The School of Sport, Tourism and Languages which wanted to examine the potential for new courses that catered for development needs of workers/employers in residential homes that care for the elderly.

> *Tom:* We have got a number of ideas of where we could develop, particularly into the professional development area. So short courses, professional development units or accredited courses or non-credit bearing possibly. Working with industry and utilizing the expertise we have got . . . . to diversify opportunities. It is also to have an opportunity for us to have a greater impact in a wider community . . . So we have these ideas but actually it is a long way from an idea to actually having anything concrete and some of the ideas you have probably aren't going to work anyway. But, it takes quite a lot of time to do the research to find out what is the potential of an opportunity.

Another stimulus was the desire to secure funding for an idea that already existed: an idea relating to a piece of academic research that was linked to the creation of new technology, that could, in time, be utilised in an educational context.

> *James:* When I saw the [SDP] remit I didn't really think it was very appropriate to the project that I had in mind. The project that got funded wasn't something written for a [SDP] funding bid, I mean it was something that had been developed for [research and enterprise funding] a year previously, it was a project looking for funding . . . . I bid for SDP funding to do essentially the same thing, it was to start building this infrastructure and then to sort of propagate it through papers, conferences and stuff like that, to kind of get it going . . .

Other ideas came through research and enterprise groups seeking to develop what they were doing.

> *Matt:* Having got a background in acoustics myself I started developing a small group in acoustics. It started out of an R&E project about three/four years ago where we got some funding to do some work on environmental noise, employed a researcher on that project and we've since employed other people in the department who have acoustic backgrounds as well and we've gradually developed a small research specialist group, acoustic specialist group that has a blend of industrial consultancy expertise and research expertise . . . One of the things we identified early on was that we wanted to go for some form of accreditation in order to be able to generate . . . an income stream. So funding by SDP enabled us to go through the processes of getting accreditation.

Another type of stimulus for innovation was the desire to develop further an existing and productive relationship so that ultimately, more value could be gained from the relationship for the University, students and the members of staff involved in the relationship.

> *Edward:* there was this relationship with an international college, which is very important to the University . . . I have been involved with that and developing that collaboration from the beginning . . . back in 1995 and I know them very, very well indeed. . . . . This particular institution in Germany has more of a focus than we had at the time on employability . . . So I had the idea which I put to them, I said, "Look we've got this SDP programme, one of the strands is employability and employability and employment are very important to you, can we do something together?" We were looking to do a project that would take the collaboration further and higher and onwards . . . . And they said "great". So I put this bid together . . . .

Personal relationships, like the one described above, provide opportunity for the collaborative development of innovative ideas that can be applied outside the institution.

> *Matt:* The project . . . . came about through contacts I had at Southampton General Hospital. A friend of mine from a number of years back is a consultant in emergency medicine there and was responsible for the training of junior doctors. Now just after the working time directive

was applied to hospitals in 2008 he came to me with concerns about how they were going to manage junior doctors' training given the restrictions on the training hours that they traditionally put in and he wanted to move into a more technological means of being able to do some of the more didactic side of medical learning . . . . We wanted to do something reasonably innovative at the time and so we . . . ran a pilot study in 2008 when we actually got commissioned by the hospital to run a pilot study to produce a couple of lectures and trial them with . . . junior doctors to look at using green screen technology to embed the presenter into the presentation so they could have much more interaction with the audience than you would get from a normal streamed webcast or podcast.

So we did that as a trial run. We got a little bit of pilot research out of it, published a paper on it and then the next stage was we decided that this was something we could expand in ways that would benefit both the hospital and the University . . . . The idea for the SDP project was to fund a research assistant to manage the production of a number of videos and the development of a website making some use of the Solent online learning platform as well to be able to deliver this material to the junior doctors, do some research as it was going along and use that to refine the materials . . . .

In one case a School had been given a steer from a senior manager that an area was worth considering.

we had a bit of a steer from above from one of the Deputy Vice-Chancellors [who said] . . . 'Well actually you know there is potential here. Can we look at it?' So we had a bit of a steer from above and also it linked into stuff we were doing anyway. So it sort of fitted our needs and the University's interests.

Local strategic plans stimulated interest in certain areas, like the use of new technology, For example, the Learning and Information Services Plan contained the objective of, 'Developing innovative ways of communicating with and providing training and skills development for students and staff through face to face activities and by using web 2.0 technologies, multimedia, myCourse and the portal'.

> We wanted to trial an instant messaging enquiry service as we felt it would play a role in achieving many of the priorities of the LIS Service Plan. *Bid for SDP Funds*

What types of change were accomplished?

Change fundamentally involves people creating new activity within which new knowledge, capability, relationships, conversations, experiences and outcomes are accomplished. Looking beyond the particular contexts and objects for change five broad underlying patterns of activity emerge, namely:

1. conducting research to gain the knowledge to make decisions about what to do
2. designing and implementing new curricular/learning experiences that are more engaging and involve students in real world experiences and are designed to make them more employable
3. creating more opportunity for learning through postgraduate study or professional short courses.
4. organising events like conferences, workshops, discussion meetings to bring people together
5. creating new technology or adapting existing technology to meet the needs of local contexts

Conducting research to gain the knowledge to decide what to do next

One of the essential tasks in several projects was to evaluate the potential of an idea before committing to a significant development process. Such research is very focused on 'what we need to know in order to make a good decision about what to do next.' The Mahara Lite project illustrated the dynamics of a research process very well.

> *Henry:* I split the project in two parts. The first part was the research basically—seeing what do the tutors want, what do the students want, is there really a market for this? And also took that out to the wider community and there are some rudimentary e-portfolio apps around but they are not particularly good at meeting our needs. One of the things that came back mostly from students was 'I want to write'. There might be all this lovely other media and audio is okay for interviews and what have you, but mostly I want to write maybe a hundred words of notes and it's in there, it's in my box, it's in the bit that I'm doing and I've pushed it up to the e-portfolio system and there it's sat in my online

portfolio and then I can organise it later. The second thing they wanted was photographs.

We recognised there is a small but valid market of key users, students and courses and then a slightly wider market, I'd say "it would be nice" audience—a desirable rather than essential audience. From that there were some conversations with the [Mahara open-source] community, the platform we used was open source so all of it has been developed by the community.

There was one school in New Zealand who funded basic photograph uploading. They've done that, can we extend that? We don't want to do the same thing again. So I talked to the developers of that and a few other people in the community and got some feedback on what other people were doing in the community cos you don't wanna reinvent the wheel. So there was one part developed and not the rest—not the being able to do writing. That was the key thing—you want to enter things into your journal, blogging's quite a popular pastime. So it was, okay, can we extend what's there rather than completely reinvent the wheel.

Having completed this research the project leader had proved that the adaption of existing technology would have educational value to users and had identified the specific functionality that would add value and the people with the skills to create the functionality.

Henry: That kind of lead up to the second part of the bid which has now been approved, which is the development of the application. Again, not a huge amount of money, not a huge amount of time. I think the bigger and also the cheaper part, was the effort of putting in the research to get the specification right. . . . . That's been outsourced to the developers of some of the original [software] there's three or four key players who have done a lot of work on this and it's one of those who've already done a lot of work in this country for the wider platform. They've got a good reputation. It's days' work rather than months' work in their terms, or maybe a month's work at the top.

The funding has given that opportunity to do the research, find a need and instead of it sitting on a wish list for another 10 years, because it's one of those projects that's not essential, it probably never gets to the top of the list. I wouldn't say it would never get done, but it never hits the essentials. There's always things that are more essential like a new finance system or a student record system or things like that. They are essential.

In some cases, knowledge development revealed that the potential in the idea was limited. In one case a School wanted to know whether employers would value new opportunities for study at Masters level.

> *Omar:* we wanted to know what our employers thought about our courses and whether there was any opportunity for us to develop new courses and if we were to develop any Masters courses, would they support us? . . . We wanted to talk to employers and talk to the alumni and then see what has gone well and how we can improve ourselves as well. So it was mainly a finding out exercise . . . We surveyed about 300 employers who have seen at least three students over the last five years. Then we did the similar exercise with the last three years alumni who have gone out from our University courses, working in the industry. Then we organised two workshops for discussion.
>
> [We discovered that] they were not keen on distance learning at all, other than for CPD . . . . and they were not keen on the idea of Masters courses although they said they would consider it . . . they didn't want us to change our courses to a blended learning approach. So that confirmed that what we were doing was satisfying their need but they were not that keen with our new initiatives like blended or distance learning. So we have now concentrated on improving our existing course rather than changing or expanding it.

In another case a School wanted to assess the potential for providing personal training and exercise training for people who work in residential care homes for the elderly.

> *Tom:* We are aware of the demographic trends, the increasing age profile of the population, increasing care needs, the work in care homes, residential homes, nursing homes and all that sort of thing. We also recognize that the benefit of exercise is huge to the quality of life for those people. . . . . But is there a demand out there for it? Is that something that the care homes would want? Is it something they would be able to pay for in terms

of staff training and staff development? Are there other opportunities that we haven't thought of? Is it also possibly an opportunity to widen the experience of our students, maybe in a volunteering sense rather than necessarily in a commercial sense? So we wanted to ask 'What potential is there here?' To be honest, we didn't know very much about it. So the innovation fund came up and it seemed there was some funding here to do some of this market research to find out a little bit more about what we might do and how we can utilize the greater knowledge then to perhaps put into place some programmes that would be of value to this community . . . . so the project was about finding out about the opportunities. It was getting out there to find out what is happening in care homes, in terms of the numbers around, the type of activities that were going on, the type of funding arrangements and so on. Also doing market research with a number of those care homes.

We came to the conclusion that yes there is an interest, yes there is a need but actually the logistics of it make it very difficult because the staff are generally very poorly paid . . . . Management budgets are very tight and they are not prepared to fund significant amounts of training or even give staff time off to do any training. They basically wanted people to come and train their staff in their care home, one or two members of staff for £50 a day.

These findings revealed that the initial idea was not viable as an economic proposition and so staff did not progress to the design stage. However, the data that were gathered were not wasted as they can be utilised in the undergraduate curriculum and by other parts of the University.

Tom: we haven't actually changed the syllabus but that market research. is now being utilized in the curriculum. So the new knowledge, in terms of what is out there, what is going on and the potential and challenges we have demonstrated, is influencing students' learning.

Tom: One of the other things we have got is quite a reasonable database which could be used by other parts of the University. Because although we were focusing predominantly fitness and physical activity there is potential, and very similar sort of opportunities, to link into something like music therapy.

Creating new curricular experiences for undergraduate students

Three of the innovations involved significant changes to the curriculum in which students were encouraged and supported to engage in challenging real world situations outside the safety of the classroom. The first involved students in mounting a pop-up art exhibition in a public space, the second the involvement of groups of students in engaging in projects with organisations outside the University. In both cases the tutors saw themselves as the facilitators of complex, high risk processes in which students had to take responsibility for their own actions.

> *William*: We saw this opportunity of moving beyond talking to students about exhibitions and exhibition making . . . to involving them in putting that work on in a public space. . . . So the course started with theory and gradually moved into looking at their work, selecting their work and putting on a show, all the thinking and the practical work of mounting and making an exhibition, and then the students were told that they were going to do it themselves in the city centre. So they learnt how to put on an exhibition theoretically and then they actually had to go and do it.

> If you ask any of the students [what they got out of it] the first thing they will say was, they didn't realise how complex it all was. They will also say that they really loved the experience of working together and making a whole show for themselves . . . and the challenge of having to put themselves on the line in a public space.

Another curriculum project involved creating opportunities for students to work with the communities of Southampton.

> *Harry:* we were about to launch two brand new units on the sports coaching development degree. In that unit students in their second year are made to go out into Southampton, into the community, research the needs of the community, establish the contacts, all that sort of stuff, and then develop a coaching innovation project to meet the need they identified.

> So it's about how can they use coaching to examine community needs and identify how to deal with an issue . . . . Then in the third year unit, if they have a good project idea, they go out and deliver it in the communities. So it's a very practical way of giving them the opportunity to go out and get involved in a community and do all this

sort of stuff while they're studying their degree, rather than studying their degree and then trying to go out and do it.

Creating new curricular experiences for professional learners

Three projects had within them the idea of developing professional courses for potential new learners in particular work settings. One successful approach used was to gain accreditation and build capacity for delivering an existing course offered by a professional institution.

> *Matthew:* we looked at the Institute of Acoustics, which is the governing body of acoustics in the UK. We wanted accreditation from the Institution of Acoustics to run their training courses. They have a number of professional certification-type courses which are rated at usually M level credits, ... and because they are very highly regarded their qualifications are recognised internationally. There are premium price products and we figured as an educational institution we [could] generate income and reputation from training, industrial and commercial training-based activities because it is very closely linked to our other teaching activities.

> SDP funding was basically to get us to the point where we'd get accreditation which we got last summer. So we got accredited . . . . to run a post-graduate diploma in acoustics and noise control and also two of their accrediting short courses and we're still thinking about and looking towards accreditation for the other short courses.

> We have the first group of diploma students, that's a one-year long course and it's currently rated by the IOA and by three other universities as 90 M level credits, so it's half a Master's degree basically. . . . . At the moment we are delivering it on behalf of the IOA. What we are aiming for next year is to bring it fully in-house so that means we're working on developing some lab facilities so that we can teach the laboratory element of the course in-house because currently that has to be outsourced to the University of Liverpool.

Another approach has been to develop professional development courses out of existing postgraduate certificate and master's courses. Staff in the Sports and Development field were particularly active in exploring the potential of this approach to varying degrees of success. One innovator wanted to find out whether the Master's level course currently offered could be adapted and offered as shorter Professional Development Units for industry. This stimulated another sort of activity.

> *Joseph:* So the SDP fund allowed for us to look at the units we had in our existing MA's and saying 'This one could be something that we could create for industry.' But it was also an opportunity for us to do something that we knew nobody did, which is put ourselves out there. Normally we are really known for inward-facing. As a major university we had an opportunity to use the SDP fund to really announce our arrival in this space, if you like.

> *Robert:* we had was an existing qualification, the Certificate in Professional Sports Management and Administration (Football), and it runs as a partner venture with the League Managers' Association.

> [The] course, which had run for about ten or eleven years was for professional football administrators—a hundred and twenty credits, six units, the equivalent of a first year of an undergraduate degree . . . . We were finding was that since the launch of the Lawrie McMenemy Centre the numbers of students studying on the course tripled almost overnight, ... additionally we were getting an awful lot of requests—from overseas, but also from other individuals who were not working in the professional game who wanted to study on this course . . .

> So the intention was to take the six units that we've got on the professional certificate and to essentially break them up into six standalone professional development units which we could run individually for those students who didn't want to commit to the full Certificate course.

A number of tangible things happened as a result of going out and talking to people. These things were not always planned, rather they emerged through the process of engaging people through SDP innovation activity.

> *Joseph:* We have new partners that have come in as guest lecturers. We have some renowned consultants in the field that are willing to come to us almost for free. To come in and say 'We want to be involved.'

> One of the tangibles also is the fact that we tried to get practitioners that came to the symposium to see some of the work that our undergrad students were doing. One person from the Foundation actually has just committed to

being involved in giving feedback to the programmes that our undergrad students are doing. They are really trying to see what the Foundation can offer, like internships. They are sending those to us and saying, 'We appreciate the kind of theoretical-driven, evidence-based approach that you are training your students around sport and development.'

But sometimes, in spite of investing time and energy in going out to meet people, and developing good relationships which seem to be bearing fruit, ideas for innovation cannot be turned into reality because of unforeseen circumstances.

Robert: we were also looking at whether or not it could be expanded beyond football and we were predominantly looking at cricket because I'd had some preliminary discussions with the Professional Cricketers' Association because they wanted to run something similarly. We'd had some pretty productive meetings with the PCA, we'd moved a good way down the road with them. Another unforeseen problem which we couldn't have accounted for was the fact that they had a major restructure in the organisation, so we pretty much had sign-off from their Chief Executive and then he suddenly left, and that meant that there was a quite significant restructure underneath of him and as so often is the case in sport, when you develop a really good relationship with somebody and then the structure completely changes overnight you have to start again.

Bringing people together for relationship building and conversation

One innovator organised an international symposium which brought an international community of educational practitioners together in an emergent field to share perspectives, have new sorts of conversation and build new relationships.

Joseph: So we had a two-day event where, you know, people from within my field which is sport and development sport and social change, came to Southampton. On the first day they basically engaged around issues of how do we evidence outcomes of different innovations, international and national as well. Also how do you begin to dialogue across the barriers that have been created within our field? So you have practitioners, you have researchers, you have end users of policy focusing on how do we begin to dialogue? We were seeing ourselves as a place for creating that platform for critical dialogue. Then that was just going to be on the first day. Then on the second day we invited those that were interested to then do a course around monitoring and evaluation and evidence. We had sixty people participating from the UK, South Africa, Sweden, Zambia, Botswana, Austria and Norway.

Developing new technology

The ambition of one innovator was to develop a new web-based platform for hosting interactive digital stories told by people who had migrated from their home country.

> *James:* I was particularly interested in exploring uses for the tablet. The iPad 1 had just been released and to me it seemed it was going to be a really significant game changer, in terms of the way people consumed interactive media . . . . So one of the things that underscored the technical development, was really making it work well in that environment . . . . at the core of it we wanted to build an architecture for online storytelling. We realised we could use the tool itself and the understanding and skills we've developed to run some new units on the degree programme. We were also offering to write new units in interactive storytelling and digital storytelling for a new post-graduate degree. Beyond that what we were looking at more of a collaborative space that would be used on an international level.

A prototype platform has been developed with a view to demonstrating the potential of the interactive technology to enhance the story telling process.

> . . . it's an iPad thing, but it will work on a PC or whatever you like. In terms of the interface, there's a tab for documentaries which are half hour television version. But the interesting thing about this is we've used Google maps to place segments. So each half hour documentary is made up of little sub-stories that are plotted in different places [on Google maps] around the world

Once the platform was created new possibilities for incorporating and using data emerged.

It's not just about video stories, it's about getting the stories to link to archives and databases, so it's not just about playing video clips and you know obviously when you're telling these kind of stories there's lots of resources that you're hinting at or you've used. So for example for the film that I'm finishing at the moment, I'm negotiating with a writer in America who has written a book called 'Waiting To Be Heard', which is actually about the Polish Christian community from the Second World War and she's gone round and interviewed lots of people about their experiences before and during the war and having left Poland and some of her material is going to go into my film, but also we're looking at a way in which this data base of recordings that she's used for the book, can be linked in to the interactive website project, so using it in the kind of web format with hyperlinks. So it's not just about playing video clips, it's also about connecting the clips to archives and records.

New knowledge and technical skills developed by the project leader are now being fed back into the curriculum. A new unit has been written for an MA course drawing on this work and the work is also having an impact in the undergraduate curriculum.

James: it's certainly had a significant impact for myself and my colleague in terms of supporting the level two students who are moving into producing work in this area . . . . So in terms of developing the understanding within the course team, I'd say it's profoundly significant for that . . . 100 students a year know we are engaged in a real project, that involves us having to work with developers and designers . . .

The work continues in order to develop film content for the website and the intention is to have it fully operational by the end of this year. But even having the prototype, has created new potential for acquiring additional resources to continue the work and created new opportunities for collaborative research.

James: because I and my colleague researched and developed some substantial small films to be put on [the website], we were able to go to the research fund for a relatively small but necessary amount of money to continue the work. So I'm scripting and editing the film that I shot last year to go on it right now.

Through the research department, I got in contact with someone in Portugal who is developing a new big collaborative project to do with migration, who is really interested and they've written our work into a bid to this Portuguese technical academic research fund or whatever it's called. So you know because we have done this these sorts of things can happen

Utilising, adapting and evaluating existing technology

Another approach is to utilise existing technology adapting it for institutional use.

Sophie: Basically we wanted to offer a chat system to enable people who were off campus and couldn't get in, to make enquiries by instant messaging. We wanted to offer them the same service as people on campus and offer an alternative to coming up to one of the face to face enquiry desks. We wanted to make sure that we are catering for different learners.

Initially, we viewed chat systems in operation at two other universities, two different chat systems. We visited Bournemouth and saw the back end of the system there and we went to King's College London and we saw Question Point which is a different system to the one we use. The one we decided to use is called VRL Plus. So we compared two different systems. We also had a look at Three Systems but they didn't seem to offer the same level of functionality as the paid for systems. And then with funding from the Innovation Fund, we got a year's subscription to VRL Plus. The training was also paid for out of the Innovation Fund.

We did a one year pilot during which we tried out the chat system. . . . . it told us that it was a valuable service to offer, that it did give an extra dimension for the students. Feedback from staff who'd operated it was that you felt to a far greater extent that you were staying with the student right the way through until they actually found what they were looking for. So if they're trying to access a journal article off campus, you're actually there with them until they achieve their aim, whereas at the enquiry desk, you send them off with the information they need but you're never really sure whether they get there in the end.

Importance of Vision

If you are trying to create something that is simple and straightforward it is easy to define the outcome in an explicit way and work towards it. But complex achievements, like for example, encouraging greater participation and engagement of students in a learning process, are less easy to visualise and define. In such situations we have a sense of direction in which we know we want to move and the rest has to be continually invented, improvised and negotiated, along the way. Complexity involves individuals visioning something in a way that is meaningful to themselves and then using this vision to propel themselves forward: it's the vision of a different, in their view better, world that drives them to accomplish difficult challenges. In bringing about such change they are making their vision concrete so that others can see the benefit and potential of their ideas.

> *Oscar:* normally you would expect your leaders to be the ones coming down and saying 'You know we got to move this way, this is where the vision is.' You know, understand the vision of the faculty, understand the University and then bring it down to my own speciality in terms of my subject area. You know, look at the circumstances that apply to myself. There wasn't anything like that, I had to continue teaching, I had to continue doing the core things that I need to do. In addition to that, then I had to do this. So there was a lot of complexity there, but I think empowerment of myself was quite strong.

> *Interviewer: Are you saying that you had a vision about where you wanted to be with this programme and where you wanted your School to be with the programme and through your innovation project you were trying to persuade your School to adopt your vision?*

> *Oscar:* Exactly, that is what I am saying. But you see my vision should not be seen as a vision which was outside [the Faculty]. My vision was negotiated already in line with what the Faculty is trying to achieve, but maybe they wouldn't see it that way. I think the SDP . . . not just funding but the SDP as the idea of trying to bring about change in the University, created an environment where that discussion could happen.

CHALLENGES

Innovation, by its nature of attempting to do new and unfamiliar things, sometimes in new and unfamiliar contexts, can be a risky business. In higher education innovation is generally accomplished alongside the day job, meaning that academics or service providers have to keep on fulfilling their professional obligations while they are engaged in innovation. SDP innovation funding provided some resource to buy out staff time, or introduce new capacity but this was sometimes insufficient to cover the real time involved developmental activity (see figure 6.7).

> as a teaching-led institution we are bound very much by teaching and teaching comes first, and we are bound by this contract for five hundred and fifty hours, so we have to be very careful in terms of making sure you've got time to do other things. So you have to know exactly how much time to bid for, and that's where we tend to start from. . . . . once you've got the time set and you know you've got time to do the project, then . . . then you can work around the other sort of non . . . non-pay supplementary elements of the bid then

Matching ambition to resources

Innovators are passionate about their ideas. They aim high and so sometimes fall short of achieving what they had hoped to achieve within the time and resources available—a situation that gets exacerbated when things do not go according to plan.

> I think also possibly there was an element of being over-ambitious in terms of the original bid to be fair. It would have been probably enough just to develop the web material within even a year time frame, rather than the kind of six months that we were left with. But the problem is that . . . you can't just go and create blue sky a story telling interface, unless you've kind of got a real story that you're really involved in researching and developing, to populate it. So you know there needed to be something quite tangible to drive the development . . . So I suppose you know in that sense it was possibly over ambitious on the part of me in terms of scheduling it, [in order] that all these things could take place coherently within that time frame.

Working with complexity

Innovation often takes people outside of their usual organisational spaces and forces people to deal with people in other parts of the organisation. For some projects people must work at a systems level, rather than a service level. Working at a systems level can prove daunting but it can also be very rewarding in terms of the experience and learning gained and feelings that what is being done is being valued.

> For me it was a massive learning experience, project management and all that side of things. I have never done that you know, scheduling meetings and talking to people and working out how we were going to do it. The major challenge was actually the complexity of the system and trying to think of all the different elements of the projects. You had the technical aspects, you had the pilot aspects, you had the feedback aspects. What was so good was that I had lots of colleagues to draw on who had abilities in those different areas who then helped me to work that out.

Coping with unforeseen circumstances

People involved in innovation working to tight time scales and work plans are particularly vulnerable to changes in circumstances that impact on their work plans.

> I lost the web designer I was working with who left the country and we were kind of back to square one . . . . and we had . . . . five weeks to spend the money, which included finding someone to build this . . . . finding a specialist skill set, I mean it was . . . a real panic. And with all of these things they kind of look really simple, they look really simple, because they are really simple, but actually getting to that point of simplicity is a really time consuming process.

Changes in the external environment

Another dimension of complexity is when the external environment changes while development work is underway. For example, one innovation team had set out to develop PDU's from an existing certificate course which they had designed and successfully delivered to a specific business sector—the League Managers' Association (LMA). But during the design process the LMA decided it wanted significant changes to the content of the Certificate course so the team decided to go back to the drawing board to re-design the course before they could create the PDU's.

> We decided that the CPS parent course needed to be revalidated. In subsequent discussions with the League

> Managers' Association we realised that they actually
> wanted quite significant changes to the course and to
> the content of the course, the LMA changed the course
> content which we'd written. So at this point we're now
> thinking is it worth bidding for more money to finish the
> PDU's or is it worth going back to the drawing board?

The course is now being redesigned and revalidated. The units have
been structured and the content is being aligned to the new needs of the
sector. Once this is done then the PDU's can be redesigned and validated.
However, other strategic considerations are now emerging.

> I think we're a fair way down the road with respect to the
> PDUs, but then I think we need to re-establish market
> demand because one of the things we're now looking
> at is whether or not the actual course can be delivered
> to those outside of football. That's an idea that's been
> mooted to the LMA which they were resistant to initially,
> but now they've changed their mind I think a bit in terms
> of allowing us to do that. So it may be that PDUs are
> less valuable because those individuals, given the choice,
> would actually rather take the full course and gain that
> recognised qualification.

This story illustrates some of the complexity in designing educational
opportunities in rapidly changing markets and some of the challenges
of transferring educational designs created in partnership with a sector
organisation, to another sector. Although this project did not complete its
objectives the innovator was still able to point to a useful outcome.

Having sat down and thought about PDUs, and having thought about their
potential and their flexibility and their usefulness . . . . having gone through
part of the process now in terms of trying to get these up and running, I
think that's been useful. The other thing that I'm now aware of is just how
long it's going to take.

The recession

There is no doubt that the recession has impacted significantly on the
opportunities that innovation projects were intended to create. For
example, one innovator had established a steering committee of external
stakeholders with the intention of collaborative bidding for funding to
supports students engaged in community-development work in sports
coaching but the economic climate meant that there was no funding to bid
for. However, other possibilities of working collaboratively emerged.

In terms of my vision when I started, the way I saw the steering group working, was that we would guide the student projects, we would mentor the student projects, we'd support them, and with the help of the industry practitioners we would be saying, right okay, this funding stream is out there, let's look at tapping into this etc, etc . . . That hasn't entirely happened, mainly because of cutbacks in the sector. It was around the time the new coalition government were coming in, and the local authority was under a lot of pressure to cut costs, the school sports sector as well. So funding was very much up in the air. So we haven't had any specific collaborative bids as such. However there's been lots of other very good sector collaboration. For example, this is not entirely due to the SDP, but some of the relationships that we've developed with industry partners across Southampton and Hampshire [through the innovations steering group] have enabled us to look at doing other really fruitful things, for example last year we ran the Hampshire Coaching Conference at Southampton Solent University.

Communication

Communication in a large organisation is always a challenge and it is often an issue where complexity is concerned.

it was a challenge having to communicate with everyone I mean it. I widened the scope quite a bit and it was a real challenge to communicate it all. Trying to get people on board with this and to get stuff done and that was the real challenge and you know communicate with people by emails to get things done, because a part of the time was spent in Germany, so that was the challenge. Actually coming up with specific initiatives and the people—and to provide a way forward and to provide some evidence of the potential of these initiatives and then getting people to consider these initiatives, read about them and persuade them to get involved, now that's the real challenge actually, which I think remains the challenge now . . . . The real challenge now is trying to get others to engage with these initiatives and also to gain more evidence [of their value].

Working with systems that are perceived to be 'unhelpful'

Engaging in innovation means working in unfamiliar territory and for most of the participants who were not in management positions, unfamiliar territory meant institutional systems and procedures. From the innovator's perspective these included—procedures for project management with a very tight and seemingly rigid time scale for delivery, too much reporting for the size of the project, overly complex bureaucratic procedures and problems with marketing. Such challenges become more acute when unforeseen circumstances intervene so that projects do not progress as smoothly as intended. Adverse perceptions of some aspect of the institutions systems or procedures, including the management of the SDP itself, appear in about 20% of the narratives. What is perhaps surprising is that this figure is so low when people are engaged in work that by its nature is likely to be pushing at the boundaries of the organisation and questioning practices that have been set up to support the routine work of the institution rather than innovation. A few examples of these are offered below to show that for some people innovation held challenges that were organisational in their nature.

Rigid time scales & financial procedures

> Well we couldn't extend the project because we have a financial year which is the end of July and basically— you can't carry over and this was a nightmare, because basically we had this delay at the start . . . . when you're working within a university funding structure, you're just coming up against. institutionalised practices that [from an innovator's perspective appear to be] anti-competitive and counter-productive. . . . . I was just banging my head on the wall, because I'd just lost a key member of my team and I had a whole load of money to spend, but nothing to spend it on . . . . It was a nightmare . . . . because one of the things that we had [to do] was that anyone external had to be . . . vetted to be brought on the books, which is all good financial practice but it all takes time which I didn't have Another innovator made a similar comment.

> we were a little bit under spent at the end of the year, so even though the SDP ran over three years, because of the University regulations, we were unable to transfer that money over into the next academic year. That's what I'd like to have done [with the] £1 to 2k left over, and in the end I had to give some of it back, whereas what's the harm in that being transferred over to another financial year so

we could use it for other developments and innovations. I wouldn't say that's the fault of the SDP. It's more the University's red tape really that caused us the problem there.

Reporting procedures

In some narratives there was a sense that communication between participants in different parts of the University's systems might on occasion have been better. Communication issues are often the source of unnecessary complexity in any organisational or administrative system. For example, the SDP team had tried to create a light-touch informal reporting procedure and few of the innovators commented on this, but for one innovator the way this was implemented was exasperating.

> there seemed an awful lot of reporting and to a certain extent it has put me off from bidding in the future . . . . I felt that I was being constantly badgered . . . in some cases you were saying well look I told you what I told you three months ago, and a lot hasn't happened so I don't know what you expect me to say, this is where I'm at. I'd rather have had a more formalised process of six months, twelve months there's a pro-forma can you just complete it.

Changes to quality procedures

A number of projects involved the creation of new Professional Development Units (PDU's) that had to be approved. One innovator felt that procedures for approval had been changed after the bid had been approved and the more complex procedures could not be accommodated within the time that had been allocated in the bid.

> Initially, when we bid for the money the process for approving PDUs was very straightforward. I'd been forwarded some examples. I think at the time we did our bid only two PDUs had actually been approved and it was a very straightforward memo that had to be put forward. Subsequently, after the money had been awarded a completely different process for the validation of PDUs was introduced . . . . a three or four—page form which required an enormous amount of checks and measures and had to be signed off by all sorts of people. . . . . So we'd planned for and bid on the basis of this system, and then all of a sudden this system became more complicated and more time-consuming . . .

No help with marketing achievements

Some innovators felt that the absence of institutional support to market what they or their students had accomplished meant that the institution failed to capitalise on the achievements that had been made.

> . . . we developed an action plan for the project, and one of the actions in there to achieve a key outcome was to try and gain some profile across the city in terms of what we were doing, because this is about social responsibility and the University contributing to Southampton. But when I went to our marketing department, the response I got was, "well this isn't very innovative". That surprised me a little bit. So in terms of the internal support to enable us to really shout about what we were doing on behalf of the University, I never got any of that at all.

Using new technology

Not surprisingly, when introducing new technology, there were sometimes issues relating to the technology itself.

> Probably the only thing I could say is that with the actual system, there were technical glitches. That was not at our end, it's hosted on an external server. But they were beyond our control, but I can't really say that other than that, there were any major issues.

The perpetual challenge of engaging students

For teaching projects one of the main challenges for teachers was to engage students in new curricular designs that put them into unfamiliar real world situations.

> The challenge was quite immense. You're dealing with second year students, and as I always say second year fine art students are probably at the most vulnerable and most undecided part of their university career. At the same time we asked them to do a lot really, I mean we asked them to think about what kind of artist they're going to be and then we say "Right now you've got to learn everything about showing your work." Well they probably don't even know what their work is so in the end there is a lot of theoretical work. But then it's interesting what happens . . . . they're quite exceptional at working together

I find, so whereas we might have gone through it ten times and despaired at somebody actually ever thinking they were going to get it, then you suddenly found that they've been working together and they've said "Oh can we have this in a corner, and can we do that and can we do that?"

In every group of students there's half a dozen who never turn up. They're told if they don't turn up they'll get their comeuppance so they might have resented it. But when the group ethos got going everybody joined in, which was interesting to me.

And

The main challenges I'd say were obviously trying to develop a programme and develop a structure that would very much buy the students in, because obviously we're reliant on students here, and students, although you can say they're probably no different to any other human being, can be unreliable at times, so we're very much reliant on students to go out, engage with and deliver this.

Working with risk

Working with complexity and the challenges that emerge in taking risks in trying to do new things often causes anxiety. About half the innovators felt that they were not taking significant risks or any risk they were taking was mediated by the support and culture of the environment they were working in.

Sophie: I felt supported by [my managers]. I had concerns that maybe people would take longer to get used to using it. That was one of the things that I thought might be difficult but in the end, the members of staff who were operating it took to it very quickly, so that was great. I felt the culture in the Library at least is very much one of trying it out, that's the important thing and I didn't feel under pressure. I didn't feel it would reflect badly on me if it was not a success. I think the attitude of library management is if you give it a try, it has a much better chance of being a success than if you refrain from ever trying anything!

About half the innovators felt that the challenges they were engaged in were accompanied by risk and a degree of anxiety which they had to manage.

Interviewer: So it's sounding to me as if there might have been some risk and anxiety around what you were doing. Is that fair?

Yeah you're absolutely right. I mean this isn't the usual stuff that you would do in a normal curriculum is it? I mean usually you do your lectures and seminars, you do your assessment, but this is way beyond that in the sense that we were doing the lectures, the seminars and assessment, but we were supporting students and facilitating the process for them to go out and work in the community. And obviously to do that they needed some resource, they needed some finance, and then suddenly you have this money to give to students going out, they're purchasing equipment, they're managing their project financially, which is innovative in itself, and there is risk involved.

Where risk seems to have been a feature of the project, innovators were quick to point out the support and encouragement given to them by the SDP Team.

I take my hat off to . . . . the SDP team, because there was a lot of encouragement, because obviously these projects are very risky, and she actually said that to me when I had the first meeting with [SDP team member] about the bidding, and she said "the whole point of these projects is that they are risky projects because what they're taking on is quite new".

VALUE OF ENGAGING IN INNOVATION

The effects on individuals of being involved in SDP innovation are considerable and deep. They engage the dimensions personal development in areas such as new capability, awareness, confidence and self-esteem.

Developing as a teacher

For a reflective teacher, the benefits are often linked to changes in their understanding because of their experience.

William: Well I doubt whether a few years ago I would have done anything like this . . . I never agreed with second year exhibitions because I think that the kids are in such a mess that they can't think straight. But I think that after this experience I can see ways of helping them with their artwork via the display of their artwork and their thinking about it because they've done it. Because one of the things we tell them is that, you know, as a professional you're not just making artwork you've got to archive it, you've got to photograph it, you've got to keep up your Twitter pages or your Facebook page, you've got to make connections, you've got to do all these things as a professional, and everything's got to be done really well otherwise you won't make it beyond the first stage. So I think probably for me there was the satisfaction of doing a good show with fairly raw material, having got the students to be sort of much more confident about how they go about their professional lives and their work,

and that's probably about it really. I mean I didn't learn anything from a gallery point of view, or from a display point of view, probably because I don't teach all the time, I got to the first stage myself about knowing what the current students are capable of doing and how they actually operate, which is probably my achievement. . . . I mean I still think it's probably a lot to ask of them, but if you do it in a certain way and you give them confidence to do it they'll deliver.

Developing as a researcher

Some innovators were using the results of their innovation work as a stimulus for their research.

> *Harry:* the biggest thing it's done, it's really sort of inspired me around my research, again with my PhD, because my PhD is all about the innovation programme now. It's about addressing a common issue in sports development, which is monitoring and evaluation, and given that these innovation projects will constitute probably I'd say, well over 50% of the sports development provision in the city, there's going to be lots of questions asked around monitoring and evaluation. So it's enabled me to connect an issue within the industry and contextualise it within what we're doing in the curriculum here in Southampton Solent University, and then also to be able to try and gain an understanding of how is this really working for the students? Does it empower them? Is it useful? And it's really like sort of putting the students on the map with industry practitioners, which is very interesting in itself. So it's been a very positive experience.

New relationships

> *Edward*: I think most of the relationships that I've established are new ones with colleagues outside of the school and outside of the institution and I think that certainly enriches the project and the potential going forward. I mean for example this second project would not have happened without having developed new relationships outside of my immediate sphere from this project.

New skills and capability

> *James*: Well certainly from the skills base, which is very linked to the teaching, a better understanding of the technologies involved, the processes involved. I've done similar but different stuff before, but you know it really was like a quantum leap into something new. From the point of view of managing the production, that's been quite a lesson in its broadest sense I suppose, both positive and negative, but certainly overall a kind of positive thing . . . I hadn't been involved in narrative film making for a number of years, because I've been doing a lot of web based material, so one of the things that I really wanted to get involved in was using cameras again and telling stories using cameras, so I was kind of picking up that, which was fairly significant for me. I mean I haven't done that for eight years or so.

> *Sophie:* I think the process of being involved in a project, the experience of managing a project, that was obviously very useful. I hadn't taken over the role particularly long when I started it, probably was the first experience of project management that I had so I think that was a key thing . . . I made use of Microsoft Project, it seemed quite a logical way of setting things out, setting out the stages of the project and then being able to share that. I updated that on a week by week basis and circulated it to other people in the group.

Professional satisfaction

> *Edward:* Yeah good question, in the first instance this is not about my own career development actually, because I could have retired two years ago and I sometimes wonder why am I still doing this, I have to say. It's just about my

professional need to do stuff that is of potential value, to our students, to colleagues and to colleagues at the BIB International College and so on and so forth. Just to do stuff that is of potential value, it's interesting to do and if it succeeds, then that will give me a high degree of job satisfaction even at this late stage of my career and of course, okay I was able of course to go out to Germany, for the core part of the project, because they came up with, you know with funding for the accommodation and so on and so forth, so that enabled me to do it. I very much enjoy teaching of course but it enabled me to get away from the day job, to do interesting stuff. It was very, very stimulating.

So my German is much better than it used to be and so on and so forth. So there have been these additional personal benefits out of it, but I think it's just ultimately to do something that is of potential value. I know it's always a personal thing . . . . but it's nice to have spice in one's working life isn't it? Surely?

Improved confidence

Emma: Confidence, absolutely. I never thought I would be able to present at a conference or have a journal article or have created with the help of others a system that we are now taking forward. I can't really believe that is where we have ended up. Yeah, it has given me confidence. I now know more people in the University. I am more aware of some other departments and things and how things are working. And just being involved with a funded project at a high level I think has been fantastic really.

Feeling appreciated and valued

Oscar: I get more hellos in the University now. You know, people are talking about me and saying 'He is doing this and that.' So I think there is more awareness, not just of me but of the work we are doing in sport and development. You know, there is that sense of pride, that sense of achievement.

James: Although it's not complete I feel really positive about the whole thing. . . . . I'm really actually quite pleased with the project and it feels a very alive positive thing for me and I suppose you know what I get from that is the value of sticking with an idea that you believe is good, it's got legs on its own, it's not about locking into a single thing.

But the answer to the question, do you feel what you have done is valued and recognised is sometimes complex and as one innovator explained, the answer is often yes and no.

I'd say there's a lot of lip service paid to it. I think the sheer scale of what this has grown into now, the innovation programme which the SDP . . . primed at the very beginning, we now have around 20 student led innovation projects that are happening in Southampton at the moment, and that represents a momentous amount of work which is way beyond the curriculum.

. . . we find ourselves not just teaching these students and developing them, but in a way managing our own small company. Ultimately we are the ones responsible for them, and one of the things that has sprung out of this SDP innovation stuff is a project . . . about volunteering and employability within the University. . . . . And that is something that myself and [my colleague] really wanted to develop further, and we were basically encouraged to develop it into a proper social enterprise, which all of these innovation projects would come into, but unfortunately we were told yeah, go ahead and do it but there's no resource for you to do it. You have to do it in your own time, and that was just something that we couldn't do.

So I think in terms of answering your question in a roundabout way, I'd say we need far more resource and time to be able to do this properly. I mean much of this has been done by ourselves as academics out of passion more than anything else, because quite easily I could say to my students when we see them in the second year, "go out, develop an initiative and go and deliver it", and have no more to do with it. All this coordination, the steering groups, running a symposium which we did on 3rd May whereby industry practitioners came in and the students presented their posters wouldn't have been done. So we're doing all this extra stuff on behalf of the students that we aren't really getting any extra resource or formal recognition for.

I'd say the people higher up the University, seem to value what we've done, [the Pro Vice-Chancellor (Academic)) has expressed quite a lot of interest. I mean every conference that we've presented at on this stuff, she's always been there. When we ran our innovation symposium on 3rd May, she was there along with . . . . other senior staff, . . . and the Dean is also fully aware of what we're doing as well, so I think it's being recognised, but the proof is in the pudding in terms of recognition turning to resource.

DISCUSSION

The philosophy of the SDP team was to create the conditions where 'many flowers could bloom'. Flowers that were grown by individuals in their working contexts that contributed to the 'garden' that was being cultivated by the SDP Team. It's clear that this is exactly what happened. The message that there was a funded opportunity was received by people who like to get involved in new things—self-confessed enthusiasts and early adopters. They had ideas that, in their view, fitted the 'call' and sometimes with the much appreciated help of the SDP team, bids were put together, with outline work plans. Once approved the innovators were left to get on with their work but members of the team monitored progress through the informal quarterly reports. For most of the innovators this seemed to be an appropriate way of working, although one would have preferred a more formal and explicit reporting structure.

Most (about 64%) of the projects were completed to a point where they were implemented, another 21% are still in the development stage ie the ideas are being turned into something that will support practice which leaves only 15% where a decision was either taken not to progress to implementation, or the project is suspended but could be implemented under the right conditions. By any measure this is a good rate of success in terms of the achievement of stated intentions.

Sustainability was an important emphasis for the SDP team during the formulation of project bids. 64% of projects are now being funded from core funds in the areas in which they were developed. A further 42% of projects have received additional funds from inside or outside the institution showing they demonstrated potential for development. Again these would seem to be good outcomes from the innovation fund strategy.

Concluding remarks

Innovation distinguished between a leader and a follower . . . . I perceive innovation as a driving force, an

> *imperative or fundamental value. It shows up in a leader*
> *as the act or practice of improvising—making the implicit*
> *explicit to satisfy a need. Steve Jobs*

This wonderful quotation from one of the greatest innovators of our time captures well the spirit of this chapter. The innovators who contributed their stories were 'ordinary' members of staff who, to an outsider looking in, would not be described as an institutional leader. But by involving themselves in innovation, by coming forward with their beliefs and ideas, and investing time, energy, emotion and intellect in their project for change, they helped lead strategic change. While many of them would not describe their role in these terms this is what they were doing each in their own way and in their own part of the organisation they attempted, and in most cases, succeeded in leading change. And at the heart of it all were two or three profound purposes—what Steve Jobs called 'need', and which are nicely summarised by these innovators.

> *Edward:* I'm always trying to do things that are relevant to and meet the needs of the faculty and the University, but at the same time of course if they can meet my needs, then everybody wins

> *Harry:* What this project is all about for me, it's not just my need as an academic leading it and getting publications out there, which is obviously something I can do, but it's about valuing students' needs and enriching their experience, and it's also buying into the needs and the aspirations of the industry practitioners in the city as well, so it's very much a triangulated approach around different needs.

The first need, was the desire to improve the education or services the University is providing—to make a difference to the lives of the students innovators are serving whether as a teacher enhancing their chances of gaining employment in their fields of study, or as a service provider improving access to services that will help them learn. Fundamentally, it is this deep sense of moral purpose that drives the innovation process.

The second need, met in a number of innovation projects, was the need to build new relationships with the community, to better meet the needs of business or public sector organisations.

Both of these needs are fundamentally connected to the strategic needs of the University as expressed in its mission and values statement which underpins the SDP.

But emerging through all the narratives is another fundamental need which is grounded in the symbolism of the word 'innovation' which comes from the Latin word 'innovatus,' meaning 'to renew.'

> *Edward:* The bottom line motivation is to do something different and interesting and developmental, above and beyond the normal stuff that we do . . . it's nice to have a bit of spice in one's academic life.

It is clear from the narratives of innovators that involving yourself in innovation fulfils the personal need of 'renewing and developing yourself'. Of making your professional life more interesting, more challenging, more engaging and more rewarding. Of putting into practice what you believe and of accessing and implementing your personal creativity to add value to the educational world you inhabit. Of achieving something that you personally value—irrespective of what colleagues around you think. This is the hidden value to a university of sponsoring and supporting innovation— it enables its staff to fulfil the need for self-renewal and self-actualisation. It enables them to become the people they want to be and become.

Appendix 1 Project Summaries

1 Information for non traditional learners

The initial aim of the project was to develop and implement a University package of information for non-traditional learners(other than full time undergraduate and post graduate learners) and customer support for sponsoring employers, to enable more effective relationships between non-traditional learners, employers and SSU. As the project developed it was clear that the task in hand was more extensive than originally thought and as a result implementation of a full package was limited. Successes were achieved in online registration and data protection, as well as gathering information and raising awareness of issues in all services in providing information to non traditional learners. Currently, this influence has been recognised by the Enrolment Working Group in the production of revised joining instructions to reflect this need.

2 Strategic evaluation of built environment courses and development of unique selling points

The aim of this project was to gain a current view of Southampton Solent's offer of built environment courses through the views of students, alumni and employers with the intention that this information would help to gain insight into developmental opportunities and assist in the identification of unique selling points to enhance the offer. Collaborations with local employers and colleges was also identified as developmental and research possibilities through this study. Surveys and discussions with employers and alumni indicated that they were broadly satisfied with the current course and graduates from the course. While there was no demand for new Masters courses there was an interest in new CPD opportunities.

3 Southampton emergency medicine education project

The aim of this project was to change the way in which junior doctors engaged with their postgraduate medical training, by moving away from traditional lecture delivery towards asynchronous delivery of material s using e-learning technology. This project follows a pilot study which was successfully developed in 09-10 which involved creating a group of short 'video lectures' on specific key diagnostic issues. Due to the success of the pilot it was felt that a more comprehensive programme of e-learning, aligned with the curriculum for Foundation training in Emergency Medicine, would be of benefit. The new learning materials were developed and they are now firmly embedded into their Foundation One Programme for Emergency Medicine training at the hospital and we're now looking at ways of developing that in the future.

4 Acoustics accreditation

The objective of this project was to develop an acoustics consultancy that would facilitate the development of work based learning to increase the employability skills of undergraduate within the Entertainment Technology programme in addition to developing external income for the University. Accreditation and membership of the Institute of Acoustics were key features in the success of this project. The project secured accreditation by the Institute of Acoustics to run a post-graduate diploma in acoustics and noise control and the first students were recruited in 2011. The group is also accredited to deliver two short courses and accreditation for the other short courses is now being considered.

5 BiB Collaboration for employability & international exchange

The main aim of this project was to research, apply and disseminate sustainable and shared best practice drawn from both the UK and Germany, in embedding student employability in the curriculum. The project expanded and deepened the relationship with the Bildungsczentrum fuer Informationverarbeiteende Berufe—Educational Centre for Information Processing Professions, a private non-profit making institution. The project resulted in new EU-funded work experience opportunities BiB to Solent and Solent to BiB planned for 2011, more industry focused activity within the curriculum using the University as a business context, an *international learning* experiment to enable bib and Solent students to work collaboratively on—line and a sharper focus on career management learning.

6 Active ageing—supporting employees working with older people

The School of Sport, Tourism and Languages recognises new educational opportunities for older people (+65 = 20% pop by 2026) with a focus of health and active ageing. The in-depth market research project aimed to identify physical activity provision in care homes in Southampton. The project sought to establish the levels of physical activity provided, who delivered the physical activity and whether those people were qualified to deliver such activity. The study went further by asking if care homes thought this type of training for their staff was desirable, would they be prepared to pay for it and if so the range of payment which might be considered feasible. The study was carried out by a graduate and involved desk and primary data collection and provides a greater understanding of potential for the future developments of provision at SSU including PDUs along with a database of key contacts in the area in the care home sector. Although an interest and need was identified in the care home sector, businesses are not prepared to fund staff development in this area and often care workers are on low incomes so are unwilling to pay for their own development.

7 Lawrie McMenemy Centre for Football Research Project

This project aimed to support the development of a series of football-related industry responsive Professional Development Units (PDU's) based upon the highly successful Higher Education Certificate in Professional Sports Management and Administration (Football) (CPSMA). The development of the PDU's is in direct response to the increasing demand for flexible forms of football-specific education from within the UK and globally. The PDU's allow students located within the professional football industry to experience elements of the CPSMA without having to commit to the full two-year course or to remain current via CPD if they have already been awarded the CPSMA. Moreover, the PDU's provide an opportunity to enter new markets including students located outside of the industry who aspire to work within it. The project delivered its main objective of designing the PDUs but due to a forthcoming review of the main programme, validation of the new PDUs was put on hold. New opportunities seemed to have emerged but they couldn't be exploited because the PDU's were not validated. Also time invested with Professional Cricket Association did not result in success.

8 Mahara Lite—Application development

The aim of this project was to research and develop a mobile friendly 'lite' version of Solent's adopted open source e-portfolio tool, Mahara. This would allow work based learners (whether on placement or studying part-time whilst working) and/or mobile students (e.g. at sea or in military service) to enable them to submit evidence where desktop computing facilities are not available. A programme of research developed the need for and potential use of such a tool and a specification has been prepared. A second stage project is being funded to commission an expert programmer to create a tool with the desired functionality which will not just benefit the University but the open source community.

9 Pilot of an instant messaging enquiry service

The purposes of the project were to trial and promote a library chat based enquiry service through a widget added to the library portal page. Through this medium students could get an instant (live) response from a member of the information team during specific operating hours. The pilot proved that the service would be a useful additional service and a library-funded on—line chat enquiry service was introduced in 2011. The project was successful involving quite a few staff, it resulted in a new embedded service, and new learning and expanded uses for the technology.

10 Reading lists and myReferences—RefWorks integration in myCourse

The main aim of this project was to investigate alternative ways of providing reading lists to students this resulted in RefWorks [bibliographic software] being integrated with myCourse to allow the creation of reading lists via RefWorks RSS feeds and a myReferences interface where students can add/edit their references and create a bibliography. The integration has been piloted with psychology and criminology students. The project was successful in demonstrating the effectiveness of the software to deliver an enhanced service and it will be offered as an embedded service from September 2012.

11 Partnership Working

The main purpose was to develop a sustained partnership between a range of employers, the students and the University. The purpose of this bid extended beyond providing student placements within organisations, and focused on the development of student enterprise. The main objective of the bid was to develop a formal relationship with employers/ organisations that resulted in their participation in guest lectures at level 5 in the BA Sports Coaching and Development, as well as providing a partnership opportunity for students to deliver their initiatives at level 6 and Coaching and Community Development unit. The project was successful in enhancing existing curriculum units at level 5 and 6 and in engaging employers in supporting and enriching the students' experiences, and the units are now being sustained by the School.

12 Pop Up exhibitions for fine arts

This project aimed to create an enhancement activity for students from the creative courses at Southampton Solent University to deliver a 'Display in the Public Domain—Pop-Up Exhibitions' project. It also included the research and development of broader opportunities for working with communities of Southampton. The purpose was to encourage students to display their work and ideas publically, utilising exhibitions spaces and other public venue. The process was integrated into the learning experience throughout the second year. It was designed to run alongside core practical and theoretical elements of the course and incorporated all of the professional development lectures and workshops. The experience encouraged students to display their work and ideas publically, utilising exhibitions spaces and other public venues including exhibitions, a live art event, performance, fashion event, public talk, publication or web-based project. The project was successful and new members of staff have now been appointed to continue running the unit.

13 Sport for Social Change

The project aimed to develop a systematic framework of PDUs whose credits can accumulate and lead to a Higher Certificate in Sport for Social Change (HCSSC). Individual Professional Development Units and HCSSC credits are recognised by the MA Sport and Development. Three Professional Development Courses were planned, developed and delivered in the 2010/2011 period. A consultative meeting was also organised involving a representative from the Sport for Social Change industry to consider professional development course for industry. Three training workshops were organised to deliver the three professional development courses and three symposia were run to allow professional development students to engage with members of the industry.

14 Collaborative Interactive Storytelling

The aim of the project was to design a website to deliver interactive video content on the internet produced by staff members which will encourage students to creatively engage with interactive technologies as a pre-requisite for working in the television industry. The project was intended to drive the teaching delivery of interactive units by aiding with skills development of the staff team. The ambitious project was partially successful in building the platform, but additional resources have been allocated to complete the work including the research and development of video content for the site. A new postgraduate curriculum unit has incorporated the technological development.

CHAPTER 7

The First On-line Course: MSc Shipping Operations

INTRODUCTION

This case study of innovation involves a development that was conceived and implemented within a Faculty-based strategic plan. While the idea for the innovation—a course for professional learners that was entirely on-line, had been in existence before the SDP—the funding enabled the Faculty to accelerate the development and also draw in considerable expertise in on—line learning from the E Development Centre (EDC) which was partly funded by the SDP. The distinctive feature of this innovation is the way in which subject and curriculum experts in maritime education worked collaboratively and productively with experts in on-line learning, curriculum design and student support from the EDC. This collaboration in turn influenced the design and development of the University's on-line platform being developed by EDC. In this way we can appreciate the beneficial interferences of trans—university, team-based collaboration for the purpose of innovation.

Background

Warsash Maritime Academy (WMA), which was the host for the MSc Shipping Operations innovation, has an international reputation for providing high quality maritime education and for innovation in this field. In 2009 when it was considering how to engage with the SDP it had already determined that strategically it had to accelerate development of e-based distance learning. While WMA had a flexible, employer-facing operation, it acknowledged that its delivery mechanisms had not kept pace with the increase in student numbers or the opportunities that technology-enabled learning offered.

However, one of the big issues for the Faculty was providing educational opportunities that met the very specific needs of seafarers who were at sea for most of their working life and could not access the internet in the same way that people who were land-based could. This began to change in 2009 when Maersk, the world's largest containership company, committed to a programme to install broadband across its fleet—this immediately began to change the communication infrastructure in a way that opened up opportunities for distance learning and support.

The Faculty's SDP proposal outlined four projects that related to its strategic intention to accelerate development of on-line learning namely:

- development of flexible mode MSc Shipping Operations
- development of different and improved support for work-based learning at sea for deck and engineering students following Foundation Degree programmes
- more flexible study modes for students working towards higher certificates
- comprehensive survey of companies to inform decisions about longer term priorities for distance and flexible mode provision.

SDP funding was used mainly to buy out the time of the Associate Dean (Enhancement) to lead the programme of work, and staff time for the main contributors to these different projects.

Figure 7.1 Development and implementation of MSc Shipping Operations at Warsash Maritime Academy

ACCOMPLISHING INNOVATIVE CHANGE

So what can we learn about accomplishing innovative change from this case study? Figure 7.1 represents the sequence of events involved in developing the MSc Shipping Operations on-line course.

Through this representation we can appreciate that the idea existed before SDP funding was available but the additional resources were able to accelerate development and enable the Faculty to move more quickly into the e-learning territory it felt it needed to occupy. It also enabled the course team to work in partnership with experts in a new SDP-funded E-Development Centre.

Origins of the idea

Like a number of other innovations described in this book the idea for an MSc Shipping Operations where learning was enabled through an on-line environment, that forms the basis of the innovation described in this chapter, had been around for a while and some work had been undertaken before SDP-funding became available.

> the idea has been around for quite a while before we got into the SDP . . . The International Association of Maritime Institutions (IAMI) that we're part of have been talking about the education of seafarers. Mostly the education of seafarers is very technical and they don't have to get a degree to become an officer. We were looking at educational needs and some of the team have undertaken a research project focused on the on-going education of seafarers . . . and out of that came the idea that seafarers who had become masters of ships might reach the point where they want to come ashore . . . . into management positions. Surprisingly management isn't something that they actually learn about, to be masters of ships, which is about command not management. So we realised that there was an opportunity for this type of education and this was where the idea for an MSc in Shipping Operations began. *Associate Dean*

The Faculty had experience of a programme of blended/distance learning and this served as the initial model for the MSc Shipping Operations.

> Key members of the team have been involved in a project which was to have a blend of learning, in a post graduate certificate in teaching and learning maritime education. This was for people who were teaching maritime training

and education in the Philippines. It was semi-distance not really online but several members of the team had been involved in that. *Associate Dean*

prior to the SDP we had developed a post graduate certificate blended learning for maritime lecturers in the Philippines, so we had started to use the virtual learning environment myCourse for delivery of that particular programme *Innovator 1*

In fact the MSc Shipping Operations was designed using the blended learning approach but it soon became apparent that the design would not work for learners.

We started out with the idea of a blended learning course and weactually went right the way through the development on that and then we found that people wouldn't sign up to it because they couldn't come here. So that's how we decided to put the course online *Associate Dean*

We were going to deliver the MSc blended learning, that was our initial thoughts, on the basis of our experience with the post graduate certificate, but it proved impossible to get the students together at the campus at any time . . . . we originally wanted to offer a couple of weeks a year where they would come and meet the staff and we would do some workshops and things like that, but it became obvious that that just wasn't going to happen because the students, as a cohort, could never come together on the same week in a year, no matter what month that happened to be. *Innovator 1*

So the decision was taken to develop a course that was delivered and supported entirely on-line—the first completely on-line course in the University and the focus for innovation was learning how to design and support these forms of learning for the particular group of professional distance learners.

The programme is innovative in terms of how it's delivered in the sense that the students never come to the University, unless they wish to do so . . . . essentially it had to be designed with the knowledge and understanding that the students are going to be accessing this through a computer and not through an interface with a person. . . . So there was no blended learning aspect . . . and the innovation came from developing ways and means of

> keeping the course alive, engaging and interacting and that, I suppose, was where our focus was on the types of activities that we developed. *Innovator 1*

Effective and productive partnership

The distinctive feature of this story of innovation is the collaboration between experts in maritime education and experts in the design and delivery of on-line learning. The development of close and supportive working relationships began with the original blended learning approach.

> when we started with the blended learning model Jamie and his team came along and give presentations about the technology and what was possible, but it wasn't until we really made the decision that we're going fully distance learning that our relationship with EDC changed . . . what seemed to happen was that this team in EDC became available to us and I think, just through the personalities that were involved, we developed a very effective partnership. We'd meet very regularly in the run up to the development of all the units, my colleagues who are teaching several of the units and we'd have [the Associate Dean] involved as well *Innovator 1*

> we had this tremendous support from the EDC teaching us all how to do it. We had weekly workshop sessions with them, bespoke work, which we wouldn't have been able to do normally with the University's normal work. If it hadn't been for having that extra impetus from the SDP to do it, I don't feel we would have got this far. *Associate Dean*

> I feel honoured really to have been involved in working with a great team of people, because I think that is the key thing with the success of that course. It has been a cross-disciplinary, cross-faculty and service co—operation. I think that was the real key to it. *Innovator 2*

Inventive process

The process of inventing the course began with the design phase in which content and process were considered from the perspectives of a) what academic subject specialists considered to be important for the postgraduate level of learning in the particular field b) the needs of learners trying to assimilate, understand and apply their learning through the on-line learning environment. The principal innovator considered this to be both and organic and a social process.

> It was very organic . . . . The process . . . . for designing it came in a number of stages. There was the initial considerations—What did it need to cover? What was the content? Who would it appeal to? What would it offer them in terms of not only of an academic qualification, but in terms of career prospects? And how were we going to divide all this content into manageable units? And how were we going to pitch it at a level that wasn't about turning them into academics but was more about providing learners with models and views that they could then apply in their own work places? So the first phase, was actually sorting out the content that was going to form this degree programme.
>
> The second phase, I suppose, was where we started to work with the development centre in terms of the tools and the technology. We had to learn what was available and we had a series of presentations from the EDC. I suppose, from there we had a better idea about what was possible.
>
> But when we got to that stage there was a bit of a hurdle to overcome. How did we as lecturers and tutors, used to the residential way of delivering, take this technology, take our aspirations of what we wanted to give the students and create something that was engaging. And that's the third phase, I suppose, where we actually tried a few things out but settled on the idea of having regular meetings for whoever could attend, once a fortnight, so very regular. *Innovator 1*

The inventive process continued into the implementation and delivery (see also Chapter 8).

> [we were] working on the units that would be coming up first in the programme and others coming along whose units were perhaps coming until later to see how we evolved our ideas and the thoughts and well, ideas that we had and which way we would end up going.
>
> And that was a process that went on, not only before the start of the MSc but also as it was running. So we were developing new units that would be coming online later, whilst we were actually running units once the MSc was

launched. And so we were able to take what we were learning from what we'd done, in terms of development and also in terms of delivery and feed it into subsequent units and that's really, more or less, the process that we're still running with now.

I was developing the course and being Course Leader and teaching all at the same time, because we never were in the position where we had everything ready before its start. We were, you know, just one step ahead of the students a lot of the time and no, I spent weekends, holidays and really long days and countless hours and it was hard going it was really hard going.

For the course team the process of invention involved a combination of generating ideas, utilising the knowledge from different team members, trying things out and seeing the results and learning new skills—like learning how to write content for this type of learner and learning context.

there were two of us whose units were up front and that was myself and a colleague and we're both get stuck in and get on with it type people and the way we found that worked best for us was that we actually learned how to write pages, write content. . . . . We were guided by Johnny and Jamie who were very good at steering us on the basis of their knowledge and understanding of using on-line technology and their experiences with other courses. I think John had worked for the OU. So they steered us into how to structure the content and we were using this book arrangement so they were guiding us on how to best structure things. I suppose my contribution was having a picture in my head of the students sat in front of the computer and using a language, a form of language, that would communicate to the student directly, not all this academic speak. So this is what you are going to learn, this is how you are going to do it, this is what you need to do, in what order and things like that.

So yes, I suppose the way it then progressed was David and I would go off and write stuff and then we'd come back. Ideas would come to us, how about doing this? how are we going to solve this? how are we going to support the students? and I drew on a lot of my experiences doing things like counselling, I did some counselling skills courses, I drew on my experiences of doing my own PG Cert in teaching and learning here at the University, and

> self-managed learning groups and things like that. We were drawing on people's experiences, but not directly involved in the development . . . I suppose, the invention was for us to translate that knowledge from the various people in the team into a product at the end of the day. *Innovator 1*

One of the issues for the innovator in the creative process was finding significant blocks of time to be able to follow-through ideas.

> The way I work is I'll start writing stuff and I'm creating as I go and ideas will come to me and if you don't have a dedicated block of time, what tends to happen is those ideas get lost and you forget where you were and where your ideas were going. *Innovator 1*

The University had set up a Usability Laboratory to test and evaluate its on—line designs and this facility helped the course team evaluate its learning and teaching strategies.

> We did use the Usability Lab not very long before we were due to start actually, we had four research assistants who have been students on a residential MSc that we ran and they were the sort of the age and sort of background of people we would be expecting for this new MSc, so we spent the day in the lab with them watching where they looked and we also carried it on for a week afterwards as if they were real students and having to do things while they were at home, getting them to write their reflections on their experiences. So yes, that helped us refine things in terms of the look, signposting and things like that, trying to make things very clear as to where they are. *Innovator 1*

> The partnership with the EDC team continued once the course had started. we still meet, less regularly obviously, but as other units came on stream, we continued the regular meetings, we probably went from once a fortnight down to on demand, mainly to support people whose units were just starting. John and Jamie particularly, if we have any particular issues with any of the technology, will help us. *Innovator 1*

Challenges

There have been a number of challenges which innovators have had to overcome. The first involves the distinctive nature of the group of professional adult learners that the MSc Shipping Operations course was serving.

> *Managing student expectations*—The people that we're dealing with here for the most part are senior people. They really expect premier treatment and . . . . if they've got a query, they want it answered right away, that could be at any time of day or night. We knew that this was going to be an issue and the eDev people were insistent that you must set the expectations but actually it is very difficult. We have found that the demands for support of that sort from students is very high and the staff's natural inclination was to attempt always to meet them and we have had some issues of overload around that and we've got to do more work on that one. *Associate Dean*

A second has been to encourage learners to see the value in both strands of the programme.

> we've got two strands in the programme at the moment, people are signing up for the safety management because they know that. The human factors side, with more of a focus on managing people, is a bit less familiar to these experienced seafarers and we've not had much take up on that yet. So we're having to build that up and get it across to people. But we've had a bit of a boost on that which will come through because the industry has recognised that human factors are important and they've actually built into the latest standards for the training of sea farers that management skills have got to be developed. *Associate Dean*

From the perspective of the principal innovator the main challenge was finding sufficient blocks of time to enable ideas to be followed through and make good progress.

> *The main challenge has been time*—we thought we've got resources, we've got materials, its just a case of sort of re-fashioning them for this particular environment, but at the same time learning how to do it and how to link things, how to put in pictures and all this sort of thing. But its horrendously time consuming and it's not the sort of thing you can do just here and there, you have to spend blocks of time otherwise you'd get nowhere. The way I work is I'll start writing stuff and I'm creating it as I go and ideas will come to me and if you don't have a dedicated block

of time, what tends to happen is those ideas get lost and you forget where you were and where your ideas were going . . . I was fortunate in that I had probably more time than my colleagues, because my teaching commitments were reduced for getting this programme off the ground, but even so . . . *Innovator 1*

During the design stage there were a number of challenges. The first related to curriculum design. The decision to build the MSc programme from free standing Professional Development Units had certain consequences.

The development of the professional development units meant that they had to stand alone so that they could be offered alone . . . . The students had to be able to engage with the material from the outset without . . . . what the MSc students who were following the whole programme would have had through doing other units. So we created . . . a whole series of advice and guidance and support materials for studying online. It also meant that we couldn't design linkages between the units for example, it would have made sense from a design perspective for the safety management strand to have linkages between the four safety related units but because we might be dealing with students that hadn't studied those other units we had to make them self-contained . . . . we had to make sure that the student had everything that they needed to, to be successful when studying a unit on its own. *Innovator 1*

The course team also had to learn to teach and support learning in a way that was unfamiliar to them.

. . . because we'd had the experience of developing a blended learning model in the PG Cert for Phillipino maritime lecturers, we had to move from using face to face elements combined with distance learning to fully distance learning . . . . That was difficult for us because it meant we had to learn to do a lecture without having anybody in front of us and without the feedback, without the opportunity to stop for questions to make it an interactive experience. The way that we overcame that was to use a programme where you narrate your power point slides So you're, in effect, giving a lecture but without the interactive element, which you add in later . . . . So being able to communicate to our students through a rather static medium was a significant challenge, yes. *Innovator 1*

> The issues that emerged during implementation were both technical and pedagogic. The technical issue brought home the vulnerability of on-line delivery, albeit in an extremely unusual situation. We had been reassured by our colleagues that our previous virtual learning environment, My Course, had never fallen over. It had never had an issue in all the time that it had been running . . . But within a week of starting the MSc we had a major power outage in Southampton and then we had floods and so in the space of a week there was no access to the learning materials for our students . . . it was quite an exceptional circumstance. *Innovator 1*

The main pedagogic challenge related to the need for learners to adopt a reflective stance on their own learning and personal development. This required them to use a particular on-line tool called Mahara.

> We had a big issue with e-Portfolios. The students just couldn't get on with them and really reacted badly to them and, you know, we recognised that we hadn't prepared them for that and partly we didn't really understand the tool well enough to use it appropriately we had only a superficial understanding. *Innovator 1*

There were clearly a number of reasons for this issue including the knowledge and ability of the teachers to support this form of learning and learner resistance to this learning.

> I don't know if it's something peculiar about our student cohort, but they were so resistant, well I think one person was sort of stirring up the rest, very concerned about protecting their identity and worried about identity theft. We were a bit puzzled by this because we couldn't think how they thought that a university educational system and course represented a threat to their identity. But he wasn't alone and they didn't see the point really I suppose, they're very used to chalk and talk teaching and seafarers doing things like personal reflection or sharing any sort of personal information that might be sensitive in any way with people is quite a scary concept for a lot of them, because its completely outside of their comfort zone . . . I suppose the Mahara tool represented all their worst fears, being public about things although public in a very select group, so that was threatening and then we didn't really know how it worked so we didn't communicate it very well to them how it worked and it's not the most intuitive

programme and so there were those problems and it was time consuming and it was bandwidth hungry, so there was all these issues that came together. *Innovator 1*

We got [an EDC colleague] to do some more guidance and videos for us on how to use it and some people were converted and others continued to not see the relevance of either using that sort of tool or personal development planning and all those sorts of issues. *Innovator 1*

As in so many of the SDP projects the principal innovator made a considerable personal investment, on top of their existing commitments to ensure momentum is sustained in the absence of additional resources when they are needed. It is this personal cost—doing what has to be done when it needs to be done—that ensures that change is actually accomplished within the time frames that have been set.

It required the goodwill of people like myself and my colleagues to work holidays and not have a break, it really did push us to the limit. *Innovator 1*

It seems that you cannot innovate in a university without this personal cost that is never measured or accounted for financially in any organisational development process. The only compensation for this type of commitment is through peer and public recognition (see later benefits).

MEETING THE ASPIRATIONS OF THE SDP

SDP funding enabled the Faculty to accelerate its strategy for more intensive use of on-line learning it also enabled the formation of a team with the right mix of expertise to design and deliver the new on-line course. But how did the course meet the aspirations of the University's Strategic Development Programme? It's clear that that the principal innovator and the Associate Dean believe that the MSc Shipping Operations on-line course has contributed to delivering some of the SDP objectives for the Faculty.

Well my understanding of the aspirations of the SDP were about appealing to or being flexible as a University to provide learning in a way in which, not just your typical student, whoever they might be, can access but can access when they're working, can access when they're overseas, can access when they've got a family. So the flexibility aspect I suppose and in terms that the students can study when it suits them and they don't have to come to us at a time when it suits us. And I suppose that's one of the key things that it offers and the other aspect is involving employers more and it's something we haven't actually touched on is that we, we encourage the students to identify a mentor within industry so they're getting a different perspective on what they're doing or the approach that they want to take with something, particularly with projects and work based assignments. So we've actually involved the employers, although they may not be their employer, in delivering the programme in a way and although they don't teach or assess, they are part of the process. *Innovator 1*

I think we're reaching out to different constituencies of students, the mature senior professionals. They can be in any part of the world, not all of them are British nationals, we know that there's probably going to be a market for this in other parts of the world, the Far East and India. It's much more flexible in terms of their ability to access it and do things at their own pace. We also have approved at the same time as the full master's programme, we approved all the units as professional development units and awards which are smaller blocks of learning and we're now moving to get that marketed so that people will take that up. And I think that that's something that we'll increasingly see, people want to do small blocks of learning that they can bank and build up for credit and then transfer into other courses and we're doing that too. We're doing it with our high level training courses at WMA now, the short courses, full masters that are not part of any particular award, we're now doing them as PDU's for credit. We'll be increasingly doing that. *WMA Associate Dean.*

CHAPTER 8

New Employer Partnership: Working with the University Hospital Southampton NHS Foundation Trust

INTRODUCTION

The chapter tells the unfolding story of how SDP funding has enabled the University to work collaboratively with the University Hospital Southampton NHS Foundation Trust (UHSFT) to co-create a Foundation Degree in Health and Social Care. The design of this programme and the manner in which it is being created and delivered is highly innovative for the University.

The story of innovation is interesting because it has been a particularly complex team effort. The narrative of this case study is constructed mainly through the voices of four different innovators (numbered 1—4).The first innovator had the vision for what eventually became the design which the second innovator put together for formal university approval with the help of other members of the team. The third innovator has oversight of the implementation of the design and the fourth innovator is responsible for the day to day operation of the programme. Innovation is occurring in real time and it is very much a pragmatic affair.

Everything about the programme is intended to be collaborative—this is the key innovative feature for the University. The key lesson from this story is how an organisation learns to innovate in a true collaboration with a partner: a partner who has very particular needs that have to be met in the design and delivery of the programme and the assessment of learning and competency for the work place.

Background

Greater involvement of employers in the co-design, co-delivery and co-funding of education and training is an important objective of the Strategic Development Programme (SDP). The bid document expressed this involvement in terms of what it would be like once the University had been transformed (Table 8.1).

This case study focuses on one of the SDP initiatives aimed at bringing about this transformation, namely the development of a new productive collaborative relationship with a major employing organisation in Southampton—UHSFT which employs over 11,000 people. Through this relationship a new Foundation Degree in Health and Social Care (FdSc H&SC), composed of numerous Professional Development Units (PDUs) which can also be studied independently, has been collaboratively developed specifically to help the employer meet its workforce development needs. The Foundation Degree is now being implemented through a co—delivery model and the first cohort of work-based learners is now being funded by the South Central Strategic Health Authority (SCSHA) to complete the course.

Table 8.1 A vision of what a transformed university would look like with respect to greater involvement of employers in the education of learners (Strategic Development Fund Bid p.xx)

The transformed university would have the following characteristics relating to employer involvement:

1. employers will be involved in developing curricula, designing, delivering and contributing to courses;
2. the portfolio will include a large number of short courses, together with internally and externally accredited professional courses to meet the demands of employers and their employees, and the wider skills agenda and a significant increase in part-time postgraduate provision;
3. employers will provide learning opportunities in the form of placements and live client briefs across all discipline areas;
4. employers will co-fund short courses and longer programmes tailored to their requirements.

Strategic alliance

Relationships between organisations begin and grow in all sorts of ways but they are generally rooted in arrangements that yield benefits to both organisations. Early in 2010, and initiated through a personal relationship between the Chief Executives of the two organisations, a new more formal relationship began to develop between Southampton Solent University and UHSFT

> The hospital's Trust has a relationship with Southampton
> University because it has the medical faculty and the

Faculty of Health Sciences there. However, our Chief Executive and the Vice-Chancellor decided that they wanted to develop this strategic alliance because Solent has different things to offer. *Representative UHSFT*

As part of the University's support for the strategic alliance SDP funds were used to enable a member of staff with an educational remit in the UHSFT to spend one day a week at the University to build a strong relationship and identify ways in which the partners could work together.

the [Strategic Alliance] agreement was made in the summer of 2010 and I started coming down here a day a week in November 2010 and it's continued since then. It was initially for six months and then a following 12 months and then this year it's been decided that it will continue until the end of July 2013. So that's without ongoing SDP funding because SSU have seen the value of what the alliance has brought and have decided to continue to fund this one day a week . . . 1

it was an interesting thing to start with because apart from the general principle of 'what we'd like to do is look at how the two organisations can work better together', there was nothing set out like these are the objectives, this is what we want you to achieve, these are the areas we want you to work in, it was very much a go out and see what you can find. 1

What I've been trying to do is to look at opportunities between both organisations looking at what Solent University offers and looking at my organisation, the hospital, so I can say this is happening at the hospital, this is happening at the University, these two things might have a relationship and in a way mapping opportunities and connecting individuals together to say this is worth looking at. 1

From the start there was an institutional will to make this innovation happen.

I think . . . right from the outset . . . . everyone who sat around the table wanted it to happen, everybody was moving in that direction and we all trusted that the other would do their bit, they would do their part to make it happen and without a doubt, from a senior leadership point of view, they were very enthusiastic and very clear to the faculty that this was a strategically important programme, that they wanted it to succeed. So I think there was a willingness to put resource where it was needed to get it off the ground. 1

In most of the innovation case studies in this book, the idea for innovation originates within the University to satisfy a perceived need. In this case study the idea for innovation originated in another organisation. From the perspective of UHSFT, the need for a new Foundation Degree had become an imperative because the existing Foundation Degree provision, with the University of Southampton, was coming to an end. Here are three different but consistent perspectives on the background to this curriculum innovation.

The first perspective is from someone who was working in a role outside the University who advised the UHSFT that the University might be the most appropriate partner for the development of a Foundation Degree.

> I'd been working both at a local and national level as Director of Foundation Degree Forward and I pointed what was Southampton University Hospitals NHS Trust at the time, towards Solent University because they had SDP funding and they were looking at flexible delivery models and with the funding changes, other more traditional Universities were moving away from that kind of delivery model. *Former Director Foundation Degree Forward*

The second perspective is offered by the University's SDP-funded, Employer Engagement Specialist.

> The Foundation Degree in Health and Social Care arose from an idea that had been spotted by [a colleague] who is seconded from the Health Trust to the University one day a week, funded by the SDP programme, to help identify partnership working opportunities driven by the needs of the Trust. She had been working with us sufficiently long to see that there were opportunities around work-based learning. In particular looking at the sorts of training they already gave their workforce. They had been in initial discussions with somebody from Foundation Degree Forward to see whether their internal training programme could be packaged as a foundation degree. They had been reassured that the sort of content they were delivering could be level four or maybe even level five and that what they needed was some contextual modules to surround the work-based practitioner-type training in order to turn it into a Foundation Degree. [My colleague] was well-primed

and had the right access to the right knowledge at the right time to spot that there was an obvious opportunity for us to be the provider of the Foundation Degree. So she initiated discussions, I believe initially with [the SDP Manager]. *2*

A third perspective is provided by the UHSFT secondee.

we had developed an internal training programme and we wanted to review it and get it validated and then offer it as a Foundation Degree. So [I said] 'is this something that you would be willing to do? It's not something you do already but does it fit, would you be willing to take the risk?' And they were very happy to take the risk . . . . at SCSHA level [I said] 'this is a university you've never worked with before as a commissioning body, we want to develop this programme with them, would you fund it? Would you be prepared to take them as a preferred provider for this Foundation Degree if people want to go on it?' And because we're a big enough organisation within Hampshire and because we said that we could get enough people together to make the course viable, it needs around 20 students, the Health Authority agreed they'd fund it and the University said they wanted to do this . . . 1

Clearly, the Trust's representative played a key role in persuading, negotiating and brokering the idea of a Foundation Degree between the University, the Trust and the Strategic Health Authority.

TURNING AN IDEA INTO AN INNOVATION

The steps involved in turning the idea for a Foundation Degree in Health and Social Care into a reality are shown in Figure 8.1. All the stages provide illustrations of the challenges involved in significant curriculum innovative for which there was no precedent and all of the stages illustrate the determination and capabilities of the individuals involved to succeed in the face of institutional hurdles and blocks. The development and implementation process shows very well how innovation challenges institutional systems, procedures and traditions that have been long established and deeply embedded in the everyday business of the organisation.

The chronological sequence of events is described in terms of: 1) Design stage 2) Capacity building and pre-course stage and 3) Implementation stage.

Figure 8.1 Timeline for collaborative development and implementation of the Foundation Degree in Health & Social Care

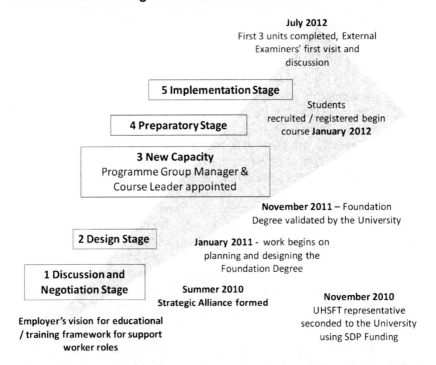

July 2012
First 3 units completed, External
Examiners' first visit and
discussion

5 Implementation Stage

4 Preparatory Stage

Students
recruited / registered begin
course **January 2012**

3 New Capacity
Programme Group Manager &
Course Leader appointed

November 2011 – Foundation
Degree validated by the University

2 Design Stage

January 2011 - work begins on
planning and designing the
Foundation Degree

**1 Discussion and
Negotiation Stage**

Summer 2010
Strategic Alliance formed

November 2010
UHSFT representative
seconded to the University
using SDP Funding

Employer's vision for educational
/ training framework for support
worker roles

Co-designing the programme

The initial step in creating a new degree programme is to design a curriculum framework, which identifies the nature of the intended learning outcomes and competencies to be developed, the knowledge content and skills that will be learnt, the learning experiences that will be created to enable learning, the resources and facilities that will be available to enable learning and the assessment that will be used to determine that learning has been achieved. Such a curriculum framework needs to be designed by people who have the necessary knowledge and skill and to be scrutinised by peers in a quality assurance process known as Programme Validation. The process typically takes six to twelve months to complete.

Because of the employer and work-related dimensions of the Foundation Degree the first university person to become directly involved was the SDP—funded Employer Engagement Specialist.

> I very quickly got involved because that was part of my job as employer engagement specialist. Actually I think it might have been [the Pro Vice-Chancellor] that spoke

to me first and said 'We need to develop a Foundation Degree that might use work-based learning' and I said, 'That would be easy to develop. It would sit quite nicely with social work' which is the programme group I used to manage . . . I could see there were opportunities with our existing curriculum to mesh with this new provision. I got the message to make it happen. To do whatever was necessary.

At the start of the design process, the Hospital Trust already had a very good idea of how it wanted the Foundation Degree to be structured based around the requirements of the support worker role (Assistant Practitioner) that was being developed in the workforce. Furthermore, its concept for a Foundation Degree was an integral part of a much bigger vision for a comprehensive education and training framework for the development of its support worker workforce (Figure 8.2).

Figure 8.2 UHSFT Health Career Pathway Options AfC Band 1-5

Band 5	BSc professional programme e.g. nursing		
Band 5	Fd in Health & Social Care		Final 2yrs BSc professional programme (to be agreed)
Band 4	Fd in Health & Social Care		Additional Fd CPD Units
Band 4	Fd in Health & Social Care		
Band 3	Advanced apprenticeship or Level 3 QCF award		Additional training/Fd CPD Units
Band 3	External delivered advanced apprenticeship or Level 3 QCF award	Additional Acute Units	
Band 3	UHS delivered advanced apprenticeship		
Band 2	UHS delivered intermediate apprenticeship		
Band 1	Induction and 'on job' training		

✓ Enables the Trust to adapt quickly to meet changes in practice

✓ Allows for stepping on and off points at all bands

✓ Allows individuals to progress at own pace to own level of competence

This is how the Trust's representative described the Foundation Degree concept.

I think to start with we'd come up with the structure at the hospital. I suppose what we were trying to think is how can we create a course which is academically sound but at the same time enables people who are part of a workforce, who are needed on the shop floor, to be released from their work in a meaningful way? But not to the point where they are away too much as it's a struggle for the clinical areas to release them. And how can we do it in a way as well which enables people to develop once they're in a role?

We'd already said to the Health Authority that one of the issues we had with other FDs is they were validated as end to end FDs and we said that just doesn't fit how we want to work, we need them in units because it's how the staff roles are evolving. Also some people who are employees, the nature of them is they're often older learners, they're people who are not always confident with learning and could find that step into higher education quite scary. So they might have done very well at their level 3 apprenticeship which we run in-house so they're confident with all of us, they know us and then we can make the suggestion 'well, perhaps you'd like to do a Foundation Degree' at the University, and their response was likely to be . . . 'oh, no, not me, I was never academic, I can't do that, it's too long'. So we wanted to create something where individuals could take that first step quite safely without feeling they'd signed up to two years and then if they didn't progress they wouldn't feel like they'd failed and feel like they'd wasted money and time and the rest of it. So by having it in units, it meant that individuals could do a very short unit, gain some evidence, gain some qualification from it and actually feel they had achieved. And then they could choose to either end there or to continue studying more units and build towards a degree. And it also would enable us to create a system of CPD for individuals once they'd finished the Foundation Degree and as they moved around in jobs, as a lot of them do, so they might start off in one clinical area but might decide to go into a similar job in a different clinical specialty. So we wanted something which was a bit more flexible and really a building block.

We also wanted to make it much more relevant to the workplace, we had to use occupational standards, so there had to be an element of assessment against the standards in the two biggest units: the 40 credit units in both the level 4 and level 5 are work-based learning units with occupational standards assessment against them as well as academic case studies in them. And that was to satisfy our need for staff to be safe to practice and to provide assurance to the registered professional clinical staff who'd be delegating work to these individuals that they were competent.

So we knew we had to do a work-based learning unit but we then said but that means we have standards against which we assessed that, it could be in any occupational area and we didn't want to create something that was just nursing . . . There's a lot of change going on across all the health professions so we wanted something which would lend itself to further development as it needed around healthcare science, technician type roles and allied health professions like the physio. support role. So the way we have founded our work-based learning means that we can add in the competencies whenever and whatever the role needs to be developed.

And then the core units were things which we found were important [regardless] of where you worked, ... and we developed those units based around what we knew would fit any occupation, whether it's health science or nursing or whatever, and those are all around communication, broader understanding of the NHS and health science, so that they got that anatomy and physiology and basic science. And in the second year two of the core units, one is around supervision and some delegation and how to supervise others like more junior support workers and also support learners in the workplace. So [learners] become assessors of our apprentices. Another unit is a project based unit which was about doing an audit where we would say to them you need to look at an area of practice where you work and think of ways it could be improved.

So those are the sorts of core things that we've built in across the two years and then we said we can develop 20 credit option units which can be the things that apply to a particular clinical role or area. [For example] we've got one for cardiac physiology which is designed for the role that supports cardiac physiologist roles . . . taught by the clinical experts in that area and delivered at the hospital so it meant no new additional resources were required here at the University.

The other thing we've planned in from the very beginning was what would be the progression routes because we were also very aware of the fact that a lot of our staff would want to progress from being assistant practitioners to becoming registered nurses or registered healthcare scientists or whatever. So we have deliberately made sure as far as we are able that the 2-year Foundation programme fits as closely as possible to the Year 1 of the degree programme for some of the clinical professional roles. And we are in discussions with other universities about people being able to complete this Foundation Degree to progress on to Year 2 of their programmes . . .

My vision is for the staff that are my responsibility to develop education and training for (support worker roles), is to create an 'end to end' [framework] from Apprenticeship at level 2, Intermediate Apprenticeship through Advanced Apprenticeship which we offer in-house through a Foundation Degree and a core option route and CPD route for those individuals as a stepping on/stepping off point. I also want progression into opportunities for registered professional training as well so they end up as registered professionals and then other colleagues in Training and Development at the Trust take on responsibility for planning the development of the registered clinical staff beyond that. But it is about creating that flow through, real roles where people can step on and step off at each point but then can clearly start to see 'this is where I fit and where I can go and how I can do it'. And by doing each of it in small blocks until you get to the registered professional bit it means people can stay in work, maintain their commitments within their family life and still be able to gain bits of qualifications they need to.

What this vision reveals is that the Foundation Degree (albeit a complex structure) is only one small part of a comprehensive and flexible framework for the development of an employer's workforce while they are in work.

From Southampton Solent University's perspective the Foundation Degree in Health and Social Care is defined as non-standard provision in so far as the design was to be one of collaboration between the University and the UHSFT and needed the coordinated contributions of university academics and clinical practitioners from the UHSFT. Because, under University rules it was considered to be non-standard provision, the design and validation process had to involve people from the University's Academic Quality Services.

> We knew from the outset that we would have to go through the collaborative provision process, which meant that Academic Services had to lead on the validation. So we effectively set up a curriculum development group made up of the Trust and myself, the head of employer-led learning in our Academic Services, another person from quality services and somebody from the Faculty. *SDP Employer Engagement Specialist*

There was an expectation that the School of Human Sciences in the Faculty of Creative Industries and Society (FCIS), would manage the programme and lead curriculum development. But because this initiative was a rapid response to a strategic partner it had never been budgeted for in Faculty plans. Not surprisingly the Faculty did not have the capacity to take a leading role which eventually fell to the SDP-funded employer engagement specialist.

> At the outset we expected the Faculty to pick up the curriculum development role. So I expected somebody in the Housing and Social Work group that I had previously managed, to be identified as the course leader in waiting to develop the curriculum and use the expertise of that group to develop units in partnership with the hospital. That never happened and as time went on we were going through the process, but nobody was coming forward from the Faculty on the curriculum development side. So I said 'I will do it.' I know enough about SocialCare because I used to manage that area, I know enough about what the hospital wants to be able to work between the partners and to develop the course documentation. 2

In the light of this strategic development the Faculty made provision for appointing a 0.5 Course Leader and a new FT Programme Group Leader in its plans for 2011-12. But the curriculum design work had to be more or less completed before these people came into post in October and November 2012 respectively.

Collaborative enterprise

Everything about the programme was intended to be collaborative—this was the key innovative feature and the key lesson from this story is how an organisation learns to innovate in collaboration with an employer partner: a partner who has very particular needs that have to be met in the design, delivery and assessment of the programme.

> There were lots of little hurdles to overcome like exams. Whereas we probably wouldn't have put exams into a foundation degree that had such a great amount of work activity we had to build these into some of the units as this would give the workplace staff the confidence that the students had been assessed in exam conditions. We might have encouraged them perhaps to think about work-based assessments. But they were very definite about that. I suppose the ethos which I found very easy was to respond to what the employer's needs were and if necessary change what the University would normally do because this was a non-standard provision. 2

The writing of the curriculum document for validation was essentially completed by the leader of the curriculum development group and two members of staff from the Hospital Trust who were on the curriculum development group.

> I ended up writing up the whole course documentation— strategic rationale, course costing, course learning outcomes . . . . The individual unit descriptors I did in partnership with the hospital authors, some of whom responded to emails and some didn't. So sometimes I just had to take a list of bullets and put it into the form of words needed for the unit descriptor. [Three of us] did the bulk of stuff even though other people's names were on the unit descriptors. 2

But it is not easy to change traditions and practices within a university and one of the reasons for the success of this innovation at the design stage was the privileged position of the person who was leading the curriculum development process for what the University describes as non-standard provision—provision that involves collaboration with an external partner.

> I think course developers [in the Faculties] are finding nobody will tell them what the answer is because no one knows what the answer is. No one is prepared to take responsibility to say 'Its new, this is the way we have to do it. We haven't done it that way at all before, but this is how you solve your problem.' I think I was in a perfect role really to overcome all of the barriers and get the thing done. I suppose the worry for me is once that role goes and the University settles back into its normal course of business that there won't be anybody that can champion this sort of development. 2

It is also clear in the curriculum design process that there was a tendency for university staff who were unfamiliar with non-standard provision, to place it within the sort of academic frameworks with which they were familiar.

> [My colleague] happened to tell me something in passing about the delivery model that was being proposed. And I said 'But that isn't what you wanted, was it?' And she said, 'No, but he said that is how we do things here.' And I said 'No, the whole point of this is to respond to what your needs are. Yes, of course we can do things differently.' He didn't know for instance that in our academic framework there was something called block delivery. He didn't know it existed. So that kind of showed me that there was a huge gap because people had not done non—standard delivery before. They just don't know what is possible even within our own academic framework. So I think that is one of our on—going issues. That yes, we have got flexibility and we can do things differently but people don't know how to do things differently because they have never done it before. If they have never looked they don't even know there is a whole range of different ways of doing stuff now. So that was an issue. 2

Another way in which the design was non-standard was in the way in which Professional Development Units had been integrated into the programme so that learners could, if they wished take the PDU as a freestanding short course.

> the PDU's were created at the same time as the Foundation Degree—the Strategic Health Authority actually said this had to be what they call a modular programme. So every unit has to be available as standalone and interestingly has to be available across the whole region. So every single unit within the programme is also a PDU and is therefore standalone which has helped with the delivery. It means that some people have only been doing them as PDUs. 2

Like all programmes that lead to a university award the programme and the infrastructure to support the programme had to be reviewed through an institutional validation event. The event itself was uneventful but an incident the day before revealed again the challenge of this innovative programme for institutional systems and procedures.

The day before the Head of Quality said 'You can't validate the PDU's as separate standalone provision at the same time as the Foundation Degree', despite that always being the plan and two people from quality being on the curriculum development group. So I suppose that is a good example of how unexpected procedural things can crop up at the last minute. So I had to go and lobby various people and say 'This is unacceptable, we don't want to drag the employer through another validation event. There is no reason why we can't do this in one go. Find out what evidence or piece of paper or whatever means that we can do it and make it happen.' So again, if I hadn't been in that kind of position of knowing who to lobby and been able to put pressure on senior people—because she was the Head of Quality, that probably wouldn't have happened and we would have just wasted a lot of people's time really. 2

But almost immediately after the Foundation Degree had been validated another issue arose because another NHS Trust expressed an interest. The issue here was with the University's quality procedures because the formal agreement that had been signed with the UHSFT limited the offer of the Foundation Degree in Health and Social Care to this Trust, in spite of the Strategic Health Authority's stipulation that the programme had to be available to all NHS employees working in the region.

we were told by our quality section 'Well our collaborative provision agreement is only with the hospital trust so actually you can't offer it to these other trusts.' And I said 'That's the whole point of it.' The strategic health authority requires us to offer it to other people. They are still working that out now, so it still hasn't been solved. So again, I don't quite know why . . . . I suppose I am slightly disappointed because I knew other universities were doing it that way. So in my mind if somebody else has done it there must be a simple way of doing it. Our motivation to sort these problems out maybe isn't always as good. 2

This story reveals how university quality procedures which regulate the University's educational business, can sometimes restrict the opportunities for business in ways that external partners, with no knowledge of the ways in which universities conduct their business, find frustrating.

Building new capacity to deliver the programme

This story of innovation is interesting because there were effectively two different lots of innovators involved. The first innovators came up with the idea and created a design. The second group of innovators turned the designs into an operational framework with systems and procedures and implemented the programme. This is probably quite a common pattern of innovation where new programmes are created but it required the people who were implementing the programme to understand what was in the minds of the designers very quickly. Building new capacity to implement the innovation design, is an important feature of this innovation and it required the University to appoint two new members of staff—a Course Leader with responsibility for the day to day operation of the course and a Programme Manager with responsibility for managerial oversight and the development of systems to support delivery.

> I arrived at the end of November right at the end of getting the Foundation Degree in Health and Social Care ready for validation . . . . I was responsible for the delivery of the programme that was due to start in January. The colleagues from the hospital who had been on that initial group, putting together the structure of the programme were all still very much involved. So it was about establishing a relationship with them and just trying to get up to speed with what their vision was, what their intention was in having this kind of programme. 3

> I'm course leader for the foundation degree. I started my contract on 11th October so course design was already well underway. It was actually approaching validation . . . there were obviously some things needed doing before it could go to validation and that was the unit descriptors. So I came in and I had two weeks to get moving on writing some unit descriptors in time for the validation at the end of November . . . those had to be completed and I only work18.5 hours a week so I didn't have lots of time to do this. I hadn't written unit descriptors before so it was a fast learning curve for me. 4

The transition into a new organisation can be a challenge as people who are new try to find out how the organisation works. One of the innovators had a mentor who seems to have provided practical help and emotional support.

> To start with I did feel like I had jumped into a pool. I had to swim around, look around and find the right people and

> think 'okay, so there is somebody that knows something
> about this and there is somebody that has got some
> expectations here.' Identifying who those people were and
> trying to understand what it was that they were looking for
> and expecting to achieve was my initial priority. 3

> I have a mentor who has been fantastic. So whenever I'm
> a bit stuck I go and see her and she's been able to help
> me and advise me and I have a good supporting manager
> as well. 4

That they were involved in an innovative programme only became clear to the innovators as they began to talk to other people who were involved.

> The fact that this was a programme that was not just
> written by the University and delivered to the hospital
> but it was to be developed delivered and assessed in
> collaboration with the employer. This was something that
> the University hadn't really done before. I hadn't realised
> that when I started. It was only as I started to work with
> them that I realised we were doing something there wasn't
> really a precedent for in the University. 3

One of the challenges in this situation is for the first group of innovators to communicate their vision for their designs and the second group to grow and take ownership for their own visions grown out of the these earlier visions. This is not something that can be achieved through the exchange of a written document. It requires a lot of conversation and discussion.

> I realised quite quickly there wasn't an articulated vision.
> I am not sure that what the hospital thought they were
> going to get was quite what the University thought they
> were going to deliver. I think as the year has gone on and
> we are delivering it for the first cohort of students, we
> are finding that out as we go along. Gradually, there is a
> coming together and we are developing a better collective
> understanding of the different roles, the different partners
> and whose responsibility it is to decide what is going to
> happen and how it is going to happen. 3

This idea of growing collective understanding as the innovation is implemented is a strong and recurrent theme in this story which developed throughout the implementation stage.

Implementing the programme—pragmatic invention

The programme was validated in late November 2011 and delivery had to begin in January 2012—but there is a world of difference between a validation document that contains a broad structure and some module descriptors and the reality of a curriculum that is delivered to students.

The major challenge of this innovation has been to develop the curriculum and the management and support systems simultaneously with delivering the programme. The two innovators who were mainly responsible for this had about two months after the programme was validated to operationalise the framework—that's to develop the curriculum to the point where it could be delivered and to have in place the necessary operational systems to recruit and register students and track their progress. Clearly, with such pressurised time scales there has to be both a pragmatic approach to development and an element of improvisation as invention becomes a more or less continuous process. Given that so many aspects of the programme were different to the way programmes were normally organised and run, the scale of the challenge was considerable.

> Every single aspect of the programme has required something different from the University system than it is normally expected to do. So how the students are funded, how they register, what days they come into the University, who is responsible for writing the assessment, deciding who is going to assess it. None of that was the traditional format. So here we are, we've got a programme that is going to start in January to which students had to be recruited, but no precedent of how that was going to happen. So we made it up as we went along. 3

The first implementation challenge was to recruit, interview and register the students. The way this was approached reveals very well the pragmatic nature of the invention process.

> We didn't have the time to think everything through and try it out in advance. We had a start date for the programme and we had a hospital that knew it needed to get a particular group of employees onto it. So we worked on the assumption that we are going to have to have interviews. We need to meet. We have got a validation document which tells us what the entry requirements are. We have got a hospital team that need to have managers supporting them, releasing their students to this programme. So we need a joint application form which meets our requirements and meets their requirements.

> But we didn't quite do it in time. So we had joint interviews between the course leader and the hospital team did the interviews together and selected the students meeting two sets of quite distinct criteria really. Our education criteria and the hospital's management and professional development criteria. So next time we do it, we know what we are looking for. But we didn't necessarily know at that point. 3

Simultaneously with recruitment, a handbook of information for students had to be put together with all the information they would need to complete the programme.

> The students actually started at the end of January. So during January we had to work very quickly to get a handbook ready for them with all the details of the course as it would look. So we had to work out the timetabling, the dates, how that would work in terms of when assessments were due in and when the exam boards would be scheduled and all those university processes in order for when the students started to say, 'This is the course you are coming on. these are the different units and when you are going to be doing them. These are the assignments you are going to write and this is when you are going to hand them in.' 3

> We needed to have the calendar organised so that we knew exactly what was happening, when it was happening and who was responsible for that. So those were the things we were having meetings to ensure that we tried to cover everything and make sure that everything was in place. So the calendars were up, and the options were up. 4

Such knowledge has to be accumulated rapidly, in this case by someone who was new to the institution.

> I needed to have all the information for students that they might need to refer to for the course and for the University. Things like understanding the way things are marked, understanding the credits, the units, core units, option units and so on and how that works. Also being aware of what they need to do as well in order to progress their studies.

> . . . . obviously I was guided by other handbooks which helped and I liaised with my mentor, with health staff and so on to ensure that anything that they wanted included

into the handbook was included. So there was a lot of talking to other people to make sure everything was there and also checking "Does this sound okay? Are you happy with this?" And sharing just to make sure before we went to print. 4

Then there was the preparation for students' arrival. There were 18 students in the first group.

Well clearly preparing for the students arrival, ensuring that registration happened, and that everybody was aware of them coming and that they were prepared and had everything in place to enrol them. Making sure we had the rooms available, and I think all of those things as well as being prepared to teach was quite a challenge and obviously we had meetings to make sure things were in place so we could tick boxes, but there was a really difficult time. Because there were so many things that needed to be in place at that particular time, that January was really hectic. 4

Developing the curriculum content proceeded in parallel with the preparation of handbooks and preparations for getting the students started.

To say the curriculum was designed, I think it was in the very early stages. It was literally the skeleton of a curriculum that was validated and then we had to work out the detail of the what and the how. 3

We had to work very quickly to identify who was going to deliver the units and be responsible for developing the detail of the curriculum content. That has been a huge learning journey for us as well because again, it is this combination between university expectations of what counts as a level four or level five qualification and the high level thinking and the academic skills that are needed for that combined with the hospital's need to develop specific competences so that the students could do a particular job. Again, we have had to be fairly reactive in getting the units ready to deliver in the short timescale. We have learned a lot by doing it the first time, about getting that balance right between a university-driven course and a hospital-driven course. And I think we will get to a point when we get the best of both worlds. 3

Well the challenges were the preparation, because I was developing a lot of content specific knowledge for this programme and I wanted to ensure that I was up to date on reading. I wanted to ensure that I could deliver in a way that the students found interesting and include various types of teaching so that it kept them interested and engaged so that they would go away and want to know more. So those were the areas that were a challenge for me. 4

The split location of the people involved in the programme, and the difficulty of finding times everyone could meet around other work commitments, makes the logistics of group meetings to discuss the programme very difficult.

Because we are on different sites even just getting a meeting where we can sit around a table is a challenge. We've had what we called operational group meetings. Not as regularly as we would have liked but they have held the thing together when issues have needed to be resolved. I think what will make it work in the long term is the trust, respect and relationships between colleagues in both organisations. We are getting there. We are getting to a point where we can say what we think our own expectations are and come to a shared understanding. 3

We have also got a strategic programme management group, which is the sort of quality overview which is due to meet only for its second time. So it is still very early days for that. Then we have . . . slightly more ad hoc curriculum development group for each new unit. They have changed depending on the nature of which unit is coming up and which group of people need to collaborate and get together on it. But again, because we are working with hospital colleagues who are all busy clinical practitioners, a lot of it is done sort of remotely and passing documents to and fro and that sort of thing. 3

The approach of pragmatic invention in order to deliver the programme leading to learning from experience is illustrated through this perspective. This is a real time curriculum development process albeit for pragmatic reasons.

Because the time was so tight when we had to deliver the first unit . . . we just had to deliver it. That raised our awareness of the different expectations of the University and the hospital and who could say 'Yes, we can include that' or 'No, we are not going to do that.' We have learnt that each unit has to have a unit leader which may not necessarily be the person who delivers it but who has overall responsibility for it. That person needs to be really clear about liaising with the clinicians who want a certain aspect in it and then to shape that into something that has got academic purpose and rigour as well. I think I am currently teaching an option unit on human growth. I think I have benefited from the learning that we have had in the other units that it is really important to seek that input to shape what it is you are going to deliver . . . . I think for the next time around it will have been a really good way of doing it because you know what went well and what didn't go well and . . . . you don't just try to imagine what ifs, you actually know what they are. 3

CHALLENGES

There have been many challenges associated with the first cycle of the Foundation Degree in Health and Social Care. Many of these challenges stem from the fact that the programme was invented as it was delivered by people who were new to the institution so they had to learn about the organisation as well as learn how to make the programme work.

The thing that I found very difficult was learning everything at the same time as implementing the course that was a real challenge. I mean even yesterday I thought "Wow!" now I totally understand that, and that's how it's been all the way through. So it has been a steep learning curve. 4

some of the challenges have been, because we've kind of run with this from the start is having the right people at the right time to teach on it. If people don't respond, because health want to be involved and sometimes you put something out "Is anybody able . . . ?" and you don't hear anything. So perhaps that's been the challenge, you think "Oh right then I need to obviously address that one." 4

The main challenge for the partner organisation was understanding and coming to terms with the way the University worked, particularly its bureaucracy.

I think the biggest challenge for us was probably understanding the way the University works, and I don't just mean this university but I think how higher education works, it feels at times quite laborious in terms of how things have got to be pulled together, the way you've got to go through the validation stuff, the due diligence is just unwieldy. You seem to have to create so much and it has to be in such a particular way and it does feel very hard work. I don't know whether it's this university or simply the nature of universities and how they tend to structure, I think it was the terminology used obviously because that's always the way, the processes that have to be put in place, the number of different groups everything's got to go through to get approved! 1

We're still struggling a bit at the moment with the due diligence . . . for another NHS Trust, it just seems to be a lumbering beast to try and get due diligence sorted, we've done it once with our hospital, we've kind of said we all have to provide this to the Health Authority anyway for all of the other stuff we do, they'll have all these things in place. So all this stuff around are they viable, I can understand it if you're talking about a small company thing, but we're talking about the health service, and the big hospitals are not small private concerns . . . 1

There were also a set of challenges relating to partnership working in the delivery of the programme.

The first unit on the social and psychological impacts of health and social care was being managed by the University. It was a challenge because neither [of the innovators] had been involved in the writing of the unit. We knew . . . what we expected to see in that unit. And there was one part of it . . . . around the wider understanding of health in a national context and a social context and how we perceive health within our community and our national culture . . . . we didn't want to seem like we were being pushy taking over but we knew there were some bits we felt we could offer as talk sessions. So to start with it felt a bit like, 'oh no, this is the University's unit and we need to teach it', but we realised that "this isn't about your need to teach all of it". We gave [the Course Leader] a list of topics we thought needed to be covered . . . and said "if you need us to teach any of this or to facilitate and get students to go and think about stuff then we're happy to help" . . . . it was fine in the end but working out how to do it was a challenge. 1

An indication of the distance travelled in learning how to collaborate in curriculum design is afforded by this example of one innovator's experience of developing a new unit in communication.

All of us sat down together and said what do we need in the communications unit because this is the first jointly delivered unit between 3 partners SSU, UHS and the new partner Southern Health NHS Foundation Trust so what do we want in it? who has the expertise to teach what part of it? how do we want to do this? and how are we going to lay out the six weeks that we're going to run the programme for? So we have evolved from this very anxious position in January when our concern was about whose bit of the world does it fit into, to now where everyone sits down and says this is what we need, I could teach this bit, I could teach that bit, and those bits all fit and where will we get this from and how can we develop that. 1

The adequacy of resources to support the implementation of an innovation in real time was also an issue for one of the innovators.

The biggest thing has been the hours more than anything else, I felt that 18.5 hours just doesn't even begin to address what's needed to implement a new course. So that's been a big problem. . . . . January was just mad. I did a lot more than 18.5 hours per week, it was impossible to complete the work . . . so I more or less worked full time throughout that period 4

There have also been a set of challenges that relate to the uniqueness and newness of the programme. The fact that it is different to any other programme in the University continually challenges a university that is used to doing things differently.

The University traditionally has two semesters. We are not doing that. So we are still . . . teaching right up until the middle of July. The way we are delivering the units is in blocks. So they do one unit and then they do the next unit, whereas traditionally in university they are doing two or three units at the same time. Another difference is that they can take a unit called a Professional Development Unit. . . . every unit in the programme is also validated to be studied as a standalone unit . . . So students can just register for a unit and then build up the units to complete the programme, or just take the units they want. So we have a start date for the programme in January, but because of the way the hospital likes to recruit people, if they want some training they want to access it quite quickly. Students can join at any point in the year at the unit they are on, do that unit, do any other units until

> January and then APEL those units into the programme
> and continue as registered in the programme. That has
> not been done in this university before. So it is a great
> model and I think we should do more of it because it is
> very responsive to employer's needs. It can be taken in
> bite-sized chunks if they want it that way. 3

The fact that students can register for the whole course or take selected
Professional Development Units is an important design feature which it
makes it very different from a traditional university course but this has
significant implications for the management of learner experiences

> tracking the people who are registered on the PDU's and
> keeping up with that, so we need to have really good
> systems in place to track those individuals as well as a
> good monitoring process. 3

Not surprisingly such flexibility has challenged some institutional systems
for example in registering students at very short notice and tracking
students through their individualised programme.

> We thought originally that we would have different points
> of entry through the year to the whole programme. We
> realised that this is actually very difficult to do in terms
> of how the University creates their records and how they
> monitor that. It is much easier to have one point of entry
> to the programme. 3

> One of the challenges has been late applications, because
> there's no set time, there was initially for the course but
> because we're running PDUs as well, it's all just in time
> you know, I could just get one tomorrow. "Oh here's an
> application for this or . . ." and it's trying to get the process
> in place for that person. And it's been really, really difficult
> because we're not set up to do that. The University is
> geared for September to July, they're not geared for
> January to December, and that's a big problem. 4

> We've had a meeting this week actually because of the
> problems with the people applying for individual units.
> Because they can't access our systems . . . they start off
> going to do this particular unit, and then it turns out they're
> actually going to do the next unit as well. What's happening
> is they're not enrolled on the next unit, they have to go
> through the process again . . . and some of the units are
> only held at the hospital, so they would never come to

the University. So that's a problem because they need to come back and enrol and they can't understand why. We have met with all the relevant people [in Registry] and said "How can we get around this in the future because this is going to be happening on a regular basis?" 3

There have also been access issues for students registered on PDU's.

I've got to ensure that they're able to access everything they need, you know, through "My Course", which has been one of the biggest problems to be honest. And I haven't always known why they can't access it and it's another phone call about the system. So until that's really sorted that's going to be the biggest problem with PDUs really, for the students to access the system. And that's what's most important for them, not so much the resources or anything else. Because all of the information is on the system, it's uploaded onto "My Course" and they need to know where they are being taught and what they're doing. It's also where we upload the assignments to be completed and any updates. Everything is on there, you know, the news forums and so on so that's why it's important. 4

To an unsympathetic observer this list of challenges and issues might give the impression that this was a problematic programme but these are the sorts of issues that emerge when you try to customise and personalise learning. It requires business systems that can cope with greater complexity of learner behaviours in order to do the things they need to do on the course. It looks as if one of the ways that institutional systems are made to change is when they are forced to adapt because there is a concrete and urgent problem to deal with. It also seems that the people using the institutional systems may not themselves anticipate the full range of scenarios that might arise, simply because they assume that business systems will be able to cope. However, when problems are raised, generally there is seems to be a willingness to address them.

Interviewer: Do you feel that in a sense the issues have to emerge in a practical sense before you can approach the University to get them sorted? and that it can't be done in terms of "Oh this might happen in the future." In other words the University has got to react to a real situation.

Yes this is how it's happened really.

Another situation has been, one student who had extenuating circumstances was unable to take the exam. And this is quite interesting because our health partners felt that, "Oh well they can do it next week instead." They weren't aware of the kind of programmes we have at university, that there's only a certain week that you can resit exams. So we felt that she could resit in the resit week, but as it turns out she can't because of the unit boards and the Progress Boards and so on. So that's another problem we've now got to address because we hadn't got our Progress Board set up, not for this year certainly.

Well I've been talking to people in registration . . . . because people have been saying, "Well you can't do this" or "You can't do that", they've been very good because they've looked for ways around things. Certainly we seem to be addressing some of these issues now but it's just that people have had the pain first, if you understand me students, you know, and it seems that's the way we have to do it because we're not always aware that there's a problem until there is some pain. 4

Interviewer: But the point you're making is that you're talking to people and you're getting responses which show that people care that there's a problem and they are trying to address it. So the University is effectively becoming much more engaged in your particular problem and there seems to be a willingness to try and sort it and to suggest short term work arounds that will allow you to carry on?

Yes absolutely and I have to say I've been quite impressed with the support that we've had in trying to address things and find ways round problems. 4

Taking risks and coping with anxiety

With so many challenges emerging from real time innovation involving students an important question is how do innovators cope with the stress and anxiety of tackling such challenges? Do innovators feel they are taking risks?

Yes I do, it is very, very risky. I think for the University it is reputationally risky and in a difficult commercial environment in higher education and in the public sector, which is what health is, it is a risk to try and do something in that field and to do it in a different way, which is absolutely the most likely way to succeed but it also might all fall badly wrong and it is a reputational risk for the University. 3

> there have been times when I've felt concerned and worried about things. Because obviously I make mistakes, I'm not anything near perfect, and obviously I do worry that sometimes perhaps things are a risk and that's that. And I have to either take the risk or not. You just have to do it sometimes. 4

In such situations innovators have to cope with the anxieties of putting themselves and their organisation into a risky situation, particularly those who ultimately are responsible for the innovation, so how do they manage this anxiety.

> I have sleepless nights and I don't like having sleepless nights. I will be glad when we have been around one circuit of it and we have begun to be a bit more strategic and a bit more able to plan rather than react. It has not been a comfortable way to work. That is the honest truth of it. We will have learned a lot, but it would have been much better if we hadn't done it this way. 3

> I suppose I am quite grateful I am not at the beginning of my working life and I feel 'Oh well, not the end of the world if it doesn't work.' If you say to yourself 'What is the worst that could happen?' well that wouldn't be so bad, that would be alright. No one is going to die if the programme doesn't succeed so let's just give it a go. And there is always a chance of something quite good coming out of it, you know, even if it is not exactly what you expect some real good things might happen along the way. 3

> I don't feel that I would be shot down or anything like that, I do feel that I am well supported. 4

ADDITIONAL PERSPECTIVES

Learning quickly

New capacity was required to introduce the Foundation Degree innovation consequently some members of the innovation team were new to the organisation and lacked the taken for granted knowledge that is acquired through being part of an organisation. Furthermore, newly appointed people lack the relationships that enable them to gain knowledge quickly— they often don't know who to ask to resolve a problem and even when they do they may not be able to get the answers they need. This issue is compounded by hierarchical structures that necessitate people referring queries up the chain of command.

> One of the key things here for me is that in a hierarchical organisation such as a university, people who are busy will only respond to what people above them in the hierarchy tell them to do. As someone who was (and is) forever asking questions—some obvious and some not obvious—getting others to engage with the questions and respond outside of their own remit and capacity was all but impossible as I didn't have sufficient hierarchical 'clout'.

Growing collective understanding through innovating

Creating and implementing something as complex as a degree programme has to be a team effort and the innovation team may, as in this example, involve people who are strategists, brokers and connectors, designers, teachers and administrators. Visioning is often seen as an important part of creating something new and in other case studies we witness examples of innovators who imagined then created their invention. In this example we see that one of the innovators had a clear vision at the start but the design and implementation process resulted in the collective development of a different sort of vision based on how the Foundation Degree programme actually worked practice.

This more practical team-based vision was based on knowledge and understanding that had to be grown through the relationships and interactions with the people involved in managing and delivering the programme.

Meaningful and productive relationships

Innovation, like that involved in creating a new programme, is an intensely relational thing. It involves creating new sets of relationships between the managers, teachers and systems administrators and between teachers, administrators and students. Innovators themselves need to find and create relationships through which they can share, develop and evaluate ideas.

> it is about finding people who you can get on a wavelength with and have ideas with and think 'Yeah, so we could really work together on this, this could really happen.' 3

> You very quickly know who are the key people that you know you can work well with them, they will make things happen. 3

Ultimately it is through personal relationships that commitment is engendered—commitment that makes it work and encourages people to go the extra mile to make it work.

> It is totally the people that make it happen . . . .

> I think we all [go the extra mile] as long as we still feel this is going to achieve the aim we want. You know I think because everyone is busy and it is not the only thing that any of us are doing . . . . I want to make use of the good working relationships as long as we are moving towards getting what it is I need from my university or they need for their employees. And while we are moving in that direction we will definitely go the extra mile. There is a huge amount of extra activity. Not just activity, but commitment to it because we have all been through these kinds of things before and realised that this is what gives you the energy to make something happen. 3

It takes time and effort to develop relationships and in the case of this innovative programme which spans two different organisations it involves spending time in each other's organisations.

> a lot of it has just grown out of developing and understanding what's going on, working out where the opportunities might be, linking with different people, and it's grown in that way really. And I think one of the things that's been a benefit is me being here a day a week because I'm here all day, people can generally find me and also that means that I get a better understanding of how the University works. 1

> I have been spending half a day at the hospital with the idea that students can access me if they want to access me because I'm their tutor and also to build our relationship with Health and I get to know the people better and their systems and ways of doing things too . . . . So that's been really, really good in developing our relationships and understanding as well, you know, their understanding in what the University processes must include and must have in terms of standards and so on and also our understanding theirs as well. 4

And one of the really crucial factors in enabling change to be accomplished, is for the people operating the programme to be able to find people who will help them overcome the barriers that are inevitable when you are trying to do new things. These are the movers and shakers, the people who can unblock things that seem to be frozen.

> I think the key thing is you need to have people in both organizations who have the strategic positions to allow things to happen, to approve things so that they can happen. You need to have them with you and on board. They don't need to know the detail, but they need to trust you to be able to say 'I need this from . . . . ', that they will put their weight behind it to enable it to happen. Because otherwise . . . you just get caught up at this low operational level, 'the computer says no' sort of level of things. Actually the computer doesn't have to say no but someone with influence has to realise and acknowledge this. So you need those people in all sorts of areas. You need them in the clinical area, you need the management of the hospital, you need the quality people here, the strategic leadership here, to say 'Actually if the computer is saying no it needs to say yes.' You need those people on board and you need them to trust you so that when you say you need something that they will use their power to support you. So these are a crucial set of relationships that you have to maintain and develop continuously 3

This situation is a common occurrence in the daily life of the innovator requiring considerable time, energy and emotion to resolve.

> this morning [I went to see someone] . . . . we have the central university and we have got the faculty. Because this is collaborative provision it tends to sit in central services, and yet everything gets approved through the faculty. There has to be communication between the two. Things were getting sort of passed around between people. So I went to somebody who I respect in the SDP project and I said, 'How do I unblock this?' and she has kindly said she will go and see if she can. It is like a circle, I just need some way of breaking into the circle to make this happen. It is about finding the person who can bang heads together and say 'you need to find a way to make that work'. 3

But because bringing about innovation is such a relational thing there is a sense that the innovation is vulnerable to the loss or destruction of such key relationships.

At the moment we have [a colleague funded through SDP] she is seconded to the University one day a week. So there is a sort of structural link. But if that ends, you know, it is dependent on individuals. I think that is a challenge for the sort of sustainability of the programme. Any of us could go and who would know what has happened and who would be able to keep it going.3

Relationships and organisational systems

Organisational systems are always challenged during innovation processes—because they were never designed to meet the new needs of the developing innovation. But systems can be redesigned, and what is important is good communication and the cultivation of a set of meaningful relationships between the innovators and the people who design and operate the business systems. There are many examples in this story of innovation of organisational systems being challenged by the innovation and a sense that change happens only when the innovator's (and affected students!) problems are shared and cared for by the people who own and operate the particular system that is causing a problem. So relationships between innovators and system owners are crucial to bringing about the sorts of changes the University wants to make to enable it to function in the more flexible and responsive ways that SDP was trying to promote.

we've had a meeting this week actually because of the problems with the people applying for individual units. Because they can't access our systems . . . they start off going to do this particular unit, and then it turns out they're actually going to do the next unit as well. What's happening is they're not enrolled on the next unit, they have to go through the process again . . . and some of the units are only held at the hospital, so they would never come to the University. So that's a problem because they need to come back and enrol and they can't understand why . . . . we have met with all the relevant people [in Registry] and said "How can we get around this in the future because this is going to be happening on a regular basis?" . . . . I have to say I've been quite impressed with the support that we've had in trying to address things and find ways round problems. 4

Leading change in complex organisational world

What also emerged from this case study were the relational dynamics and forms of leadership and devolved decision making necessary to make complex forms of education, training and professional development spanning two different organisations, work. It provides an experience-based model for other co-delivery relationships the University might want to develop.

Innovators who are trying to make things happen in the way that has been described in this case study are leaders of change—not just any change but change that contributes in a fundamental and generative way to the change the University wants to make. Through their daily experiences they become acutely aware of their role and of the qualities and capabilities necessary to make things happen, without the power and authority that senior managerial office provides.

> I think [leadership] is about seeing what you want to achieve and getting people to come with you to achieve it. it is not just an individualistic thing. I mean this vision was handed to me, but I shared it. You know, I think this is exactly what we should be doing. This idea of getting education out and making it collaborative and using the theory of how adults learn best, it is the right way to go. It is also much more commercially viable in the new world of higher education. I am very excited about that. so I share that vision, I have got that vision and I can see exactly how we can make it work. So it's kind of getting the conditions around you to be able to . . . I am very keen to make the changes, but I need the sort of conditions to enable that to happen. 3

Underlying this personal concept leadership is a strong notion of empowering people to do the job that is necessary and not simply to replicate practice that might be appropriate in another context but which is not appropriate for a new emerging context.

> I think it is about inspiring and empowering people and getting everybody on board. It's a corny, clichéd old story about when you interview the janitor at NASA and you ask him what he does for a job and he says 'I put a man on the moon.' But that is what it is about for me. We are all trying to achieve this thing and we all need to be open minded enough to say what it is that I need to do in order to achieve that thing. I think a big structure like a university finds that extraordinarily difficult to do. 3

> I would say it's a leadership and cultural thing . . . . The reason why people follow the pro forma for 'This is what I do and I register somebody on a course,' is because they have been given a pro forma to do it. Whereas if they said 'You are the person who registers people on this new collaborative course. You find out the best way of doing it and you get on with it' then they can do it. I think it is sort of self-fulfilling really. 3

But you can't empower people in a climate where people believe they will be publicly criticised for taking justifiable risks in order to try something new.

> I guess you need a senior leadership team who are going to say we are prepared to take a risk and prepared to unblock where there are blockages, problems, where there are structural things which have become a 'this is how we do it'. [Leaders need to] give the teams out there the confidence that it's okay to change what you've done, to take a risk as long as it's justified and there's an understanding of we're not going to do this but we're going to do that instead so we still think it gives us quality, and I guess it's the confidence that those teams have wherever they might be that if they change or do something that's not part of the norm that they're not going to get beaten up because it's not how it should be, because the minute that happens people get very defensive. So it's about how much are you doing to give your staff the freedom to do things even if they might make a mistake, how willing are the senior management team to take a risk. 1

But there is also a sense that the organisation itself damps down this spirit for a more empowering organisational dynamic.

> The question is where does that level of lack of feeling of support come from? Is it from [the top] or further down in the middle . . . . for some people . . . change is quite a threat, particularly if those managers in the middle aren't very confident at taking it forward, so even if there isn't a big hammer at the very top which is going to come down, there's lots of little hammers which are constantly knocking it back and in the end people don't bother, but if you change that middle layer sometimes a completely different ethos emerges and then people become empowered . . . 1

So how do people empower each other? This innovator believes it's to do with how you treat people and engendering a positive and optimistic climate in the workplace.

> For me and the way I find the most effective way to get things accomplished is to constantly believe it is possible to have a sort of can—do attitude and to assume other people have also got a can-do attitude and to treat them as if they have. On the whole I find that I get more productive responses if I do that. But it involves huge amounts of diplomacy and of trying to establish and sustain relationships, really. We want the shared goal, don't we? How do we together make that happen? Sometimes you just want to say 'For goodness sake, get on with it and do it.' Yeah, I think its masses of flexibility, respect, grace and diplomacy. 3

But innovators themselves need to connect to people who can sustain them in an optimistic and positive way. This is another set of relationships that innovators need to develop to sustain themselves to literally create their own supportive environment.

> it is identifying the individuals that get it and will be supportive. I think I am still identifying who those people . . . . still being new. It is not necessarily the obvious people . . . it is not a functional role. It is people you think, 'If I happen to bump into you at a workshop or a meeting or something we were at and we got what we were talking about. If I needed to run things by you, you would be somebody I would come to.' It is that sort of ad hoc stumbling across people that you see, 'Yeah, you get where I am coming from and I can sound you out about something and I know you will help and encourage me.' 3

Finally, these devolved forms of leading have to be supported by devolved forms of decision making, something that strongly hierarchical university organisations find very difficult to do.

> I think the localizing of decision making is absolutely critical to making things happen quickly. Giving people the power to make happen what it is you have the shared vision for. I think universities find it extraordinarily difficult to do that because they are sort of bulky. 3

Complexity requires brokerage

Boundary spanning innovations are inherently complex. There is so much communication, liaison, explanation, discussion, negotiation and persuasion required between the constituent elements of a complex system in this form of innovation that individuals assume the role of 'broker' to connect and bring people, visions and ideas together to try to create new things, to make things happen—solve problems and resolve situations that are inhibiting progress. Indeed, it seems that brokers were instrumental in helping at the start of this initiative.

> I think what the employer wanted was some reassurances from an external independent and trusted person that if they made more noises towards Solent they were going to get what they wanted. And they have. So that comes back to that kind of brokerage role being an independent broker who didn't work for a University. So employers would take that advice because they would feel, well you know them but you're not representing their interests. *Former Director Foundation Degree Forward*

Brokerage was also involved in selling the idea of the Foundation Degree to the Strategic Health Authority and in promoting the programme to other NHS Trusts.

> Through our conversations with colleagues in other trusts, the idea of this has been diffused quite quickly because they absolutely get how it's been developed . . . . we met with a couple of colleagues from the Isle of Wight on Friday and they said "one of the things they like about the course is that it has been developed by people in practice because we know what we need". So that's much more attractive than thinking it had been developed by somebody at the University with a bit of input from people in practice. 1

And brokerage was also involved role during the design stage.

> Now because I worked in the SDP I had direct access into Academic Services. Because of [a colleague], that task wasn't that hard. The consequence that I am now seeing for colleagues who are trying to do similar work in the Faculty is that because they don't have that higher profile they are still encountering barriers and difficulties and they can't martial all the different people they need to get a non-standard provision easily validated and approved. 2

Importance of feeling valued

Having taken risks and put lots of effort and energy into creating something new, do innovators feel their efforts have been valued? All too often this is an unanswered question because they have not had the explicit feedback that would enable them to make a judgement on the value of what they have done to others.

> I think the senior strategic people in the University definitely do [value me]. I think they definitely want it. They are definitely grateful that there are people like me who will try and make it happen. But of course I don't really hear that or see it. I think there is a way to go . . . . I am not blaming anyone for it, but there is a lot more that could be done to spread what we have done in an on-going way, I think you don't always know when you are beavering away in a risky situation and trying to make things happen and trying to make the University adapt its systems. You think 'What is all this for?' But this is a challenge which is worth giving a go to. I am not looking for external reward for it, I am just hoping it works and that will be my reward

BENEFITS

Sense of achievement

And what are the personal benefits of involving yourself as a teacher or course organisers in demanding and difficult work? For a teacher the value is often in seeing the results of their work reflected in the development and performance of their students.

> Achievement? I suppose the fact that it's up and running, that more people are coming and learning. And it's quite exciting actually that other Health Trusts are now getting more interested and wanting to send more students, so I think that's really quite something and it's fulfilling to see the course taking off as it is. So for me achieving that and seeing students developing, I mean that's been amazing. And being involved with Health, I mean just recently they did presentations at the hospital for the unit that they'd just completed and it was amazing to watch and listen to the students. The level of presentations, the standard was just very high. That alone in itself you think "Wow!" This makes it all worthwhile. 4

Becoming a leader of change

Given the challenges, demands and frustrations it is perhaps surprising that anyone would want to become an innovator. From a professional perspective, for some innovators their involvement provides them with an opportunity to develop themselves so that they can go on to perform in similar complex situations.

> [ultimately] I would like to be able to make use of this experience to lead others and other similar collaborative, innovative, risky things. To sort of say 'Look I've done it. I've been through the nitty gritty of making this happen from the big vision to the tiny—like this student can't submit their assignment. It's possible and let's do another one.' That would be great. I suppose that keeps me hanging in to think if we can crack this, there are lots of other possible places in the University where they might want to have the benefit of my experience. So that is a personal benefit. 3

And that is the message for the University ultimately? To help and empower people in positions like these innovators who are trying very hard to bring something that is radically different into existence, to do the job that the University wants and needs them to do.

> It's given me an insight into how a university works because I've always worked for the NHS my whole working life. I've worked with universities and colleges as part of my job role, but you're on the outside looking in. This has enabled me to be in and really get behind some of those things and how and why it works. What's been quite nice for me is being involved at the strategic level and being able to go between the strategic and the operational, learning more about things which are completely outside of my experience . . . . it's given me confidence that I've got transferrable skills and transfer it into another organisation and that I have things to offer another organisation that they see as valuable.1

Organisational learning

The scope and nature of the learning derived by the active participants in this process is enormous—knowledge that they value and which can be brought to bear on future situations. This is personal knowledge but for it to be useful in an organisational sense beyond the individuals there has to be a way of diffusing the knowledge into other areas. For one innovator the extent to which this learning was being shared within the host Faculty was a concern.

> I think [innovator 3] can definitely see how she can work differently with other employers around some of the social work courses, and . . . what would be interesting to know is across the rest of that faculty, has it made a difference or is [what has been leant] very much contained within these few people working in the social work area? 1

The benefit to the university would be in applying this learning in other parts of the university to develop new relationships with employers. There are signs that this is now happening. For example,

> [We have developed] a model, . . . of a Foundation Degree which is adaptable and as [innovator 5] is doing now with Southern Health, they're doing an FD in administration. And they're amending and adapting, they're bringing in units we've created as part of the FD. The good thing about this is the constant adding to, amending, collaborating, building relationships. 1

Another perspective was provided by the Head of Programme Development—a central role within Academic Services with a remit for finding further opportunities for employer-university partnerships. Here is a good example of the University creating new capacity to make good use of the learning the organisation has gained through the process of creating the Foundation Degree.

> I think the learning from that for me has been start off with a good product where you have a relationship that is mutual and get something piloted and out there. And then use your partner as the advocate for going and talking to other employers because effectively, that's then peer to peer or business to business, rather than the university selling the idea. So that whole area has grown and we've now got some business opportunities with the Business School around Strategic Management and Business Administration. *Head of Programme Development*

Employer-designed curriculum

The final word in this chapter should, quite rightly, rest with the employer who had a very clear idea about the type of curriculum they needed to develop their support worker workforce. The Foundation Degree also had to provide progression routes to into a comprehensive framework of opportunities for the further development of this workforce. The benefit to the employer is in achieving these aims.

> I think it's about developing a good working relationship and come at it with a view that you really want this to be truly collaborative . . . . This whole notion of Foundation Degrees when they were set up is they're employer led and I would say, in terms of how we've been involved with other universities in the past, mostly the University drove it and we were asked our opinion on it and we were asked to lead inasmuch as have an opinion on what was in this curriculum. I would say that this Foundation Degree has been 'employer designed'. We came to the party with a design in mind and I guess the University has partnered with that expertise and enabled us to fulfil our ambition . . . 1

> For us as a Trust it has meant we can now develop our support worker workforce to fit a workforce plan in the future to create a change in skill mix to make an affordable workforce but do it in a way which enables those individuals in our support roles to progress from apprenticeships through the Foundation Degree to the role we need them to play. 1

CHAPTER 9

Working with the Community: Sport Solent Schools & Colleges Partnership Scheme

INTRODUCTION

This case study offers a number of perspectives on innovative change that are different from the other case studies. Firstly, this is a story about innovation that relates to the University working in partnership with the local community to provide a social benefit to school children. Secondly, it is a story about expanding opportunity for university students to gain valuable practical experience in a field that is relevant to sports-related academic study. Thirdly, it is a story of how a successful development opens up further possibilities for development. Fourthly, the innovation demonstrates the value of involving non-academic departments in the Strategic Development Programme and the value of collaboration between a non—academic Directorate and a Faculty.

Background

A network of School Sports Partnerships (SSP) was established with the aid of Government funding throughout the country in 2000. There were a total of 450 partnerships in England, involving every primary, secondary and special school, as well as dedicated sports colleges, in the state sector. The primary role of the SSPs was to provide young people with opportunities to develop and demonstrate their creativity, health and fitness levels, civic pride and social responsibility. The scheme provided opportunities for thedevelopment of natural talent and increased opportunities for engaging in competitive sport. Each partnership was coordinated by a full time manager working with dedicated organisers at secondary and primary schools in their area to encourage increased participation in sporting, fitness and health-related activity.

Unfortunately, this worthy scheme became a casualty of the recession. In the 2010 Comprehensive Spending Review the Government announced that all direct funding for SSPs would be cut from 2011. Consequently, many of the SSPs across the country have ceased to exist. In the Southampton region there was strong support from head teachers and teaching staff for the SSP to continue. All 450 SSP hubsites were given funding to employ a School Games Organiser. All secondary schools were given funding to release a PE teacher from timetable for one day a week to co-ordinate activity within their feeder schools, but there was no funding for a manager.

SDP funding bid

This story provides the background to an SDP-supported innovation that has been led by 'Sport Solent', a Directorate within the University offering a comprehensive range of competitive and recreational sports, coach education and coaching opportunities, healthy lifestyle expertise and talented athlete support.

With the loss of Government funding for the Southampton, School Sports Partnerships (SSP), the Director of Sport Solent recognised the opportunity for the University to take over the running of the programme and a bid was made for SDP funding to pump prime the venture.

> When we heard that the School Sports Partnerships were being knocked on the head by the government in about November 2010, our first thought was we could do that, we as a department could take that on, it's not a ridiculous concept so let's look at it. As always it came down to yes, okay, but who's going to pay for this, and this is how the SDP team became involved. We went to [SDP team leader] and said, 'is this the sort of project that would fit into the SDP remit?' And she was very supportive and very helpful in actually putting our bid in to the right format and terminology *Director Sport Solent*

The argument advanced in the bid proposal was that Sport Solent already provided after-school coaching in 20 local schools, and operated a talented and gifted development programme for local young athletes. Furthermore, there was already an infrastructure to enable some of the SSP functions to be delivered within areas of existing expertise.

The proposed innovation had the potential to enhance and expand contacts with schools and colleges within the Southampton area and support the University's widening participation and progression targets by building greater awareness of the Solent offering amongst teachers and college lecturers, and developing stronger relationships between the University and school and college students. The other aspect of SDP that the innovation addressed was improving opportunities for university students to gain valuable work experience—specifically in the area of coaching.

> We've sold it [to the University] largely on the basis of the work placement because the University made a commitment when we settled our fees:

> our offer includes guaranteed work placement for every undergraduate student and that's quite a big task to take on, and we see this as very much a part of helping us deliver that promise. We currently have about 1,000 students on sports courses, they're on the course in the Faculty but the Sport Solent remit is that we find meaningful work placements for the students, which use and enable them to build on their qualifications. *Director Sport Solent*

The strategy outlined in the SDP funding bid was to recruit a suitably qualified and experienced post-holder who would raise funding, recruit appropriately qualified students and staff, and use these resources.

> to develop, in partnership with local schools and FE Colleges, a sustainable programme to transform the provision of sport and well-being among the young community of Southampton. *SDP funding bid p2*

The essential capacity for delivering the programme in schools was to be provided by undergraduate students from FBSE's School of Sport, Tourism and Languages including students from eleven different programmes.

Students from these programmes would be placed in schools throughout their course, on both a voluntary and paid basis, and there would also be scope to deliver a range of sport-related projects, helping them gain valuable work experience in such roles as coaching, mentoring, sports development and event management.

The £50k bid for start-up funding was to fund a 12 month fixed-term post for the manager and support for delivery of the programme. It was envisaged that the programme would become self-funding after the initial 12 month period, as new and existing income streams were introduced. The bid was supported by the Management Board.

> The main champions in the VCG are the Director of Resources, my line manager and the Vice-Chancellor. I think people at all levels bought it, the Faculty obviously bought into it, because at the end of the day it's students

from the faculty that we are servicing. *Director Sport Solent*

We acquired SDP funding for the post of the Partnership Development Manager and subsequently took on the existing partnership manager on a 12 month fixed-term contract, which ran out in July 2012 but we've now secured funding through the University as a permanent post and programme. *Director Sport Solent*

The main risks envisaged related to the failure of schools to take up the service and for the service to be unsustainable. The bigger picture was to position the University as the main organisation for developing and delivering sport strategy for young people in the city and the architects of the bid could see future potential to develop and expand this initiative on a wider geographic basis, and the possibility of further developments with the Local Authority.

Without that kick start, we probably wouldn't have that and probably wouldn't have taken over the sports development unit from the city council either, so it's actually generated a lot of business for us, a lot of confidence for us in being able to take those type of projects on. *Director Sport Solent*

Figure 9.1 Development and implementation of School & Colleges Partnerships

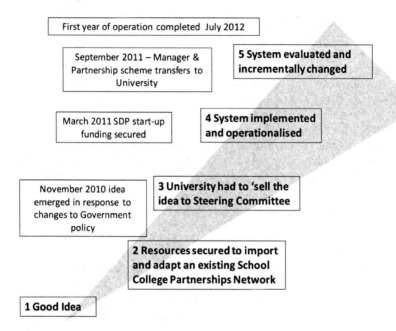

ACCOMPLISHING INNOVATIVE CHANGE

This story of accomplishing innovative change has taken place over about 18 months. Figure 9.1 shows the steps in the change process. The idea was born out of a change in the external environment which created a new opportunity. The fact that the opportunity was first appreciated and owned by the Sport Solent Director perhaps made it easier for the sponsoring department to be proactive in taking the idea forward.

Implementing an idea

The first step in the development and implementation process was to appoint a Manager to help maintain and develop the network of existing relationships with schools created under the School Sport Partnership scheme and coordinate activities with schools. The role of the manager was to implement and operationalise the idea. In any innovation initiative having the right person or people is crucial to the success of a project. The right person means someone with the right skills sets, attitudes and capability, but it also means someone with the right knowledge and experience and with a very short project that has to be accomplished within a year—insider knowledge is essential. The School College Partnerships initiative was fortunate in being able to appoint the person who was already in the role under the previous funding arrangements.

> She'd been doing the role for about 7 years under different funding streams . . . and part of the attraction was that she was the person doing it and she's really good and she has a very good reputation in that field. It wouldn't have worked as well if we'd got the go ahead and she'd not been interested, we'd have probably made it work but it would have been harder. She hit the ground running because she was carrying on what she was doing rather than having to start from scratch . . . her work rate and her output are unbelievable and she's a very valued member of staff now. *Director Sport Solent*

> Contacts are vital and she'd been in Southampton the last four or five years so she knows all the head teachers, she knew the people at school that made it tick so you know, at a certain school we don't speak to the head teacher, you speak to X, that's the person . . . And it gave the schools confidence in our ability to deliver this, because if we'd have just said we're taking over the school sports partnership as an entity, we'd have had to start from scratch and win the confidence of schools but we were able to say we're taking on what already exists, we're employing Julia, and all the schools were saying, 'that's brilliant, thanks for doing that, that means we can just carry on with what we're doing', and that's how it's happened. *Director Sport Solent*

INNOVATOR'S STORY

But what has it meant from the innovator's perspective? Was it simply a case of importing an existing partnership model into a new organisational home? What were the consequences of bringing the scheme into the University and what new opportunities emerged from the new situation?

The innovator

In the seven years prior to joining the Sport Solent team the innovator had been Partnership Development Manager for Southampton School Sport Partnership which was a government funded project. The role involved working across primary and secondary special schools predominantly—

trying to increase the amount of physical activity that children have access to and are engaged in, working with those that tended not to participate to try to change their attitudes and trying to encourage them to take part. The role also included working with more gifted and talented young people and providing pathways, advice and encouragement to enable them to participate in their sport beyond the school day and into communities as well.

In this role the innovator had already established a good working relationship with the Faculty of Business, Sport and Enterprise (FBSE).

> I'd done a fair bit of work with FBSE . . . They saw the benefits of being able to access schools easier. They needed students to be able to be placed and to gain experience. We were in the schools. We had built a relationship over a seven year period with schools and were fairly trusted and had a good reputation. Through our network . . . . we were able to link the University to the schools to be able to provide the work experience [for their students].

The innovator also had links with Sport Solent who were also involved in supporting sporting activities in schools

> Sport Solent . . . had funding from the city council to provide after school activities within the schools as well so there was a bit of a cross-over in terms of our work too . . . . We tried to ensure that we worked together so that we could provide provision across the city fairly and equally so that we weren't both in the same schools at the same time etc . . . .

The news that the Government was going to cut funding for the school sport partnership scheme came as quite a shock. It was big news at both a national and a local level but the Director of Sport Solent saw an opportunity that would benefit the community and the University.

> [The Sport Solent Director] was very proactive [he called us and said], I'd really like to have a conversation with you to see if there's anything that we can do to try and help maintain this infrastructure that you've got across Southampton and maybe talk to you about possible ways of making this continue for the benefits of us and obviously for the benefits of the young people in the city. So that's how the initial conversation started and that was quite early on. As soon as the announcement was made— which was good at the time because we had also been given direction by chair of our steering group to get out

there now and start talking to partners [to see what could be done to save the scheme.]

Given that, at the time, the only way of saving the partnership scheme was through the University's intervention it should have been easy to negotiate the transfer of the scheme but some members of the Steering Committee were suspicious of the University's motives.

> It should have been. To me it felt like it should be extremely simple, but we had a school sport partnership steering group with members from different backgrounds within the city that all had a passion or a commitment to PE and school sports . . . . nobody else [was] jumping up and down and saying, we also want to save your partnership and we want to save this infrastructure, because we can see the benefits . . . . So it should have been simple but there were a few members of the steering group that said, I don't know, why Solent are wanting to do this? They want to put in a lump sum of money to fund a position, why? What are they trying to get out of it? They were a little bit sceptical about it.

So there was a persuading job to be done before responsibility for the schools sport partnership scheme could be transferred to the University.

> Representatives from the University came to the steering group meeting and explained why they were wanting to do it and I think it put people's minds at rest. Everybody said, well look there's no alternative, let's give this a go, let's see what they produce within a year's time and see what it feels like.

Eventually, the Steering Committee agreed that it was in the best interests of the schools and their pupils for the University to take over the resourcing and management of the scheme and the network was brought into the University through employment of one of the existing partnership managers using funding provided by SDP. Managing a transition like this, with a change of responsibility for a set of existing relationships can be tricky, but—thanks to the personal good standing of the Manager, bringing all the schools over seems to have been successful.

> We very much saw it as a transition year and I was hoping to bring everybody with me lock, stock and barrel which I did more or less. By the time I joined Solent I had 60 of our 65 primary schools signed up to a service level agreement. The project itself has always been very primary focused,

so secondary schools will maybe argue there wasn't as much in it for us, all the programmes seem to be primary schools, they get all of the support in terms of CPD etc— which is not a fair account of it.,

We have 12 secondary schools in Southampton. I had managed to get five signed up to the programme. I'm fairly happy with that . . . . The five schools that didn't sign up to the primary school SLA were from one cluster. It was very political.

I'm in the process now obviously of getting all these schools signed back in. We've gone out there with a slightly new looking SLA which reflects some of the other work areas that the University different departments can offer the schools which I don't think the schools are fully familiar with, I definitely wasn't prior to coming here.

So we've gone out with a new looking SLA, pretty much the same, asking them to sign in for two years rather than having to do this process every single year. I think schools are fairly happy with what's been achieved this year. It's been a very smooth transition and I think they've seen the benefits of this partnership, so people will vote with their feet. I've had three schools that weren't signed in last year come over to us and one secondary school that wasn't in it last year also come over. . . . It's been difficult having all of those meetings and trying to get people signing in. I've not had one negative email or phone call so it's looking pretty good . . .

Service Level Agreement

Each school has a Service Level Agreement (SLA) outlining the services that are offered. There are separate SLAs for primary and secondary schools. The SLA is currently £1.40 per child and schools receive a two hours, six week block of either gymnastics, games or dance facilitated by a qualified practitioner. They work alongside a class teacher providing high quality gymnastics or dance to the group, but also equally importantly providing CPD to the teacher as well.

one of the things that the schools have hugely benefited from—and whenever we evaluate at the end of any academic year CPD comes out top always . . . Schools will look at their timetable and say we've got an NQT

> coming in, we'd quite like her to have maybe 12 hours worth of coaching.

> It helps them with their schemes of work, it helps them to plan their lessons . . . . That's one of the most valuable things that they get, the six times two hour blocks.

Schools get a free place on the annual PE conference which was merged with the University's 'young Hampshire coaching conference'. They also receive regular weekly emails and newsletters and they also have opportunities to access funding that the innovator is able to attract.

> I put in applications all the time for different funding pots, different funding streams that are out there. I'll get the money in and then it will be a blanket email out to all of my schools in the SLA asking them who would like to access it?—we've got coaches in the area, who would like this etc?

Schools are also offered a menu of 10 different projects from which they can select three. This menu is now benefitting from the scheme now being located in the University. Two examples of projects are outlined below.

> Some of the new things that we added were the innovation projects like 'EduMove' which FBSE are responsible for. So they have groups of students that are looking at different projects that have an impact on young people in Southampton. I have about 10 groups of students that all came to me and said, okay we're thinking about doing a project that's going to impact on Key Stage 4 girls, widening participation for argument's sake. I say, right okay let's hear what you're thinking. They go through it and we tweak it a little bit. We have an initial meeting where we get an idea of the project and go and talk to these people and have you thought about this, etc?

> They go off and do some work, they come back and then I find them a school. I go to one of my schools and say, right I've got a really great project happening. It's all about trying to increase participation. I know you're interested in that in this school. Why don't you meet these students and we'll see whether we can do some work with you. So they come in, deliver six to eight week projects and it's a win: win for everyone.

> We also have the EduSport—EduMove . . . and that's just fantastic. I got so excited when I heard about this

project. It's all to do with teaching cross—curricula, so numeracy, maths, history, geography but using physical activity as the vehicle. The groups of students have done some amazing work, produced some amazing resources.

I had an initial few conversations with head teachers in the primary schools. I go back to the ones that I know are more proactive to start with to just test the water and see how they take to it. Then I met with the group of students that were looking at numeracy for Key Stage 1 and we went into an infant school and talked to the learning mentor there because that school said, I quite like the sound of that project, I think that could really work well with some of our children.

We came up with an outline of opportunities for the students. So they're going to go in there and shadow a Year 1 class so they can get an idea of what level these children work at. They're also looking at the curriculum for next year so that when they do come back in to do their delivery say in Autumn they know that they're going to be basing their physical activity around fractions, for example, because that's what they're doing within that year group at that time of year. The children that are struggling to get fractions, a small group will come out, work with the learning mentor or the teaching assistant with our group of students and they will have an hour's session once a week for an eight week period around fractions, but within a physical activity . . .

The innovator's role

The innovator has built a network over a significant period of time and has productive and meaningful relationships with teachers and head teachers in schools. She has also developed strong links with members of staff in FBSE and Sport Solent whose roles involve them in gaining work placements in schools. The innovator plays the role of connecting schools to the student resources within the University.

I'm a bit of a middle person really. I'm advocating the good work that the students are producing, and negotiating work placements for them. From our point of view it's a work placement it's an experience that they've got to get. From my schools' point of view I'm ensuring that my schools are getting the best out of this opportunity as well to make it

> a win: win. I've got a very good understanding of what my schools want and their needs and requirements but then I know I am gathering a better understanding of what our students' needs are too, working with FBSE colleagues and having those conversations with the students as well. I can see what they're trying to achieve. I know what they need from a school placement. I'm marrying the two up so I'm a bit of a match maker I suppose.

Because of the relationships and communication structures that have been built the innovator is continually developing knowledge about the University she has been able to build new relationships and extend this connecting process to other departments.

> The other big project that we've put into the SLA is something that our university partnership team do. I had no idea, until I joined, that the team have a remit for primary school aged children and they have to engage with a certain number of Year 4s, Year 5s and 6s and they have a menu of activities that they offer. I was thinking if I didn't know maybe a lot of my schools don't know as well. I think what they offer is invaluable. We've packaged it up as gifted and talented provision. It doesn't have to just be sports gifted and talented, it can be academic too. So we're trying to encourage the schools to take that project so they can bring a group of students down for the day so that they select whatever activities they prefer from this menu . . . . One of my schools has selected this as a project. I'm now going to have conversations back here and say, I've got a school and they're really keen to bring some children in throughout the year and what can we do to help?

> Again, I just see myself being this link person . . . . It's just helping the University partnership team they've obviously got their links out there anyway, so it's just linking them with a few more schools.

The sharing of information is a two way process.

> The partnership team have been great here because they've given me their contacts within each college too so it's been quite good. I have my own contacts too, but sharing information has been very beneficial.

From a university perspective one of the most important roles of the innovator is to help course leaders place their students in schools, and from the students who are needing placements to match their aspirations and talents to the needs of schools.

> I speak to secondary schools on a weekly basis. I have a good rapport with them. I also link with each course leader. They've all got slightly different needs . . . I met with [a course leader] and he told me how many students we had and the percentage that would like to go into secondary PE, and the percentage that were interested in teaching PE in Key Stage 1-2 primary school. We also look at what those students have in terms of qualifications and experience. From my schools' point of view, I want to give them the best student that will meet their needs to. For example, if we had a student that had an extensive background in gymnastics and I had a school that was trying to develop gymnastics, for example, I would most likely put that student there to help them. Or if we had students that were very strong in rugby and had done lots of rugby at a high standard we would look at that because they're looking to develop their after school club programme. So it's been a bit of a win: win as well . . .

In a sense the innovator is acting as a knowledge broker providing course leaders with detailed knowledge of individual schools and their interests and needs so that a much better match can be made between students who are aspiring to develop and gain experience in particular ways and schools that would like support in developing in particular ways.

The innovator is also extending the opportunities available to students.

> We've got 350 sports students here. We're providing them with opportunities, not just after school activity but community provision. We're doing a lot of work with the NHS groups. We have students on a regular basis going into the local hospital to provide coaching for sick children, because whilst they're in there they still need to be physically active.
>
> We also have a very good group of students at the moment that really want to specialise in sport for young people with disabilities. I can access training through my networks so instead of me going on the training or a couple of my coaches, I've offered it to a group of students because

they've shown me that they are keen to work with these people so we've offered them the training.

The innovator is also able to broker links with sports clubs in the local community from which university students can benefit.

I have also brought with me my links with the community, community clubs and other providers in the city. Some of our students need performance placements. These are the students that are going to be coaching out there in the community. They need to have a high quality placement. They need to be working with a coach that is of a certain calibre, where I've worked with a number of clubs across various sports and worked with national governing bodies across various sports I have a good rapport, I have a good relationship with them.

I helped interview all Year 1 students quite early on— October/November 2011—which was great because I got a real good insight into each student's aspirations. I got a really good understanding of each young person and I was able to then think, right okay then I probably need to link you up with—I will talk to so and so about that.

It's quite exciting. For example, we've linked with the diving club in the city, probably one of the biggest clubs in the city. We've got the GB coach, Lindsay Fraser there. We have Peter Waterford diving from there, a very prestigious club, providing high quality coaching. We've started a placement with them. We have four students placed with them. They're going through a journey with them. They're being mentored by coaches in the club. They've all just completed their National Governing Body Level 1 in diving. They're being given opportunities in the schools to go out there and do some talent ID through diving.

Those kind of placements and those experiences that we're being able to offer, that I'm able to arrange. It's been quite valuable I think to the students.

The innovator is also proactive in seeing and converting opportunities into tangible results.

The school games organisers that are still part of this government initiative project. In Southampton we were two partnerships—Redbridge and Bitterne Park. They employ a school game organiser three days a week to provide a school games position which is basically providing competitive opportunities in sport for young people.

At the eleventh hour come September 2011 when we were supposed to have these people in place the member of staff that was going to do the role found a new job. Because of my relationship with Redbridge I went to them and said, we're in trouble now, we've got nobody to start this academic year in terms of this role. Had a conversation back here and Phil said, we can do it can't we? It was like, probably can yeah.

As a result we managed to secure the funding from Redbridge and we've provided that service on behalf of Redbridge partnership this year. Because the funding has been guaranteed now from the government until 2015, we've secured the funding for the next few years so we're able to appoint somebody on a fixed term contract based within our department working across the city—so working and managing that role too. So the school games organisers have played quite a key part in bringing all of this together as well, as a part of my team working with young people.

The innovator is also entrepreneurial in her outlook and actions—identifying new sources of funding and new partners for bidding that can be drawn into and connected with the services provided through the Schools and Colleges Partnerships scheme.

I've got access to resources beyond what the University is able to provide. There are funding streams that I can access and do access and then we provide a service with those resources . . . .

I've got lots of things on the back burner—there's another government project called National Citizenship Services, which will sit superbly within this environment. It's about University team mentors and providing opportunities for young leaders . . . . There's always pots of money all over the place and, to be honest, if we had another person—not me—sitting there looking at all these different funding streams and all these external opportunities that are available, we would probably be able to do considerably more than what we are currently.

The innovator quite clearly sees herself in the middle of everything she has created and is trying to create.

> I'm very much in the middle I think. I have an obligation to my schools, as part of an SLA, to provide them with a service. I equally have an obligation to the University to provide our students with opportunities . . . . I feel very much a part of a jigsaw really. There's lots of different aspects to what I do but I feel very much in the middle of everything.

Challenges

There have been a number of challenges associated with the innovation. The first relates to persuading the University that this was the right thing to do. The fact that the Director of Sport Solent, is a member of the University's Senior Management Team, the support of members of the Vice Chancellor's Group and the support of the SDP team, were all influential in this process.

> The first challenge was probably convincing the University why, there were no examples to say let's do this because x, y and z universities do it, we were flying the flag for a new idea really. So the first challenge was internally to the University, why should this get SDP funding compared to other bids?

Having overcome the hurdle of securing the funding and appointing the manager, the main strategic challenge was, and still is, gaining the trust and buy-in from schools. The fact that the newly appointed manager was already known and trusted within the school community was an important factor in securing participation.

> But there was still a persuading job to do. I went to some of the initial meetings with the schools and they were very sceptical, probably the same reason as the University because they all listened to what we said we were going to do and Julia's going to carry on doing it and now she's going to be backed by Solent University and no one's going to say that's not a good idea on the face of it, but most of them thought there's a catch here, they said that, 'why are you doing this?' As always money comes into it, because there's these pots of money that were available and they were suspicious that we were using it as a way of creaming off money for ourselves and things like that . . .

there's still schools out there that have got a basic problem with us doing it, schools in Southampton who don't buy into it and do their own thing and send out messages to other schools that we're doing it for the wrong reason. We've had that battle but we're up to about 90% of buy-in now and I'm quite comfortable with that, I never expected 100% anyway but we won over most of them *Director Sport Solent*

The third type of challenge is logistical in managing the bureaucratic demands of the system and in ensuring that a quality and reliable service is delivered.

There's also the logistical challenge but that's an operational thing, but when you've got however many students we deal with going through these programmes, 250 students or something every year, just the CRB checks alone are a challenge *Director Sport Solent*

You also have the logistical challenge of getting students to the right school at the right time and teaching the right sport and having the right equipment and that sounds as though it should be straightforward but just the sheer volume means it's not.

So we have people who do the logistics.It can be a nightmare because we have to get our students to a particular school, typically straight after school and usually lectures finish about a quarter of an hour before. On a typical day in February there'd be 14 taxis waiting out the front and the students just pile out of lectures and go off to schools all around Southampton with kitbags ready to work as soon as they get there. *Director Sport Solent*

The fourth challenge is maintaining and enhancing the quality of the service.

And then I think the hardest challenge is just sustaining something like this and keeping it fresh, because it's easy to say yes, we've got that in place now, we've got a continual stream of students so we're covered for three years, but you've got to keep refreshing it and come up with new ways of doing things because otherwise it'll just get stale and then people get complacent and things will start to go wrong.

Having implemented the scheme the fifth challenge is to sustain the enterprise. In fact sustainability was designed into the bid for funding as it was presented as a pump priming opportunity in which once established the initiative itself would generate sufficient funds to be self-sustaining.

> Very early in the 12 months, we realised that we had to start making the post permanent because there's not much point in doing that for 12 months and then saying well, that's okay but that's it. It was always intended to be just a pump prime exercise to get the post into the system so we had to prove to the University that it justified itself. There's all kinds of ways of justifying a post and a project but if you just look at it in financial terms it actually brings in income that matches what it costs us to pay somebody, so it is a break even situation as well. *Director Sport Solent*

BENEFITS OF INNOVATING

Why do innovators innovate?

One of the questions we are trying to answer in this study is why do innovators do what they do? Especially as they know it will involve them in extra work that they will have to do on top of their normal responsibilities and may involve them in challenges and possibly even conflict. This innovator was offered continuity of employment so it's perhaps not surprising that she wanted to be involved but beyond this we can see that there was a passion to continue building on what had been achieved and a desire to maintain an important set of relationships through which the programme was shaped and delivered.

> I absolutely loved the whole thing about the project and what we were about and what has been achieved in the last seven years. So when I heard that it was being slashed I was devastated and then to hear that somebody like Solent were keen to keep it going for me was just fantastic. But it's more than the job? It's about maintaining something that is making a difference to many school children. Also we had a very strong network. We used to meet regularly, half a term, to work on projects together or to go through things together. Everybody felt exactly the same about what we've achieved over quite a small period of time so I wanted to keep that going.

Personal rewards

As with other innovators involved in the SDP, the rewards for working harder, taking risks, suffering frustration and perhaps engaging in a degree of conflict with colleagues in order to bring about successful innovation are not financial or material. Rather they are psychological and associated with a sense of achievement and professional satisfaction as they witness the beneficial effects of their industry and enterprise.

> Just seeing the impact that we make on the children that we work with, the young people that we work with, the students that we've helped to gain the necessary experiences. It's just a very rewarding job from start to finish. Being able to support teachers to be able to deliver better quality lessons in PE.

Benefits for the University

There are perhaps three main benefits to the University brought about by this innovation. The first relates directly to the aspirations of the Strategic Development Programme to improve students' employability—the innovation provides new and better opportunities for work placements in the fields of coaching and increasingly in other aspects of student enterprise. Secondly, and again in relation to the SDP objectives, the innovation improves the University's ability to engage with employers—in this case schools as the employing organisation who need to employ competent coaches and PE specialists not only to help in the classroom, but also to provide professional development for their staff.

> the faculty will say we've got these students who are looking for placement, we then take on that task of placing them . . . . we've got somebody whose job is specifically to do all the administration of student placements, ensuring their CRB checks and qualifications are in place and organising the timetable of placement, so that is a role within the department. Because of the School and Colleges Partnerships I think we've got about 90% of the schools in Southampton signed up to the programme . . . .
> *Director Sport Solent*

Having demonstrated the capacity and capability to manage and deliver an effective service to the local community other opportunities have presented themselves. The credibility of the organisation has led directly to new contracts to provide services to the local authority.

the most recent large development from Sport Solent's point of view has been the addition of the Local Authority Sports Development Unit. The Local Authority decided a year or so ago to outsource its Sports Development Unit which has the remit to look after all the sports development of clubs in Southampton: it's the conduit from the national government bodies of sport, how they get to the community through the local government. They decided to outsource it and we bid for it. Again, no other university had ever done anything like this but the School Sports Partnership initiative put us in the position where we could bid for this because the Local Authority have got the confidence in us through doing that well. They knew that we could deliver.

We were bidding against commercial suppliers but we won the tender back in November last year and we took over that department and staff in December . . . So we now have the remit for sport provision in Southampton from schools right through to clubs and of course our main one which is the University. So it's evolved quicker than we would have planned, not just the facilities but the supporting mechanisms we put in place and that needs a lot of essential growth as well like marketing and things like that which we now need to build into it. I think I can safely say that we are regarded as the people that run sport in this city now, that's how people refer to us anyway, Sport Solent look after sport in Southampton. *Director Sport Solent*

Successful innovation in a field leads to enhanced reputation and opportunities to influence a wider practice community or system. The Schools and Colleges Partnership Scheme has attracted interest from other universities as the distinctiveness of its approach has become widely recognised.

we were prepared to put head above the parapet and say all these other schools' sport partnerships all over the country, 400 and something of them were all floundering and we said okay, we'll take it on, and very few have done that still now, a year on, there's very few that survived. They've got different models, some took it on a management buyout, they've gone commercial and some have a commercial backing but there's nobody that really has the model we have, and a lot of people are looking at it now and saying we want it to be like that. And we're telling other universities, we're going to the BUCS conference, British University and College Sport, we're going to the national conference tomorrow at Exeter, [our Vice-Chancellor is] making the keynote speech at the opening session. That's largely I would say because of the reputation that we have now, not for sport on the field, but for all the other things we've done around it. And these sorts of initiatives, the bigger sports universities don't do and they're looking quite enviously at us . . . . so we've got members of our team making presentations at the BUCS conference about how we did it. *Director Sport Solent*

The innovator also believes that what she is doing is of interest at a system—wide level.

I think we're probably the envy of a lot of other areas within county and nationally. I had a phone call from somebody in Sheffield saying, I've heard a little bit about what Solent University have done locally for you. How did that come about and how did you manage to secure some funding to do that? What have the benefits been for the University and what have the benefits been for your old partnership etc?

I think we're being spoken about nationally and I'm really keen to try and get us on the national stage if you like. We have a conference every year with all the old school sport partnerships. There's lots of awards for innovative projects and work in different areas. I think what we've achieved here is a great example of where different partners in industry can work together to provide a good service to schools. *Innovator*

INNOVATION THROUGH PARTNERSHIP

The innovator attributes her success to her effectiveness as a developer of partnerships, creating, maintaining and developing relationships and partnerships with people and organisations. This type of innovation is entirely dependent on the integrity and commitment, actions and relationships of an individual who is able to see opportunities, make connections, tap into resources, persuade and negotiate as well as coordinate and manage an operation. These types of innovation are not accomplished overnight and this story illustrates well how new opportunities can be created in the moment, when value systems and understandings connect.

I've sat in this Children and Young People in Southampton meeting for three years now. It's got a real big health focus. We have various partners from the City Council there. We've got a team called No Limits which I think is the sensible drinking team. We have a sex education team. We have a smoking team there, a mental health team there. It's very NHS dominated. I've sat there for three years and I give my little bit on PE and school sport. I get five minutes at the end of this meeting and every meeting I come away thinking, I'm wasting my time but I've continued to go . . . once a term

A couple of meetings ago they said, you've obviously moved now . . . . can you give us an update on what you're doing? So I did . . . . I just mentioned a project that we have access to at the moment and it was called the 'Living for Sport Project'. It was all about engaging with Key Stage 3 and 4 young people at secondary school that were disengaged at school, who were not attending, misbehaving and just completely going off track. Using sport as the tool, as the vehicle to try and get these kids back engaged, back in school, back learning etc.

There was a great example of one lad—lazy, didn't get out of bed in the morning, constantly late into school, poor attendance, smoking in the corner of the playground at lunchtimes etc. They brought in a professional boxer and did some work with the kids, put them through a bit of a circuit etc. This professional boxer said to this young lad, I really see potential in you, you're something special you are, you remind me of me at that age.

This kid was interviewed and he said, "that was it for me. Somebody saw potential in me, that was a turning point for me. That was it, I stopped smoking instantly. I was in school every single day using the facilities, using the gym, I got engaged in a leadership programme. I started to go into primary schools to see if I could make a difference to some of those naughty lads in there."

I gave this example and all the members around the table went, "wow that's fantastic." I thought, well I've been doing this now for six or seven years but you've actually given me more than five minutes on the end of the agenda so I could tell you what we do. The whole group said, right

I think we could probably work with you. Great, so the penny's finally dropped!

STRATEGIC VALUE OF SDP

This story of innovation demonstrates how all parts of the University have the potential to contribute to the SDP objectives. The Director of Sport Solent recognised the importance of SDP funding and encouragement from the SDP team to turning and opportunity into an advantageous position for the University.

> when the SDP was first offered to the University by HEFCE, it was very much aimed at the academic departments. As a department we didn't think we could put in a bid because it was quite clearly an academic programme. It was only when the opportunity came up and we looked at the School Sports Partnership scheme and talked to the SDP who were very helpful in showing us how it could fit in with the SDP aspirations, mainly around the two strands of student work experience and building better links with employers. That's how we managed to tie it in with the fund and I think from that, it has developed into a project that fits many of the SDP aspirations. . . . I think it's fair to say that without the SDP, this probably wouldn't have happened because all parties wanted it to happen, there had to be the funding to get it going. The post for partnerships manager has now been secured so a 12 month initial trial which the SDP enabled us to undertake has now become a permanent and important part of the University's work. In that respect it's been a big success story for the SDP because it's worked for the University.
> *Director Sport Solent*

CHAPTER 10

Solent Creatives

INTRODUCTION

One of the interesting features of the Strategic Development Programme (SDP) is the range of ways in which its objective of engaging employers was achieved. The idea for Solent Creatives grew out of the Faculty of Creative Industries and Society's (FCIS) engagement with the Strategic Development Programme. The concept was to create an organisation within the University modelled on the idea of a 'job recruitment agency'. The agency would aim to connect local employers in the creative industry sector, who were searching for freelance workers, with appropriately skilled students who were interested in freelance assignments.

This approach is helping to improve the employability of students and helping the University to meet its target of providing or facilitating professionally relevant work experience in all programmes. It is engaging employers and encouraging them to provide opportunities for professionally relevant work for students, and it is also promoting entrepreneurship and creating opportunities for students to start their own companies in a supportive environment.

Rationale

The creative industry sector is a competitive one where traditionally self-employment or short term contracts are the norm. By offering students the opportunity to work on short term commercial assignments rather than through more traditional work experience the agency would be helping to prepare students for the types of working environment that they were likely to encounter when they completed their degree.

Traditional work experience is very valuable but it is not an entrepreneurial experience and the student often undertakes routine tasks over an elected period. Freelance working offers students the opportunity to engage with worthwhile projects to be completed relatively quickly so a student might work with a number of clients over a period of time on a variety of projects.

In this way the agency would be encouraging students to develop their entrepreneurial capability and self-sufficiency. It would also raise their awareness of the importance of building a relationship with a client and managing their assignment efficiently, in a professional manner, within time constraints. Developing and demonstrating these complex capabilities would be valuable to any student entering the professional world.

IMPLEMENTING THE IDEA: PRIMARY INNOVATION

Figure 10.1 shows the steps in establishing, piloting and refining the Solent Creatives employment agency. The agency was created in about four months and launched in March 2011. The organisation was set up within FCIS, mainly for the Faculty's communication and media students, but it is open to students from other Faculties provided they have the right skill sets.

The first year was treated as a pilot and following and evaluation in mid 2012 some new initiatives will be introduced in the 2012-13 academic year.

Figure 10.1 Development and implementation of Solent Creatives

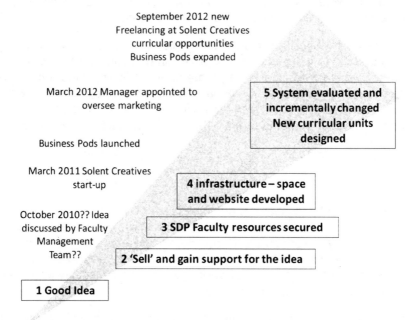

Origin of the idea

In the second year of the SDP (2010-11) the innovator was given responsibility for leading the Faculty of Creative Industries SDP work.

When responsibility for the SDP was passed to me, it was my job to align the Faculty's SDP work with the SDP objectives and because employability and enterprise in the curriculum is something that I'm interested in and passionate about and something that we already do to a certain degree on all of our courses, I wanted to take our work a step further.

The idea of an agency to promote student enterprise had been in the mind of the innovator for some time, but the idea was reinforced by the Dean who had seen an agency operating in another university, in another country.

I've always had the idea of creating an agency for enterprise and always wanted to do it and the Dean had seen something very similar at a university in Spain, when he was an external examiner. So it's something that we'd spoken about and had said you know, wouldn't it be great if we could do something like that. *Innovator*

The idea seems to have been well supported by senior managers from the start.

I'm very fortunate that when the idea was mentioned, the Dean was very supportive and took it on board and also [the Pro Vice-Chancellor (Academic)], was very supportive. No one thought it was impossible. So with that support we were able to take it forward.

I think I've been very lucky in having a Vice-Chancellor and Pro Vice-Chancellor (Academic) here who could see that it was something that would enhance the student experience.

The principal innovator acknowledged the challenge of establishing the agency. In this response she reveals her attitude to getting on and doing it.

> starting it up was very difficult. Our Dean . . . . would say that I just got on and did it and there was an element of that, but it was hard work.

Creating a space and place

The concept of an agency required a physical space where students could meet and interact with business clients. A space that is dedicated to an enterprise, especially if it is distinctive and attractive conveys the message that this matters to the organisation. The creation of a physical space is also a tangible expression of an idea and creates a sense of organisational identity.

It was important that it was visual. We could have done it possibly from a staff office and on a much smaller scale. But I think it was important to have the space almost for it to become real, so students had somewhere to go and we could have that interaction with businesses.

But space is in short supply in any university. The innovator's tactic was simply to appropriate some spaces that seemed to be underused and hope that it would be acceptable.

> We used the rooms that were quite dull classrooms, and in fact although the rooms were at the front of the building nobody wanted to teach in there. So we took them off the timetabling system and began to transform them.

> I began with the front classroom and then once that was up and running . . . there were two very dull classrooms next door, which were poorly lit, so we took those as well and we've opened up the business pod space. And the cost of refurbishment, was next to nothing—the carpet was already there and the walls were already painted, and [the Pro Vice-Chancellor (Academic)] funded furniture and computer equipment.

> The rooms are ideally located at street level at the front of the campus so they are very accessible to the public and people can walk in off the street to make enquiries.

> Its located in a good position on the main road, so that it's visible and it looks out into the community. So Monday to Friday we're open for business. Businesses are coming in all the time, so people will come in off the street, or they'll ring or they'll email with projects that their businesses need undertaking.

The risk in appropriating the rooms paid off and the Faculty felt that what had been created was an effective and productive way of using its space.

Creating a website

The second piece of infrastructure needed for the agency to operate was a website: indeed, without the website the agency could not function. The Solent Creatives website (Figure 10.2) is the shop window for the agency's work. It enables businesses to advertise their freelance job opportunities and students to register their interest in working with a business and also to register their interests and skills. The website therefore is underpinned by a database of students and their interests for example in logo design, copywriting, promotional support, film making, animation, illustration, market research, journalism, public relations, web design, social media, advertising campaigns and event management.

But creating a website offering a university service is not a simple matter. Solent University like other universities has strict design protocols to protect branding and reputation.

Because of the difficulties of doing anything that is different or out of the box, we made a website ourselves. We knew what we wanted and we knew how we wanted to interact with businesses. We also had to do this quickly so we had to do it ourselves.

Figure 10.2 Solent Creatives website home page

Students register their interests by completing a simple on-line registration form, once registered they are encouraged to upload a personal profile and check out the assignments in the student opportunities section. If they find an assignment they would like to take on they can make an application via the website to the placement team. The whole process has been designed to encourage the students to be pro-active and take responsibility for engaging with employers.

There is a student database where students list their skills and they can either be skills that they've learnt on their course, or they could be skills that they already brought with them. So they list their skills and we hold them on the database and when the jobs come in, they go on the website, the students can apply and we match them.

Businesses representatives register their contact details through the website and provide information about job opportunities or projects they are interested in finding students to assist them with. There is currently no charge for this service.

Once a business has offered an opportunity a member of the Solent Creatives Team contacts the business representative to discuss what is required and explain the conditions for employing students. If the agency is able to help one or more students are identified with the requisite skills sets suitable for the freelance work.

Payment is entirely at the discretion of the business as long as it is more than the specified minimum hourly rate to be paid directly to the student on successful completion of your project. An estimate of the time is written into the assignment brief at the first meeting and a suggested total provided on completion. Charitable organisations and internal projects without funding are accepted. There is an expectation that employers will always cover students' expenses.

The online application process in place for business has enabled the agency to monitor the businesses being helped i.e. by size, industry sector and the type of projects they apply for help.

The majority of requests from businesses are for multiple projects e.g. logo/ brand and website design. The team then has to agree one prioritisation with the employer with a fee for any future work paid direct to the student.

About seventy five per cent of applications are from micro-businesses, with less than ten employees. This in itself is a challenge as they are not always clear as to what their business needs are in terms of media support and they often require a great deal of support from the outset. Such businesses often lack a well defined marketing strategy and this is not helpful to working with students, as not all are mature or experienced to advise business owners, and this has required further support from staff.

From January 2012, the agency experienced an increase in requests from larger businesses, some national and international e.g. Sainsbury's, Sodexo, B & Q, BAE systems and IBM are in this category. Public Sector organisations have also made enquiries like the National Health Service, Hampshire Police Authority, Hampshire Ambulance Service, Southampton City Council and Hampshire County Council. A number of charities have also shown an interest. If a business enquiry is declined the team tell the employer and explain the reason why.

A job finding agency that supports student development

The main difference between Solent Creatives and a commercial job agency is the care and attention given to preparing and supporting students to undertake their commercial assignments. In other words it's not just an agency for finding students work, it's an agency for helping students to develop so that they can perform effectively in the world of work.

When students register with the agency they are provided with a short induction course. As the students are acting as freelance workers they are introduced to their Tax and National Insurance obligations and other subjects that are relevant to being an effective freelance worker.

> So at the start we do a little bit on tax, we had two gentlemen come in from the tax office that were very good. We also introduce them to intellectual property, we have an expert here and he's given us his time. We do some kit induction, so if they are just level one and their skills are not quite what they should be with some of the camera kit that's going to be needed, we do a little bit with them on that. But mainly induction is about teaching them how they should engage with business and how to behave in a professional manner, how you complete a timesheet, and how if you say something will be done by three o'clock on Friday, it really has to be done. A lot of it, to you and I would seem fairly obvious, but to undergraduates, even at level three sometimes, it isn't.

The agency tries to match students to business clients and then meets the client with the student to ensure that they are treated fairly and that they can meet the expectations of the client.

> Because the level of work is such we need someone to help with the matching and we now have a manager and an intern to support our work. We match the student skills to the business and we have a match meeting in the agency. We don't send students off anywhere until we've

> seen the business. So the business comes in and we sit with the manager, we've just got to a position now where we've got members of staff involved also. So this morning for example, we've had a PR job that's come in, so the PR member of staff was there, who teaches those skills. I was also there together with the manager of the agency and the student. So at that first meeting we support the student as they negotiate how many hours the job will involve and what they'll be paid and also the business talks them through the brief and what they'll need to bring to the job, and it's about matching those expectations.

There has been considerable demand for students' services; since the agency opened in March 2011 over 600 assignments have been completed. The defining characteristic of the agency is that it has at its heart a mission to help student s develop themselves and members of teaching staff provide support on a voluntary basis in key areas.

> We don't turn anyone away and it's open to level one students as well. So even though students who are just coming in, who really need a lot of support, we don't turn them away. We'll sit with them and I don't quite know how we do it, but we will sit with them and we'll help them do the project and bring them on.

> For example we've currently got seven level one film students working with us and they've recently been to IBM and done quite a lot of filming there. That was really challenging for them, but we didn't want to turn them down, they were very keen and they are good, but if we can work with them and grow them, by level three they are going to be fantastic. But at the moment they need a lot of looking after. So a member of staff from the filming team helped with all the security clearances, which they wouldn't have been able to do on their own, and she went along with them to IBM to support them.

The agency also provides an incubator service for a small number of student companies.

> Creative entrepreneurship is a unit at level 6 where we've taught 40 students some business skills, so those creative students who've got a good idea and want to start a business have access to a business pod. We're just coming to the end of the second 20, and we've got seven start—up businesses and we're going to move some more

in soon. We've got one firm called Britkids that are doing high end children's clothing, a fashion designer, two film editing companies and an event management company and we've also got two lads who are working on computer games, who are really very talented. We're just helping them to get started.

To gain a place in the business pod which comes with free office space and a start up grant of £2000 is highly competitive.

When they have completed the unit, they produce a successful plan and pitch it Dragon's Den style for a place in the pods. They pitch to a panel, [including a senior manager who is responsible for the HEIF budget] and an outside business consultant, who we couldn't have done any of this without. She's been amazing and mentors the start-up companies one to one in the pods. So they pitched their idea and business plan and then seven were offered a place for nine months and they get £2000 to support them and one to one mentoring from the business consultant and from someone from the background that they are developing in.

Challenges

There have been a number of challenges associated with the innovation. The first relates to persuading colleagues that setting up an agency within the University would spoil existing relationships with local commercial agencies. Here the tactic was to risk trying it and to see what would happen.

When the idea was first suggested some members of staff weren't particularly keen, because they felt it would impact on local agencies, who offered similar sorts of services, some of whom we have very good relationships with and they already write live briefs for us. But in fact they've been very good about it, and one agency came along and actually opened it and they've been great. I think the reality is that if you want a full service job, you're still going to go to one of those agencies anyway. So I think the larger businesses who do use us, are engaging with us as part of their corporate social responsibility to the University. Businesses like B&Q, Sainsbury's, and the NHS, are quite large employers. They have done it because they've been quite keen to give something back.

The second challenge was to set up the website. Ideally this would have been within the University's existing website structure but this was not possible to achieve in the short time scale that was available before the agency's launch date. The issue facing the innovator was twofold— access to space on the University website and compliance with the design specifications of any website offering university services.

> There wasn't room on the University website, so we developed our own. It has to work from both the business and student point of view, and we have updated it again recently to ensure this is the case. It works well. We just couldn't have operated as an agency without it.

Again the innovator took a risk by operating outside the University protocols in order to achieve something that needed to be done quickly if the innovation was to be launched in time. This tactic did cause a fair amount of friction with the marketing department, which was difficult to resolve. Here is a good example of someone trying to innovate and solve a tricky operational problem in real time meeting considerable resistance from within a central university service.

> One senior manager was very upset about the website and members of the same team weren't happy about its development. If they could find room on the main portal, we could link up, but at the time this wasn't possible and we can't operate without a website it just wouldn't have worked. I understand that senior colleagues were worried that we might develop something that would embarrass the University, but everything we have done, we have planned carefully. It has all been thought through, so there was no question of us doing something that would damage the University's reputation.

Staffing the agency was also difficult but here the solution was to create a job opportunity for an intern.

> Staffing the agency was an issue but we were lucky because we came at a time when the University was about to have interns, so we bid for one of those interns and we got one.

The fourth challenge was operational and related to the difficulties of accomplishing change where current university systems were not set up to support the enterprise. For example,

> the NHS came in and there's been a dip in health visitors recruitment, so they wanted us to make a film that would

> help with that. So we made something called 'Grumpy Baby' and now we've got other jobs on the back of that, but one of the things there was, they came in with £5000 to pay the student and we had nowhere to put it. So all the time it's challenging the University systems if you like, so we did sort that one, but I'm sure there will be other things that come along.

There are also a set of issues relating to student involvement. The solution to these challenges generally involves students taking on responsibility to do more.

> Although there is a natural lead from the application form to the personal profile the students are not promoting themselves either individually or as teams. Very few have the confidence to highlight their skills and this comes across through the application process. We may receive a number of applications from the same course but only one or two will add their knowledge and skills although encouraged to do so. Students are relying on the placement team to source assignments. In addition, there is a reliance on the team to arrange meetings and write assignment briefs. The team also spends a considerable amount of time chasing and checking up that they are working to the agreed timescale.

One of the objectives of the pilot was to test the employer market. Marketing commenced three months before the launch through selected local intermediary business and sector groups and business recruitment has been highly successful.

However, the demand created through the employer engagement strategy quickly outstripped supply identifying the need for the agency to have a larger bank of students with a broader range of skills briefed, registered and signed up to the principles and opportunities available through the programme.

These challenges and the uncertainties that arise from them are a considerable source of anxiety. But worrying about specific issues and the thinking it provokes also leads to new ideas as possible solutions are considered to tackle perceived problems.

> It's been a lot of work, especially on top of teaching and running the school, and a lot of worry as well. I worry about it constantly. My main anxiety is about reputation. My two biggest concerns are firstly, that we won't be able

> to meet demand and secondly, where do we go with it? I feel it's my responsibility to make it sustainable in the long term, which people are now saying to me more and more, of course.
>
> One solution to this is embedding it in the curriculum, that's part of it, but it's not the whole answer. You know, I think we need a proper charging system, where possibly we could pull some of that funding back in, I don't know, I haven't sorted that out in my mind yet. Do we open it up to staff talent as well, so we could offer staff expertise and take a small cut from that? Do we encourage local creatives to get involved? With the economy the way that it is, could we offer work to them and have another arm to the agency, where we can start to strengthen creative skills in the business sector. These are the things I think about constantly.

One creative solution to sustaining the enterprise is to embed the work of the agency in the curriculum so that fee income can be brought it to underpin the work.

> Because it has to be financially sustainable in the long term, I've written four units called 'Freelancing at Solent Creatives', so students can pick that as an option. I validated it across the whole faculty and we've got around 90 students who've chosen it. So what that means is they complete assignments, and at the end of the project, they are assessed. At level five they have to have a portfolio of work, a reflective log, and at level six it's a portfolio of work, a reflective log and a personal development plan that helps them prepare for when they graduate. So it means I can pull the funding stream back through those students doing that unit and use it to help fund the other work of the agency if I need to. This will give us some sort of financial sustainability to continue the work.

Managing the anxieties that emerge from innovating in this way is a challenge for an innovator and support from colleagues is very important. In this case support comes mainly through conversations with the Dean.

> I talk to the Dean. He's very good and again from a practitioner background, so I tend to talk about it and where we're going to go. He is very good at offering advice and has been extremely supportive.

Innovators are never short of ideas and are usually thinking ahead.

> I'd like to do a publishing house attached to Solent
> Creatives and it would be a place where staff work and
> student work could be published to the outside world.
> We don't have one of those at the moment and to do it
> digitally does not involve huge start up costs and is very
> cheap to do. So we've got Solent Creatives the agency
> and the business pods and then we'd have this publishing
> attached.

SECONDARY INNOVATION

Once the innovation has been created and the prototype has been piloted (primary innovation), a second stage begins in which the innovation is refined, adapted and perhaps entirely new features are added.

The issues and challenges that were thrown up during the primary stage of bringing an idea into practical existence provide the context for the secondary stage of innovation much of which involves fine tuning and marginal improvement of existing systems or procedures. A number of improvements of the existing business model have been identified for the coming year (2012-13) including:

1. An induction clinic for new student registrations. The induction should include guidance on the tools available to them through the website, the importance of meeting the expectations of the client once involved in an assignment.
2. Individual post assignment debriefs to ensure that students are given the tools and support to market themselves and increase their client portfolios outside Solent Creatives. This could be in the form of a questionnaire followed by an interview. It should also include an introduction to the business start-up programme and its benefits.
3. Agreement to extend a recruitment campaign across the University but only to recruit from degree courses where we have a skill mismatch.
4. Increased support from course leasers, we monitor the source of student registrations and course leaders have a huge influence on sign ups. The registrations vary considerably across the Faculty and it is likely that providing information back to course leaders on their students' take-up will enable them to become more involved.

Another area for incremental change is in the forms that are used to register the skills that are on offer. Here a newly appointed Manager, with a commercial background, was able to find a better way to represent the skill sets of students.

> There were a lot of skills on the project application forms and the corresponding student application form that I didn't think were ones that we could either offer at the moment or that businesses want. So I got a list of all the courses in the faculty and started to map all the different skills that would be taught within the degrees and I generated a spread sheet that had a list of all the skills and the degrees that taught that specific skill so that we could see where our strengths were likely to lie.

The key communication infrastructure—the website has also been revamped, again because the newly appointed Manager who had a commercial background in design and marketing recognised that there was scope for improvement.

> When I started, the first thing I noticed was that the website didn't scream a creative agency to me and I wanted to get more emphasis on the agency's portfolio of work that the students had undertaken. I'm still working on that with one of our students to develop our website in this direction. I've managed to pull together a lot of portfolio items for the agency which we didn't have before. I've also added a customer management system and a new database so that we can manage all of our projects and all of our contacts properly. We've also developed our own marketing over the last two weeks with a student graphic designer. I've worked with him to develop brochures, flyers, posters, banners, online stuff all the kind of things that we need to start pushing ourselves out there to both the businesses and the students.

The databases underlying the website have also been revamped.

> we had a variety of databases but they were quite unorganised so both myself and the current intern worked on getting them all into one software package and linking up all the students with the projects that they've undertaken because whilst it had the names of the students on the projects, it wasn't clear and it wasn't easy to see a list of the projects that a certain student had worked on so that was something that I was quite keen to implement. The software package we used were off-the-shelf but we had to create the databases within it and work out how to link

them all up in a way that was easy to understand and that we'd be able to generate reports from. So that was something that we did within the first month of me being here.

More radical innovation in the second stage relates to marketing. This is an area where new organisational capability was required so a Manager was appointed to develop a marketing strategy and campaign and oversee the production of promotional materials. This is where he is making an original contribution and participate in inventive rather than adaptive processes.

> one of the reasons for my role being created was because they hadn't had a chance to do any marketing before and they needed someone to come in and start to push out the agency more, even though by doing a little marketing they had got a lot of projects in. Part of my role is to increase the amount of requests that we're getting and increase the amount of student sign ups as well.

The business pods have also proved to be successful and the number of pods is being doubled during the secondary stage of innovation.

> At the moment we have seven businesses in the start-up space. The second batch of students have just pitched for a place in this incubation space. So when they come back in September we should have about 12 to 15 small businesses.

Another area of inventive (rather than incremental) second stage innovation is in the way the principal innovator has continued to create curriculum units that afford learners the opportunity to gain credit towards their degree through working on freelance assignments. It is through the process of embedding the work of the agency in the undergraduate curriculum that the innovator is creating a sustainable and an expanded future for the enterprise.

> When it first opened, the units and the work coming into the agency were an extra to the studies students undertook. But now we have written units so that students can work on assignments, claim credits towards their degree and be paid. So from this September 2012, students at level 2 and 3 can take an option called 'Freelancing at Solent Creatives' and this is where they can pick up a number of assignments, work on them with the support of staff, gain credit towards their degree and build a portfolio that will help them when they leave us.

Why do innovators innovate?

Innovators innovate for all sorts of reasons but in higher education teachers innovate to enhance the learning and development opportunities for their students. Some of the tangible benefits of Solent Creatives to students and to the University are elaborated below.

> at level one it's helping to build their confidence and getting them to work in the real world and to negotiate with real employers. Even if on that creative entrepreneurship unit they don't go in to start up their own business, those skills that they are taught, I mean no one is going to stay in any one job now, so you know they've got those life skills where they can pitch for the best contract. They can negotiate money, because money is very difficult to talk about and you know some of the students that we have, who do lack confidence, that's something they need a lot of help with.

> So I think the growth in confidence, in getting them to see what skills they already have. They are very reluctant sometimes to tick skills that they have and have already demonstrated, so I think that's important. Engaging with employers, because by doing that it's a way of us keeping our curriculum up to date, so if we're working with them regularly, we know which areas of the curriculum we need to change and I don't mean by offering freelancing at Solent Creatives, I mean you know by what they are doing, so what the ad agencies are teaching currently with the new digital advancements. If our students are working closely with them while they are in, we get all that information and we can use it to update ourselves, so I think that's crucial, it builds our links, it's now developing into partnerships, which hopefully will then move on to knowledge transfer. So it will just start to build and also you know the jobs that they go on to get at the end. It definitely improves their chances of employability at the end.

The School also benefits from having a distinctive and innovative asset in Solent Creatives which can be used to support the mainstream curriculum—for example in course validation processes.

> Recently we've re-validated our titles—we've gone for professional accreditation on some courses, so on sports journalism and multi-media, we went for accreditation from the BJTC. On magazine it was the PTC and last week we

> validated a photo journalism course, so of course I did a
> session in there with all of those validation panels and
> they were all amazed at it and I'm not saying that because
> it's anything special, it's just what we've done, but you
> could see the course teams were really pleased to be
> associated with it and of course they got their validation,
> so that was nice.

For employers there are economic and relational benefits.

> For charities, they are getting work done that they wouldn't
> otherwise be able to do. For the small SME's, that's the
> majority of our customer base, 69% are SME's in the city
> or just outside, so again there the students are making
> a real difference where they wouldn't otherwise at the
> moment be able to afford.

From the perspective of the innovators the rewards for working harder, taking risks, suffering frustration and perhaps engaging in a degree of conflict with colleagues in order to bring about successful innovation are not financial or material. Rather they are psychological and associated with a sense of achievement and professional satisfaction as they overcome challenges, solve particular problems and see the effects of their creations grow.

> I've learnt not be put off by colleagues who claim that
> things can't be done. There is usually a solution, so it is
> best not to give up, to just keep going and find a way round
> all these obstacles.

It also means that they have new experiences through which they can develop themselves

> It's given me skills that I didn't have before and it's given
> me a chance to develop some of my existing skills to new
> levels. In my previous role in marketing and promotions, the
> campaigns I would work on were very short term, whereas
> when I started here I created a marketing campaign for the
> whole year. And then alongside that I'm currently working
> on an impact report as well, which I wouldn't have had
> experience with before. So it's given me quite a lot of new
> experiences and opportunities to develop my skills.

Ultimately the rewards are linked to the sense of pride and satisfaction as the students who have been involved enter the real world much better prepared to embark on their chosen career.

> Talking to level three students who have just left and
> were very involved with us from the start, its seeing the
> difference [Solent Creatives] has made to their CVs and
> to their portfolio as they go out and get jobs.

Perhaps the most significant achievement is that the innovator has demonstrated that not only does the approach work, in the sense of achieving university SDP objectives, it can and is being sustained through Faculty funding and expanded. In this respect it provides an important practice model which can be emulated in other parts of the University or exported to other universities.

CHAPTER 11

Warsash Superyacht Academy

Introduction

This case study differs from other case studies described in this volume in that the idea for it did not emanate from a Faculty's SDP strategy or a response by individuals to the opportunities of SDP funding. Rather, the ideas for innovation emanated from the longstanding belief of an individual that his idea for innovation would create a new way of representing and communicating the opportunities for learning and development in a particular industrial sector.

The idea was for the creation of a new virtual organisation—a Warsash Superyacht Academy. That this idea born out of an individual's insights, interests and passion, and was not part of any grand plan, was highlighted in a comment by a senior manager.

> I would never have thought of a virtual Superyacht Academy as a project idea . . . . A colleague brought it forward as an idea that he was really interested in and mentioned it when I went for a conversation with a group of people in that Faculty. His enthusiasm for it was absolutely tangible, you had to listen . . . . you could see there was something serious there. It is being aware at a moment like that that there is something that wouldn't necessarily have been in any grand plan, something really quite important and someone who wants to carry it through and who believes it will work and who knows enough about the conditions in that part of the University to know it will work if it is given a chance. *Pro Vice-Chancellor (Academic).*

As we will see, the idea for a Warsash Superyacht Academy had been in the mind of the innovator for over a year but the strategic development programme provided a context and resources within which it could come to fruition. This Chapter is based on the innovator's own story of how the innovation is being accomplished.

Background

The global superyacht industry has a multi-billion dollar turnover annually, including yacht design, build and repair, services, berths, crewing and training. The superyacht fleet has doubled since 2000 and there are now more than 4,000 yachts > 30m length, while orders for superyachts have almost tripled in the same period. While the current economic downturn has caused a softening of the market for smaller superyachts (30m-50m length), there has been little impact for larger vessels.

Expansion of the superyacht fleet has also increased demand for "quality" yacht crew at a time when there is a shortfall in personnel supply, and 9% of the worldwide fleet (29% of EU fleet) is registered in UK and complies with UK Maritime and Coastguard Agency (MCA) certification requirements.

As in many other strategic development projects, the first step in the process of change involved gathering and appraising information so that good decisions could be made. In 2009-10, Warsash Maritime Academy (WMA) submitted a bid for SDP Funding that made provision for undertaking a programme of market research that was relevant to its educational and training provision.

The bid was successful and as part of this programme of research, WMA's Business Operations team reviewed different aspects of the international superyacht industry to determine the potential for developing and advancing the current levels of yacht education and training (YET) provision offered by WMA, together with the associated income streams. The study included consideration of available market research, evaluation of market demands, feedback from attendance at the Monaco Yacht Show (the international yacht industry's premier sales exhibition) and discussions with interested parties including the UK's Maritime and Coastguard Agency, Viking Recruitment, UK Sailing Association and other organisations.

> Warsash Maritime Academy is the commercial maritime arm of Southampton Solent University and provides education and training for the main merchant navy shipping sectors, including cargo, containers, cruise ships, tankers and ferries,. It also supports the offshore market, port authorities and commercial yachts. Commercial yachts had been a relatively small element over the previous ten years or so. We tried to nurture it a little bit but there was some organizational scepticism about future engagement with the commercial yacht sector. I therefore initiated a review of course viability, costing and pricing models and market predictions etc. Through this review I identified that course provision for the commercial yacht sector was

definitely viable, with relatively good returns on the cost of running the courses. It is also quite an affluent sector. *Innovator*

The study revealed that WMA already achieved about 6% of its annual income from its yacht education and training (YET) provision. The income was mainly derived from two sources, namely the commercial Yacht Deck and Marine Engineering Certification courses and STCW safety courses like fire fighting and medical first aid that students complete during their time on campus. The study considered the current extent of the University's YET, specifically WMA's range of commercial yacht certification courses, the Faculty of Technology 's degree-level courses (i.e. Yacht & Powercraft Design, Yacht Production & Surveying), and Sport Solent's RYA-level provision (i.e. power boating and jet skis). The study also revealed that there was little interaction between WMA and Sport Solent's yacht-related course delivery on the Warsash campus.

The innovator concluded that the University would benefit if the YET course provision was brought together through the creation of a virtual umbrella organisation, and the idea of the Warsash Superyacht Academy was born. Underlying this story of innovation is the innovator's strong personal vision for a unique global institution in terms of the scope of its course provision, the facilities and expertise that were available to it, and the opportunities available for business development and third stream revenue generation.

> The vision was to develop a unique umbrella organization for the worldwide commercial yacht sector, and no other organisation in the world today can currently compete with what we are about to launch. There are a couple of FE-level providers in the south of France and Florida that do small segments of the provision, particularly at the lower certification level. However, they don't have the supporting resources of a university organisation, they don't have a £3 million ship handling centre at Timsbury Lake, and they don't provide the full merchant navy certification programmes required for larger yachts. This is ultimately a collaborative venture to provide something that the commercial yacht world has never seen before, and it is really about the whole being greater than the sum of the parts. In terms of how you project the branding, Warsash Maritime Academy already has a good name internationally, but how you capitalize on that reputation, how you expand into other areas and how you generate more opportunities like additional courses or third stream income activities is what this initiative is all about. So that is the essence of it really. It is how you take what is

already in our portfolio and how you get better visibility, better profile and growth in student numbers and income by presenting it within the form of a virtual Superyacht Academy. *Innovator*

It was this deeply held personal vision for a virtual Superyacht Academy that motivated the innovator to pursue its development over several years, even when there was some scepticism within his Faculty about the future potential of the superyacht industry.

Scoping study

The outcomes of WMA's SDP-funded study reinforced the belief of the innovator that there that there was merit in conducting a more comprehensive scoping exercise to evaluate the viability of establishing a Virtual Superyacht Academy, which would connect yacht-related provision in different Faculties under a virtual umbrella organisation. Such an organisation had the potential to enhance brand value, market awareness, student numbers, revenue and business development opportunities.

A small project scoping group subsequently undertook this exercise and also considered potential collaborations with external organisations to achieve business synergies and extend both the umbrella organisation's business markets and its range of provision beyond current offerings.

The project scoping group concluded that creation of a 'Warsash Superyacht Academy' was viable and a paper supporting the initiative was then presented to senior management for their consideration, approval and allocation of appropriate resources. It was envisaged that the timeline for project development, partnership consultations/agreements and infrastructure creation would be completed by early summer 2011. This would then facilitate a formal launch of the Warsash Superyacht Academy at the Monaco Yacht Show in September 2011.

Infrastructure and support requirements were considered to involve:

1) High specification website with upmarket appeal, which would provide a portal to provide easy navigation and access to the underlying activities. For example, a prospective student selecting certification courses would be directed to relevant WMA web pages, while selection of Interior & Hospitality courses would link to Interior Yacht Services' related web page and yacht degree courses would link to FTEC.
2) A co-ordinating unit to have oversight of Warsash Superyacht Academy activities and to handle initial postal/telephone enquiries

before onward referral to the appropriate faculty/service/external organisation for further information and course bookings.

3) Adequate marketing and promotional support, possibly co-ordinated by the Marketing and Communications Service (MCS) with supporting finance being derived from a mixture of central funding and pro-rata contributions from faculties/services/external organisations.

Turning an idea into reality

In spite of the good business case that had been made through the initial market research, the exciting idea of a virtual Warsash Superyacht Academy, and recognition within the SDP Team that the idea had good potential to fulfil SDP priorities, the idea could not be progressed in 2010-2011 as a number of organisational issues had to be resolved prior to and following WMA's merger with FTEC to form the new Maritime & Technology Faculty (MarTec).

> Although I had written position papers, held lots of meetings and given a number of presentations, we got to the stage where the project had to be put on hold pending resolution of organizational issues. I also think there was a small element of risk aversion, with some people perhaps not quite understanding the market that we were trying to tap into. *Innovator*

> Superyachts have been a relatively small part of our business up until now so there was some scepticism from a number of people at WMA and in other parts of the University about the true potential of this area. It is a fairly bespoke market sector, not mainstream yachting, and I think some people underestimated just what the actual potential was as they didn't really understand the market. *Innovator*

> It was only really when we merged with FTEC in March 2011 that we were able to take a fresh look at everything. At the first management away day after the merger, there was discussion around how are we were going to make the new faculty work and did we have any flagship initiatives to help us? I said, "Yes, I've got one, its ready to go and I can launch it quickly", and that was the point at which we were able to move it forward. *Innovator*

With this project, timing was everything and the creation of a new Faculty created the conditions which enabled the idea to be progressed so that its potential could be realised.

> It was a case of this project was good to go. It was already scoped out and the project plan was there. All we were waiting for was the green light to go out and recruit somebody who could be dedicated to managing the project. It was 'off the shelf' and everything was ready to go. The only thing we needed was project funding and organisational motivation to proceed. *Innovator*

From the outset, the SDP team had been strongly supportive of the Superyacht Academy proposition, which had grown from the initial market research that had been funded through SDP, but by March 2011 the SDP was approaching its final year and funding was being redistributed to support major organisational change initiatives. The SDP Team and a senior manager did however support Higher Education Innovation Funding (HEIF) funding bid for the Superyacht Academy, which was successful.

> The original intention was to gain SDP funding. I initially saw an opportunity through joining up the University's strategic dots in terms of developing flexible learning, employer engagement, and a maritime hub, and I then referenced the bid to the 2008-13 strategic plan as I thought this project ticked a lot of those objectives too. However, it was agreed that we would hold off on the project due to management issues at WMA at that time so another year went by until we were into the MarTec merger. It was only really after the merger when we were looking for a project that was ready to go that I flagged up that the Superyacht Academy was already scoped out. In the end we were lucky enough to get some HEIF funding for the Business Development Manager post. *Innovator*

At the start of the development process the innovator had to provide all the information necessary to create the new virtual organisation system. The information was however based on numerous interactions with the people in the University who would be contributing to the virtual organisation.

> When we launch it, we will market a comprehensive range of courses. Eventually it will include everything needed to work on super yachts, whether it is interior hospitality training, a safety course or a personal development programme. WMA will cover the higher level certification programmes for professional yacht and merchant navy

officers, all of the STCW safety courses and much of the CPD work like ship handling. We are very lucky to have a £3 million ship handling centre at Timsbury Lake, one of only five in the world and certainly the best. Leadership and management for the maritime industry is another area of strength and then you have SSU's specialist undergraduate and post-graduate degrees, and Professional Development Units (PDUs). I think PDUs will be a major growth area in future . . . . what I eventually see [on the website] is a drop down 'menu' of online or blended learning PDUs so that someone working on these yachts can say, 'This week I want to do a unit on "Introduction to accounting and finance' or 'Introduction to marketing' as part of a personal development programme.' We have got a number of PDUs that we have already developed but there is still a lot of work to be done there. *Innovator*

A second task involved the creation of partnerships and agreements with external organisations who will offer their courses through the virtual organisation.

We look to external partners to fill the gaps in the provision that we don't have and don't want to do. The main one being for interior hospitality where we are in the final stages of forming a partnership agreement with Interior Yacht Services (IYS). The key player is the CEO of IYS who was instrumental in developing a suite of hospitality courses accredited by the Professional Yachtsmen's Association (PYA), now that the industry is maturing and they want to focus more on quality. So having the PYA kite mark is important and we are going to be the first organization to actually run these courses. *Innovator*

Figure 11.1 Screen shot of the Warsash Superyacht Academy website

A third important task in establishing the virtual organisation has been the creation of a visually attractive, easy to navigate, high quality website which acts as a portal to the opportunities provided by the virtual academy. Content has been created primarily by the innovator and his team while the designs, branding and web development have been completed by the University's marketing and e-development teams established through the SDP to provide support for new forms of flexible delivery.

> At the core [of the virtual academy] is this high spec website. They won't take you seriously in this industry unless you have the right standard of website . . . . everything about this is trying to achieve a high spec feel. Stunning photographs, good design and simple navigation. If students already know what they want, they can just type in what it is. If they want to find out about us, our courses, career options, services, CPD opportunities, that is all easily found on the top navigation bar. Nice and simple so they can see straight away what they can do. Our new logo is also very catchy, produced in-house by our design team within MCS. *Innovator*
>
> [The website] is effectively a virtual front for the underlying activities. If somebody is interested in a WMA course,

they will click through onto our course booking pages. But if they are looking at interior courses, they will go through the initial web pages and then click through to the IYS website to complete their booking. Likewise if they wanted a business service from Regs4Yachts it would jump to their website. So that's what I mean by a virtual front. It's a shop window for our courses and services. *Innovator*

I knew what the website had to look like and what the core course portfolio was going to be. All of these things had been prepared in outline because I couldn't wait for [the Business Development Manager] to start on the project due to the tight timescales. I had initially mapped a lot of this out three years ago and then kept updating it in terms of courses or where the extra revenue generation was coming from, the type of approach we needed to take with industry, and the sort of collaborations needed to make it work. All of this information was needed at the start and I had to develop it myself as I didn't have anybody else in place until January this year. *Innovator*

Once the project manager was in post, some delays were initially experienced in integrating Marketing and Communication Services [MCS] and the e-Development Centre staff into the project schedule but these were eventually resolved. It has still been a challenge but we will be ready for the launch. The website is going to go live with a 'soft' launch on 20th August 2012, one month before the formal launch at the Monaco Yacht Show on the 20th September 2012. *Innovator*

The current task is to launch the venture and then to mount an effective marketing campaign.

We are already raising the brand and market awareness. We haven't even announced it formally yet but the industry is quite well aware through its grapevine of the Superyacht Academy initiative and there is already a buzz going around. Having the website live a month beforehand will only help that and we are also getting a lot of positive feedback from various supporters. Draft plans are also in place for the launch ceremonies and associated promotional activities. *Innovator*

Pamela Baker, Norman Jackson and Jane Longmore

One of the important roles of the innovator is to demonstrate the value in a new concept by creating new forms of organisation. It is only when new structures are in place that others will see the benefits and potential in the idea. It is clear that the innovator is looking beyond a portal to enable people to find courses or CPD opportunities; he is looking to a future where the virtual academy provides access to a comprehensive suite of on-line learning opportunities. With the help of SDP funding, WMA has recently developed a completely on-line MSc programme, designed so that the component parts can be taken as freestanding Professional Development Units (PDUs). It is the first example of a fully on-line programme in the University and it provides a model for future course delivery through the Virtual Superyacht Academy.

> The MSc Shipping Operations concept is very applicable to the maritime industry because it is an on-line programme and most of our customers are on ships for eight months or so each year. So it is a question of how you make it easy for people in this situation to participate through flexible learning or even fully online learning. And we do need to apply that to other courses, other programmes that we have. That needs to be an ongoing development project.

> Everybody had been talking about PDUs but how do you make them work for this particular industry? It makes sense to have them on-line, and of course most of the PDUs in our current collection are available in that form. So somebody on a yacht in Monaco or the south of Florida could do it without coming to the University. If you are able to generate enough of these PDUs it would benefit all of the faculties in the University. It will also open up new markets. But the problem at the moment is we haven't gone far enough with developing those types of PDUs. I think the University would have to invest quite heavily to convert the materials into the right form and then start to market them. But hopefully this will set the ball rolling. *Innovator*

The innovator's creative process

The innovator used the terms creativity and creative on a number of occasions and so it is worth exploring the innovator's perceptions of what was meant by these terms.

> I think it was a case of taking a fresh look at something and trying to find another way of doing it. From the original concept of a Superyacht Academy, it was then about trying to find a way of getting the project funded and

- 258 -

looking at how to make it work, and that led me back to the university's strategic plans and then evolving the idea to make it fit better. The original creativity was just seeing an opportunity and after that it was a case of how it could evolve to fit in with the university's plans, make it viable and secure the funding to make it happen.

The idea of 'seeing and recognising new opportunities', and 'joining up the dots' emerges over and over again in conversation as a key aspect of the innovator's creative process.

You're picking up information left right and centre and I do spend quite a bit of time watching the news or reading the maritime press to find out there's any new innovations that could or could not be good for us. So it is a case of trying to sift through all this data and take the bits that we need to make sure we move forward. I think that's where the Superyacht Academy concept came from because when I first started looking at this it was to determine if superyacht training was viable at all or should we just forget about it and reallocate the associated resource elsewhere.

But it was only when you got into the detail that you started to see the potential with the growth figures in terms of the number of yachts, the number of personnel involved against the backdrop of shortages of quality personnel in the whole maritime industry. When you join those dots up you suddenly realise that there is going to be quite a significant increase in course demand, and then you have to work out how to harness that demand and drive it forward in other areas. *Innovator*

The development of a virtual Warsash Superyacht Academy is an interesting story because it reveals the continuous search, by the innovator, for the ways and means to bring his idea into existence. Key elements of this creative process of turning ideas into reality are elaborated in these extracts from the interview with the innovator.

The creative side of this was driven by me trying to find another way of positioning superyacht business because I knew I had to grow it [superyacht education, training and services] as a segment to make it more visible and I needed to overcome a certain amount of resistance to the fact that there was business here. I was convinced of that but I had to find a way to do it and to gain the necessary support and resources.

I started to join the dots that tied in with things we were already doing. Before SDP there had been a lot of talk about cross-faculty collaboration so were there other areas of the university that could be connected? At that time the Faculty of Technology, as it still was, had things like the yacht design degree while Sport Solent has certain RYA level yacht courses so there were other bits that could be connected.

Then I started to think a bit broader than that. We already had the vast majority of the technical course provision in our portfolio but we don't do hospitality and catering. As the university doesn't do it either, the challenge then is to get the right external partner? So I was trying to map out what the portfolio would look like if we fully exploited the potential of the overall concept and the SDP helped me do this through the market research.

I had already configured the idea in line with the university's strategic plan and objectives, but I then reconfigured it because of the way that SDP was being positioned. Then it was a short hop from there to say 'Well look, if there is money available for innovation and strategic development, this is an ideal project.'

What this story reveals is the dogged determination of the innovator to bring his idea into existence and his creative process attempting to do this in the presence of some scepticism and resistance. Through this story the innovator reveals his creative process as one of building a compelling business case to meet the strategic priorities of the University, by 'joining up the dots' of what already exists, and thinking creatively to exploit the potential of the idea by adding new elements to the provision that currently do not exist through partnerships with external providers.

The story also reveals the interplay between the creative enterprise of an innovator trying to accomplish what they value and their interaction with supportive agents in the organisation who appreciate the potential of the ideas in achieving objectives that are of strategic value to the organisation.

There was a meeting about new initiatives and taking them forward. That was when I threw the idea on the table. The Pro Vice-Chancellor (Academic) liked the idea, although she didn't have a handle on the whole concept. That led in short order to the contact with the SDP Project Manager who I hadn't met up until that point but she helped me to position the project scope through our conversations. So if you are talking about champions, yes, without a shadow of a doubt they have been very good in supporting the project and helping to move it forward. *Innovator*

But joining up dots to create an interesting idea and conducting an appraisal to evaluate the worth of an idea are not enough to bring an idea into existence. The ideas and their potential value have to be sold to the people who need to support the idea if it is to be implemented. This is another area requiring a degree of creativity to communicate the idea in ways that will be understood and accepted by people, some of whom may well be skeptical or lack the knowledge that would enable them to appreciate the value in the idea.

> I think the main thing I did was selling it to people. I have lost track of the number of presentations I had given to the point when we actually got the go-ahead in March last year. But that was in terms of talking to staff in each of the Faculties, the marketing and finance teams. It was really about building a consensus because there was some scepticism and I had to overcome that. *Innovator*

> I don't think the business model was difficult to sell. I just think the idea didn't really fit with how others saw things evolving. I think there was also a lack of detailed understanding of the superyacht industry and the potential to develop our provision for this sector. But eventually we got past that and so here we are. *Innovator*

Clearly there was some resistance to the idea and it could have deterred the innovator from pursuing the idea further but will and determination to turn the idea into reality sustained the innovator's involvement until a successful outcome was secured. Here we see the importance of a positive and determined disposition to accomplish change fuelled by a belief that change was, in the innovator's mind, quite achievable.

> I am quite motivated and determined but with this project I couldn't see anything to lose. It was a simple project and didn't need a lot of resource. It didn't have high risk because I wasn't really inventing or creating a brand new portfolio of courses. All I was doing was taking the existing portfolio, repackaging it and then extending it. So, low risk. And for the university it ticked all the boxes. If you look at the 2008/2013 strategic objectives and go down the list you can pretty much tick most of them to some degree.

> I guess my belief in it helped though. It would have been easy to park it when I hit various roadblocks along the way but I just kept persevering and the right moment came. We got the go ahead and here we are almost ready to launch.
> *Innovator*

So the innovator's creativity was used to see opportunities and come up with an idea to exploit the opportunity—an essentially imaginative process, but then to sell the idea to significant others and persuade whoever needed to be persuaded that this was the right thing to do. But once the idea had been accepted by the organisation the idea had to be turned into practical reality. There were two other ways in which the innovator used his creativity to achieve this goal. Firstly, there was the need to secure the necessary resources—here the innovator is behaving as an entrepreneur.

> The HEIF funding itself is only actually covering the cost of the Business Development Manager's salary for two years so I then had to find other resources elsewhere to cover the rest of the project development. We've used some operational funds where we've needed to, to support additional work to bring it into its full form. Everything else is either being covered by existing expenditure that is targeted at superyacht promotions and supporting activities or from reallocation of operational non-pay budgets to finance the website development work.
> *Innovator*

Once other people become involved in a project, design, building and delivery become a co-creative process.

> It's not just been my creativity, a number of people have also been involved in the creative process since we got the go ahead. I did a lot of the work myself up front as there was only me at that time and I had to scope out a number of elements, whether it was a rough idea on what the website should look like, the type of course portfolio that we needed, the approach that we were going to take with business service partners. Those sort of things were pretty well mapped out before we got our Business Development Manager in post and before we really engaged with the e-development unit for web development and the design teams within MCS. Since then though, the small group of people working on this project have helped each other enormously. For example, it's only been through our Business Development Manager's discussions with the e-development, and MCS design teams that we were able

to see different opportunities and identify better ways of doing things. So the creativity element has very much been a team effort since we actually started creating the website. *Innovator*

But the co-creative process also has to be managed in a way that enables the ideas and capabilities of team members to be harnessed in a way that achieves the innovator's vision. Here we witness the role of the innovator as holding a group together to perform the development work in a manner that achieves his goal.

In the past six months I've had to try and keep project development on the right track and aligned to the original concept, reminding people that this is going to be a commercial platform. It's not just about the look, feel and aesthetic value of the website, it has to be the right standard and do a job in the commercial world. *Innovator*

Challenges

The innovator encountered a number of challenges which had to be overcome or worked around during the process of bringing about change.

Getting the go-ahead was the first big challenge. That is more down to individuals than organizational inertia. The second big challenge was getting it off the drawing board and getting the funding sorted out. But then it proved difficult to move quickly. I come from a commercial background so I'm used to projects being resourced quickly if they are viable, whereas here it took a little longer.

Unfortunately I didn't get my project manager in post until January and he had to get up to speed in a hurry but since then he's being going flat out. So it certainly put quite a bit of pressure on me personally to keep the project on track, to get the work done and make sure it stays true to where it needs to be. Hopefully once the Superyacht Academy is up and running though, the University will see the benefit. *Innovator*

As in many of the SDP projects the innovator clearly makes a considerable personal investment, on top of their existing commitments to ensure momentum is sustained in the absence of additional resources when they are needed. It is this personal cost—doing what has to be done when it needs to be done—that ensures that change is actually accomplished within the time frames that have been set.

Rewards for innovation

From the perspective of the innovator, the rewards for working harder, taking risks, suffering frustration and perhaps engaging in a degree of conflict with colleagues in order to bring about successful innovation are not financial or material. Rather they are psychological and associated with a sense of achievement and professional satisfaction as he witnesses his ideas being turned into concrete practices, and in time for these practices to yield the anticipated results and influence others so that similar practices are grown in other parts of the University.

> The reward above all has been seeing the concept evolve from its original form into how we have managed to develop it since then. Seeing it come to fruition in this form and knowing now, just from the feedback we have already received and the fact that the partners that we have engaged with are so enthusiastic about the project, that the concept has such enormous potential. The sense of satisfaction now it is about to launch and that I can see exactly how it's going to work. That is the real reward. That some idea I had in the bathtub three years ago is all of a sudden about to happen. I think reward will also come from people in other parts of the university starting to think, 'How can we do something similar to that'? *Innovator*

> I think I've had good overall support from the organisation and personal support from key individuals, particularly at the VCG level and the SDP team leader in particular. *Innovator*

> I just had a meeting with the Vice-Chancellor and the Director of Finance and Resources to talk through progress, and the feedback was very good. In fact, since this project was given the go-ahead, everybody has been very supportive. *Innovator*

Through these perspectives we can appreciate that personal rewards for this individual are linked to the achievement of his vision for change and the recognition of the value of his ideas by enthusiastic supporters, partners and senior managers. Ultimately, his reward is the confirmation that the beliefs that have sustained his engagement with the challenge over a considerable period of time and in the face of scepticism and challenges, have been justified.

CHAPTER 12

Develop People and Organisational Development Will Follow

INTRODUCTION

Transforming the University so that it was more engaged with employers needs and provided more flexible curricular and delivery arrangements that could meet these needs called for underpinning administrative processes that could rapidly adapt and flex to accommodate and exploit new situations rapidly. This required that administrative staff needed to develop confidence and harness their latent capability to respond and do this for themselves. The essence of the intervention was to develop capability rather than focus on very specific issues, learning by doing, mirroring the SDP process across the University. However, internally the University both lacked sufficient depth of expertise and resource capacity to deliver the mentoring and support to achieve this in a short time horizon. Bringing in an external organisation was necessary but a risk; would their intervention work (it was new), would they be accepted by the staff, would Faculties let them work with their teams, could they work with the programme methodology and not try to impose their own, what would happen after the programme finished?

This chapter describes an evolving relationship that has been an important element of Southampton Solent University's work on strategic change. In particular, it illustrates the important role external consultants can play in mentoring and supporting action learning, and the value to both consultants and the University of a longer term relationship.

In early 2010 Southampton Solent University began working with an external learning and organisational development company which specialises in Higher Education. Initially, the company delivered a series of development workshops to academic staff on techniques for successful employer engagement. Since then the relationship has grown and developed to the point where a particular elements of organisational development have been outsourced to the external company. This chapter describes and illustrates the growth and development of the relationship, the organisational development activities that have been undertaken, and explores and analyses the conditions for success, the benefits and the challenges.

FROM SUPPLIER TO TRUSTED PARTNER

A road map of the organisational development activities described in the chapter is provided in Figure 12.1.

Figure 12.1 Evolution of the relationship between the consultant facilitators and Southampton Solent University Organisational Development programme. Specific projects involving the external company are shown.

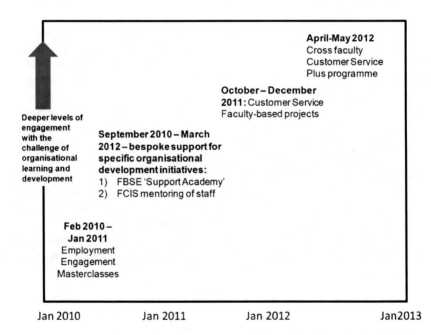

In 2010 a mainstay of the external company's portfolio was a series of employer engagement masterclasses which were designed to help staff to work successfully with employers. Titles offered included 'Designing and delivering a curriculum for employer engagement', 'Using real work for assessment', 'Quality assurance for work-based learning', Understanding your market' and 'Accrediting employer learning'. Southampton Solent University initially booked one workshop to offer as a staff development opportunity for those (mostly academic staff) working or aspiring to work more in the area of employer engagement.

Feedback from the initial workshop was good and three series were booked. Workshops were typically customised for individual institutional clients so several detailed discussions took place between the directors of the external company and the University team responsible for commissioning the workshops. Also the workshops were designed to allow participants to learn from addressing their real employer engagement challenges during the sessions and to receive advice from the expert practitioners running the sessions. This meant that over the period of approximately nine months that the workshop series were delivered at Southampton Solent University, the directors became familiar with and advised on several key issues that the University was working on in relation to the development of their existing and prospective portfolio of work with employers. Issues that were discussed ranged widely and often beyond the initial employer engagement remit, such as the service standards that must be achieved by all departments of the University in direct contact with employers.

It was during this period that the relationship between the University and the consultant facilitator *changed* from merely providing a standard service that fulfilled a general organisational development need to one in which members of the SDP Team shared their thoughts and aspirations on deeper forms of organisational engagement and development. Through this process the consultant was able to identify further ways in which value could be added to the University's organisational development process.

Discussions arising from the employer engagement workshops led to a further commission to undertake work with specific individual and small teams at a point where these were "engaging" with employers to ensure that they were supported in developing effective and confident relationships with their targets.

This work took two forms. Firstly, working with a team of lecturers from the Faculty of Sport, Business and Enterprise (FBSE), facilitating their Support Academy. Secondly, mentoring two academics from the Faculty of Creative Industries and Society as they negotiated accreditation by Southampton Solent University of two employers' existing learning programmes.(More analysis of this work can be found in part two of this chapter where it is examined as a case study). Through this process the consultant was able to demonstrate in a concrete way the value of working with teams/individuals on a "just in time" basis on practical problems to build capacity.

July 2011: New approach to organisational development

The external company had recognised that the new student funding regime would mean that proven excellence of student experience could provide HEIs with competitive advantage. In response to this situation the consultants devised a customer service programme which to a certain extent built on an understanding of the excellence of service standards that HEIs needed to achieve to work effectively with employers. The programme is explicitly aimed at HE administrative staff and work teams. It recognises that to enhance the student experience the administrative role requires increased professionalisation and administrators need to work more collaboratively with academic colleagues to deliver a seamless service to students. The programme is totally work-based and delivered over approximately eight weeks with the main focus being one week's intensive collaborative learning. It provides the opportunity for teams of administrators to work on the real challenges of their role with advice and support from external experts. It is also set up so that senior managers can direct the programme to address specific organisational challenges and then harness the power of the administrative teams to find creative ways to address these challenges.

October—December 2011: Introduction of Customer Service Programmes

In the summer of 2011 Southampton Solent University decided to offer the customer service programmes to each of its faculties to support administrators in taking a pro-active and engaged role in developing and improving all aspects of service standards for students, traditional and non—traditional. This was an important aspect of organisational change driven by the Strategic Development Programme. In commissioning this work the University was seeking an approach that was not traditional L&D but supported a very different approach with staff in a way that would enthuse, engage and most importantly, empower the administrative teams, creating the basis for a continuous improvement culture.

Each Faculty Manager agreed an overarching element of their practice that they wanted their teams to focus on for the customer service programmes. They then worked with the external consultants to agree small group projects to work on during and following the intensive week's study. Across all three faculties administrative project teams selected and pursued projects which had real organisational impact for the University. A summary of faculty projects can be found in Appendix 1. Through their involvement participants demonstrated how keenly aware administrative staff are of the fundamental challenges affecting the University in terms of student experience and also that they have a wealth of ideas about how to offer solutions to service related problems. They also showed a real enthusiasm for changes in practice and a commitment to continuous improvement which had potentially far reaching implications.

The nature of the intensive, contextualised programme experience meant that the external delivery team quickly gained deep insight into the challenges faced by each faculty administration team and also the innovative approaches they were testing out to address such challenges. Being external, the directors were able to recognise similarities and contrasts between individual faculty practice and draw together the expertise from all three faculties in suggesting improved ways forward in offering excellence in student experience.

By December 2011, when the customer service programme had been completed, regular reporting and discussions with the Pro Vice-Chancellor Academic (PVC) and those responsible for organisational development had allowed a relationship of trust and openness to develop, which enabled the externals to offer insights on how to draw together separate initiatives within faculties and suggestions for solutions to problems from the HE community beyond Southampton Solent University.

Outside SDP the external company was also undertaking work commissioned by Faculties. A review of low performing academic modules/units with unit leaders and development of action plans provided a vital insight, for the external team, so, where low performing units were affected by poor student attendance, for example, it was possible to link up the work of academics and administrators and work out how both groups of staff might work collaboratively to address this issue.

April 2012: Using the model across faculties

In reflecting on the successes of the faculty customer service programmes the University realised it could use the same model to address institution-wide issues. A cross—faculty approach would have the additional benefits of providing an opportunity for collaborative working between different parts of the University. Using the customer service approach again would also help embed the processes and show how it could be used in other contexts by other groups.

Considerable time was spent defining and setting the parameters of the overarching challenge administrators were required to address. The University wanted the external programme's participants to look at ways in which student participation could be improved. This programme is designed to give as much autonomy as possible to administrators taking part: a strong framework ensures those delivering the programme can use a sure but light touch in guiding the selection of projects. This was achieved through discussions involving the external consultants and senior university staff including PVC (Academic), Head of Student Operations and the three Faculty Managers to discuss and negotiate an agreed approach to improving student participation at Southampton Solent University. Faculty Managers then set up meetings for the programme and joined project groups of administrators as they chose their specific topics.

A description of topics from the cross faculty customer service programme can be found in Appendix 2.

This cross-faculty programme took place over two intensive weeks in April and May 2012. It was led by the Head of Student Operations and Assistant Faculty Managers, Team leaders and Student Support Network Officers from the Faculties.

There were two notable features of this second iteration of the externally-provided customer service programme.

Firstly, two of the groups addressed issues that could be seen as potentially controversial and difficult to address organisationally. The second notable feature was in the way administrators chose to address their selected topics. Most were considerably more evidence—based than the topics they had pursued in the individual faculty customer service programme and demonstrated a strong understanding of how available data within the University can be used to explore a problem and help generate solutions to challenges.

A key element of the way programmmes are designed by the external consultant is to give a voice to administrators who can sometimes find it hard to use the typical channels, such as university committees, through which change is often managed and directed. Because of this, the final stage of the intensive week of the programme is a session in which participants present their projects to a wide and influential university audience. For the project presentations for the cross-faculty customer service programme a wide audience including several senior decision makers was attracted. This allowed the changes in practice being suggested by participants to have as much influence as possible in changing the way in which Southampton Solent University sought to improve student participation.

After an initial slightly hesitant start, probably because the customer service programme looks very different from other staff development interventions that people had experienced, the teams embraced it and welcomed the fact that it empowered them to make changes to both their own working environment and most importantly to the administrative teams, that it helped them to offer a better and continuously improving service to students. A summary of some of the skills that administrative staff developed as a result of the programme are shown below.

- The ability to analyse and evidence a problem and understand how to measure the effectiveness of possible solutions.

- Techniques for working in small faculty or cross faculty groups to tackle a problem including sharing and delegating workload taking account of competing workplace commitments
- Confidence in presenting ideas and solutions formally and in a way appropriate to promote decision making within the University
- A developing ability to understand nuances and sensitivities in presenting ideas for changed practice within a university.
- The ability to work quickly in available time to make things happen effectively.

The benefits have yet to be fully realised but already Faculty Managers can see that progress has been made in getting more involvement of their staff in bringing about change in the University.

Staff did find it hard work, demanding and challenging. It felt like an extra thing to have to do in the midst of an already very busy working life. Fundamentally it was about teaching staff to learn new ways of behaving at work and helping to move us towards being more proactive and less reactive. It is empowering which gives staff confidence. They also gained confidence because throughout the various service plus projects and presentations they were listened to by senior staff. As a manager it's given me a new realisation about my staff. I will never forget their presentations at the end of the intensive week; so many of them conveyed the message 'I want to be more involved.' *Faculty Manager*

As the external team has understood more about the University's direction and aspirations it has been able to customise the interventions it supplies to support them. As relationships and trust have developed with the senior team managing organisational development, more opportunities for the external team to provide a useful external insight into future direction of organisational development for the institution have arisen.

CASE STUDIES IN ORGANISATIONAL DEVELOPMENT

Some of the ways in which the external consultants worked with university staff to support organisational development at Southampton Solent University are examined in more detail below. These demonstrate how short term external support can be used effectively to promote immediate change and also kick start longer term change and development. The final case study explores how the relationship between the external company and the team responsible for organisational development at Southampton Solent University has grown and developed and how this has enabled interventions which were initially quite separate to connect and have influence on Southampton Solent University as a whole organisation.

Building staff confidence in new areas of working

The Faculty of the Creative Industries and Society had been approached by two organisations who they already worked with, both of whom had shown an interest in Southampton Solent University accrediting work—based qualifications that the organisations already delivered. The initial request had come to the Head of Department and she was looking for appropriate members of staff to lead this activity and with the experience they gained to then lead other similar initiatives. Although the faculty did not have staff members with this experience they had two academics, a programme leader and a senior lecturer who had worked with the interested companies, had the necessary aptitude for working with employers and were interested in doing more. The external consultant worked alongside these two staff members to develop their skills in the specific area of accrediting employer learning and also mentored these staff as they progressed through the accreditation process working alongside employers.

Initially a member of the external team worked with the two members of faculty staff to prepare for the meetings with employers and a BR team member attended the meetings with employers alongside the Southampton Solent member of staff. They also reviewed and informally reflected on each meeting with university staff. A first meeting with each employer was held to find out more about the learning programme they wished to accredit. This was followed by requesting relevant paperwork about each learning programme and then reviewing it to see the extent to which it would 'fit' existing university quality systems, its potential size and shape and in terms of level and amount of credit. Decisions must also be made about the assessment regime and its match with university requirements. Th external company worked side by side with the two university academics, with both parties reviewing the employer programmes and in one case visiting the people who delivered the programme for an in depth discussion of delivery methods.

The next step in the process required the member of Southampton Solent University staff leading the work, supported by the external team, to negotiate the accreditation process with representatives of faculty quality management and academic services This was the most complex and delicate aspect of the role where the University staff must be seen by the employer as their 'sponsor' with the institution, but also be seen to be upholding the rigour of university quality assurance. To some extent the expert quality teams at Southampton Solent were also new to working with employers in this way so the presence of the external team in the background who had done this before at other institutions offered reassurance.

Alongside the core issues of quality in the accreditation process, several peripheral but nonetheless critical processes needed to be carried out within a timescale to fit the client's needs which were more demanding than typical university timescales. For example, contracts needed to be written, costs needed to be agreed and official documentation such as unit descriptors had to be completed. The external team kept a focus on the whole picture to ensure small but critical elements did not get forgotten.

As well as the successful accreditation of one employer programme and the kitemarking of another, the outcome of this process has been the transfer of knowledge and expertise on all aspects of accrediting employer learning to the two members of staff from the Faculty of Creative Industries and Society. More generally additional expertise has been gained in Academic Services, associated with quality assurance of such programmes and also in departments such as Finance and Contracts who have dealt with non-standard payments and contracts. The role of the external company in this process has been one of an experienced, critical and supportive friend. The learning which has taken place as a result of this work for both the two members of staff and the wider university has been both embedded and context related making it easy to re-visit and extend as they repeat the process with other employers.

Harnessing staff ideas and energy: Faculty—based customer service programmes

The Faculty based programmes were explicitly designed to harness the energy of ideas for continuous improvement and changes in practice from administrative staff working at all levels. The external programme recognises in its design that those who have the keenest sense of processes and procedures that need to be changed and improved often have the most difficult route to get suggestions for such changes recognised within the University hierarchy.

During the faculty-based customer service programmes administrative staff were asked to work on small scale projects to address things they would like to change. Participants had a free hand in choosing projects, but were encouraged to focus on systems or procedures that frequently challenged or exasperated them and would improve both their service to students and their own working life if they could be changed for the better. Projects fell roughly into two categories each of which had different outcomes. Firstly individuals chose projects which were very specific, had clear and easily definable outcomes and involved reasonably small numbers of people. An example of this is outlined below.

The emergency panel

One participant had been reflecting on the recent handling of a recent major system failure at the University. As a team leader she had taken a front-line role in managing the dissatisfaction of students at the problems they were experiencing. Although as part of the response to the failure, senior decision makers met with front line staff, the participant felt this process could be handled more systematically and more effectively in giving students better service, if a major system failure occurred again. She put together a draft process for a more effective way of using the expertise and experience of front line staff to handle students' concerns in this type of situation. After the programme a senior decision maker took responsibility for taking the participants plan to the Risk Committee, ensuring it was recognised by the appropriate University decision making body

Some small groups decided to tackle less defined, and more complex projects which were affected by and influenced large staff groups. The organisational issues addressed by these groups were probably more important and far reaching than the more limited project topics above, but the complexity and interdependence of outcomes made it harder to reach a neat and quick solution. An example is outlined below.

A timetable of administrative deadlines for academic staff

Within each faculty team, small groups decided it would be a good idea to try and prepare a chronological timetable which identified when academic staff needed to meet deadlines for submission of specific documentation such as exam papers. The aim of this process was to give academic staff warning of what was required of them so that they could plan their workload more effectively and also to avoid administrators spending disproportionate amounts of time chasing documentation. Although good progress was made with this task during the customer service weeks it has proved much more difficult to draw to a conclusion. This is mainly because taking this project into the mainstream requires a complex and interlinked web of communication and decision making. So administrators must seek buy-in from the academic team, agreement from other departments about appropriateness of deadlines (timetabling and quality office) and a consideration of what (if any) sanctions might apply if deadlines are not met.

The three faculty-based programmes demonstrated clearly that administrative staff, even those in junior roles, have a huge range of ideas about how the organisation can work more effectively. They showed a real sensitivity to student need, probably because administrators see the results of problems with study at first hand often dealing face to face with students who may be upset and angry. Participants used their detailed knowledge of how university systems and procedures work in practice to analyse problems and suggest workable solutions that took account of their knowledge of the special culture and ways of working that each individual institution has. The ideas of this group, who are not often asked about how they think things should be done differently, are both refreshing and by virtue of being built on real work experience, sure footed and sustainable.

> The Programme provided my colleagues and myself a way to voice our opinions and share ideas in a constructive and useful way. It enabled us to work together, look at different challenges we were all facing and implement these changes and agreed outcomes. Having been involved in two of the Projects, both with close colleagues and then networking with colleagues from different faculties, I personally felt that it helped me develop further my own team working and brainstorming skills. Having the chance to work on a project away from the day to day norm was refreshing and being able to take ownership and responsibility has made me realise more of my own potential. When you can see that your idea has made a difference it gives you a new found confidence to voice your ideas and opinions and help make not only working life that little bit easier but also aid in bettering the student experience. *Programme participant*

Using the external programme to support this organisational development has had several benefits. Having an explicit staff development event encouraged people to focus clearly on ideas for just a short period of time which concentrated the effect of their work. The external team was also able to use contacts with the senior team at the University to help participants present their ideas to decision makers who would welcome and be receptive to their enthusiasm and initiative. They were able to connect similar ideas which had occurred in individual faculties to ensure maximum institutional benefit was achieved and helped staff to retain focus on deadlines when they were challenged by competing priorities and activities

As always it is the voice of the participants that really matters because they are the ones that make change actually happen.

> An interesting experience, very different type of staff development for me. It was hard balancing this around the normal workload but satisfying once the week was completed. It did make me open my mind more than usual, perhaps due to the fact we were encouraged to look at the

bigger picture . . . . at our own jobs/tasks and the way that they impact elsewhere. I found looking for 'areas of good practice' to share with the faculty and the wider University encouraging and also slightly motivating!

Overall, it has been a valuable experience, teaching me to learn from others and share ideas however small or large they are. It was also worthwhile and interesting to take part in the cross faculty projects as it is nice to be able to work with staff from other areas and hear their ideas and ways of working. I also feel I gained confidence particularly at the end of the cross faculty project as we had to present to very senior staff in the University. It was good to get the feeling that they were actually listening to what we were suggesting and taking comments on board. It was also nice to be able to answer their questions at the end of the presentations—again, confidence building resulting in heightened motivation in my own role as well as the staff I look after and the tasks we undertake. *Programme participant*

Working across internal university boundaries: Cross-Faculty Customer Service programme

Southampton Solent University, in common with many other HE institutions, is organised on a faculty basis with administrative and academic teams in each faculty working independently of the other faculties. Although some of the major institutional processes and procedures, for example those associated with quality assurance, are operated in the same way across all faculties, almost every element of administration has aspects which are done differently in individual faculties. This is sometimes because of the nature of the academic programmes delivered within the faculty—so for example assessment processes for media related courses are different from those for engineering courses, but sometimes also simply because processes have evolved differently historically. In most cases the focus of the work of faculty administrative staff looks inward and administrators may simply not be aware of the differences between faculties.

The purpose of the cross-faculty customer service programme was to encourage teams of administrators working across faculties to consider approaches to improve student participation. This approach took account of the fact that suggestions to improve participation were likely to be effective across all faculties. It also recognised that faculty administrative teams had expressed an interest in working with colleagues from other faculties to stimulate new ideas and share good practice. Small project teams were formed by encouraging people to work in groups depending on their interests. In general, cross-faculty coverage was achieved in groups and where this was not the case input was sought from colleagues from the faculties that were not represented. Working across faculties seemed to encourage groups to take on really substantial challenges that had a fundamental influence on student participation. Below is an example of a project topic.

Helping students to make contact with academics outside class time

This project recognised that sometimes students find it hard to access academic members of staff outside class time when they need particular support or have a specific query. The availability of this ad hoc help for students can be really important in helping them to engage with their learning and keep motivated when things are tough. A wide variety of methods that were currently being used to support access were identified including set surgery times, or a timetable on an academic's door. The most challenging issue for administrators occurred when a student was seeking a particular academic and administrators were unable to provide information about when the academic would be available. The project team proposed different ways that academics could inform the administrative team of their availability to students so the administrative team could advise students much more accurately, so solving a problem which is likely to influence participation.

This example illustrated typical findings for a cross faculty project. Practice in relation to this issue across faculties was broadly similar with each experiencing the same problems of receiving and holding detailed information about academic availability. The way in which decision makers viewed this problem and the priority which they were prepared to give it varied a little, but project leaders were able to use a similar mechanism— an approach to Faculty Management Team—to get it recognised and on to the faculty agenda.

> The programme was designed to incorporate personal development opportunities, whilst identifying improvements that could be made to processes, especially service improvements that could enhance the student experience. We started as individual faculties, but it soon became clear that there were common themes emerging. This led to cross-faculty and cross-University collaboration and networking, and some good, practical projects have resulted. As a manager I already knew about the capabilities of our staff, but the programme allowed them to showcase their skills and abilities to colleagues across

the University, including the senior management team. There is much wider recognition now about the talent pool that we have at Solent. It has allowed all members of administrative staff to have a voice, and more importantly be listened to by decision-makers. *Manager involved in Programme*

The advantage of addressing this issue at a cross-faculty level is that this approach encourages participants to engage with challenges that have university-wide significance. This is particularly important as it sends the message that the contributions of staff members at all levels are valued, and can influence management thinking and impact on the big issues in the institution. Realisation of this power has encouraged some members of administrative staff to take a much more pro-active approach to their roles, regularly making suggestions for things that can be improved rather than seeing problems as being insurmountable or not able to be influenced by junior staff.

The external company played two key roles in the cross-faculty programme. Firstly they managed the organisation. This was much more logistically complex than the individual faculty programmes and perhaps indicates why cross-faculty initiatives are not common within the institution. The second important role was to ensure that key decision makers were informed of the work of the project groups so that they were prepared to pick up initiatives after the programme ended. Both these roles could be undertaken by an internal university department but using an external company avoids the complexity of fitting in a large volume of work over a short time alongside an existing workload. The novelty value of an external organisation also to certain extent glamourises and legitimises the staff development opportunity.

Managing the reporting relationship

One of the potential challenges of using an external company for substantial elements of organisational development is that the commissioning institution might find it hard to make the best use of learning gained about the organisation itself from development interventions. To make the most of development opportunities it is important to have someone in a position to 'join up' findings from working with different areas of the institution and relate them to the way the institution seeks to develop as a whole. Achieving this overview can be a challenge for whoever undertakes it— whether internal or external—but if an external organisation is responsible for it, then it is essential that robust and sensitive communication lines are forged between the external provider and the institution.

The communication system between the external company and the University has grown over the period of their working together. Initially most communication was with those responsible for running the University employer engagement programme and followed a typical relationship between supplier and client. However, when the programme was introduced, the external company started to report more widely and at a senior level. The reporting was both formal and informal. Formal reports of each programme were supplied to each Faculty Manager. These were given verbally at the end of the intensive week and then summarised in writing after the intensive week. The SDP Programme Director was also aware of all of this activity, attending the presentation sessions at the end of each intensive week.

More informal reports were regularly made by the external team to the SDP Programme Director and the PVC. These provided the opportunity to draw together findings and conclusions across faculties and also between the work being done with both academic and administrative teams. The opportunity for communication was always two-way. When given insight into a particular aspect of performance that the University wished to focus on the team was able to emphasise this in their planning and customisation of delivery of learning programmes. As their knowledge of the institution developed the external team were also able to suggest different approaches to challenges that expressed an innovative approach from an external perspective.

The success of this communication, which allowed the University to make the most of these organisational development opportunities, relies on a considerable level of trust and sensitivity to confidentiality between both parties which has built up slowly over a period of nearly three years. The SSU organisational development team must trust the external company with information about their aspirations and also the challenges their organisation faces. They must trust the company to deal with this knowledge sensitively when it is disseminated to different institutional groups. For the company the challenge is to ensure the University gets the most benefit from learning about organisational development, derived from these programmes, they must be confident that they will receive a sensitive reception to information shared and a willingness to act on it appropriately from the University team.

The working relationship developed between the external company and Southampton Solent University is probably closer and more reactive than a typical consultant/HE institution relationship. The nature of the relationship has heavily influenced the way the company has worked with the University. As a result of the way the two parties have worked together, the company has been able to anticipate and suggest solutions to internal challenges rather than wait to have these highlighted by the University. They have also been able to design interventions that mesh with both existing and embryo policy and strategy developments.

CHALLENGES

It is important to recognise that in choosing to use an external provider to deliver organisational development an institution realises certain challenges may be encountered. In this final section some of the potential challenges are highlighted together with suggestions for how they might be managed.

Sustaining organisational development

When using an external provider to deliver any element of an organisational development programme it is essential to recognise that to make the most of any learning achieved a planned handover of the ownership of the learning must be achieved. This is particularly important in the case of the company's programmes as the nature of the programme is that it delivers its learning over a relatively short term—usually within an eight week period or less. There are several reasons for this choice. Firstly organising learning over a relatively intense period gives it impact. Participants are encouraged to see how much progress they can make over a relatively short period of time which by inference suggests they could make bigger changes over a longer period of time. Secondly, administrative teams often express the view that they are so busy it is almost impossible to 'get their heads above water' to see what changes they might make to their practice to improve it. The short, intense nature of the programme helps to persuade them that they can find time for change. The way in which it is delivered and the fact that is it perceived as an external intervention illustrates the importance of efforts to ensure the learning from the programme is strongly embedded and owned by the staff of the institution.

Recognising the importance of the handover of learning, the external comapny designed the programme to ensure staff from the institution are strongly involved in the customisation and delivery of the programme. At Southampton Solent University, Faculty Managers and Assistant Faculty Managers took an active and participative role in the customisation and delivery of the whole programme to ensure that they could support projects into mainstream provision where appropriate. In one faculty the transfer of knowledge was demonstrated when they undertook a 'Lite' version of the programme using their own staff who had experienced the initial programme as mentors to the staff who were new to the approach. The external team also took an approach which allowed them to withdraw slowly from projects, offering support with practicalities where necessary, such as setting up meetings across faculties and monitoring progress with a light touch. Albeit occasionally hesitantly, these projects have made it into the mainstream of university service delivery, supported by university staff. The close and ongoing nature of the relationship between the external company and Southampton Solent University has meant that a member of the team is always available for advice and to pick up the reins of a project for a short period of time until a member of Southampton Solent University staff can manage it if necessary. The movement of projects into the mainstream is also supported by the fact that each project is practice and problem-based and therefore often supplies a solution to a real and tangible service need.

The nature of the reporting relationship also allowed the external team to alert appropriate senior team members if progress of a project was being blocked or needed a little additional support.

Transferring skills, knowledge and learning to the institution

An external provider is likely to bring new skills and knowledge into an institution, however to make the most of this learning it is important that plans are made to ensure that skills and knowledge are transferred to the institution and can be used after the external provider has gone. The design of the majority of the organisational development work undertaken by the external team has been explicitly made to transfer knowledge. As the relationship with the University has developed, the delivery of learning has become less formal, moving from workshops to learning through coaching and mentoring and facilitation of real work experiences to enable university staff to practice new skills in context while the external team are on hand to advise. The programme is designed to be handed over to the institution for delivery once they feel confident to 'go it alone'.

This blurring of the ownership of teaching, learning and knowledge transfer requires an excellent relationship between provider and client to be successful as it has the potential to make the relationship between the two more complicated. Often what is purchased from the provider may be hard to define at the outset, each next step being dependent on the one before. This requires an element of trust between both parties as it does not fit comfortably with the usual pattern of a commissioner identifying what they require and a supplier outlining what they can supply and how much it will cost. That trust must also extend to a transparent appreciation of intellectual property so that an agreement of how material belonging to the provider is used is made. It is important for the provider to plan and agree how knowledge is to be transferred to the provider at the outset rather than as an afterthought.

Making the most of learning from institutional development when using an external provider

When an institution decides to undertake organisational development activities it should, of course, experience the planned benefits from the activities themselves. But in the circumstances at Southampton Solent University, where funding has allowed them to pursue development with many different groups of staff there are also benefits to be gained from drawing together understanding and learning from the different organisational development activities when considered together—a clear example of the learning from activities being more than the sum of their parts.

The fact that the external team has worked on diverse activities has given them the opportunity to draw together learning from work with different teams. So, for example, the work done on underperforming units with academic staff, where ways to encourage students to attend teaching sessions were considered was informative for the parallel programme considering how to manage the administrative side of student attendance. To make the most of this 'joining up' of activities, the external partners must be sensitive to what information will be useful and relevant for the institution to know and be pro-active in passing it on. The Deputy Vice-Chancellor and her team shared information with the external company about elements of performance that they were keen to develop in the institution. The growing understanding of the organic way that Southampton Solent University seeks to develop has helped the external company to know better what learning and conclusions to pass back to the organisational development team and also how to use this understanding to shape future interventions. As their understanding of the University's organisational development agenda has grown they have also been able to suggest new ways to progress the agenda linked to the development work currently in delivery.

CONCLUSIONS

The other case studies in this volume have been accomplished by University staff working on their own developments.

However at times external assistance may be required to help an organisation develop new capacity for change. The value and success of the relationship described in this chapter has been as much about the way of working and shared fundamental principles concerning the way organisational development is delivered, as the technical capabilities delivered.

Shared principles

- A belief in the ability and potential of staff at all levels to be the drivers of change and improvement in their own work
- Staff develop greater capacity by "doing" in a supported, learning environment, not by just attending courses.
- "Organisational Listening" drives when the most productive interventions can be made. An external provider with a grand plan wanting to impose a timetable will probably not produce the best results (In this programme, Faculties were "invited" to take up the service, not told they must.)
- A commitment to the transfer of knowledge to those who will continue to use it, an underlying approach which has been essential in allowing the development of such a successful working relationship

As the complexity of the development work has increased, the relationship between the external company and those responsible for organisational development has also deepened to a point where communication is more spontaneous and focuses on the underlying themes for development identified by the University as much as on specific interventions.

Interventions arise out of "conversations"; inherently the parties understand the endpoint—what will the University look like—but timing, sequence and type of intervention is not planned in a programmatic way.

This deliberate lack of longer term planning with firmly specified dates and teams to be involved potentially presents a significant challenge to consultants, but in forging a successful and effective way of working together the external company and the University have been able to override the possible challenges that outsourcing elements of organisational development might bring and benefit from the flexibility, control and economies which working extensively with an external provider, who can share the world view, will give to an institution.

Much of the success of the relationship has depended on the development of a strong ethos of open communication between the external company and the University which has taken time and trust from both parties to develop, but has allowed each to benefit from an in depth understanding of the way the other works.

Of course the fundamental question is, will these interventions make a difference? Will the process of developing people in these ways have an impact on the University in future? The answer to this question must reside in the participants themselves, be they administrators or managers it is their will and agency working together that will make a difference.

It is not obvious within tasks/roles/jobs the difference that this made at this point in time other than the confidence built and the satisfaction of having completed the two intensive weeks. I strongly feel that the Faculty and the University will see the difference in time as some projects suggested are being progressed and rolled out. I also think that I am more likely to make suggestions to senior staff if I think something could be done differently in future. *Programmme participant*

The benefits are yet to be fully realised. As managers we do have to put effort into practising these skills which we intend to do through utilising the Programme approach. I have certainly tried to involve staff more. *Faculty Manager*

Appendix 1 List of projects from Faculty Customer Service programmes

Faculty of Maritime and Technology
A recently reorganised team of four worked on pinning down key areas of work for their jobs and examined how they could describe what they do with a particular focus on preparing materials that could be used for inducting new members of staff. One member of this team looked at potential improvements to the counter service and designed a method for monitoring traffic at the counter.
The SSNO for Martech reviewed how her work meshed with the rest of the academic support team and worked to define the cross over point between her work and that of the rest of the administrative team. She also examined how academics could be encouraged to share information with her informally about students who were having difficulty with their studies.
A team from the assessments office are devising a 'one stop shop' information source about assessments designed to help academics to access the information they need to support students in this process and provide timely information to the academic team.
The admissions team created an information sheet for students and their parents who are considering choosing Solent as their university. They will be monitoring whether use f this sheet cuts down on simple telephone queries to their team.
Two members of the administrative team are piloting a new process to simplify and streamline how academics approve exam papers.

Faculty of Business, Sport and Enterprise
A group of three staff focused on ways in which they could support postgraduate students more effectively. Their project comprised three strands. Firstly they worked with the faculty quality team to explore areas of the regulations relating to postgraduate students where their team were unclear on how regulations should be implemented. Secondly they decided to work on a document for administrative colleagues to help them to answer typical questions from postgraduate students. Thirdly they investigated whether it would be possible for the University to produce a dedicated handbook for postgraduate professional students. One member of the team also explored ways in which he might support blended learning students more effectively using the MOD as a case study.
One member of staff developed a rationale for a group made up of staff who are particularly experienced in the delivery of student services who could be used to support decision making about implementation issues in the event of major system error. She also explored how this group would work, the potential benefits to the University of such a group and who might be members of this group if it became a cross faculty entity
One member of staff devised a project which explored the possibility of sending out standard emails to students at particular times to support them in the management of their learning.
This project was designed to ensure academic advisors could make the best use of assistants' time to support their work. This team designed a spreadsheet to allow advisors to book in work that they would like assistants to complete for them. As a result of this project the team also investigated the possibility of the administrative team using electronic diaries. This would help the counter team to offer a better service to students, advising accurately when colleagues would be in the office if they are not immediately available. One member of the team also compiled a list of FAQs to help staff who had to take over counter duties
A team of four staff prepared a detailed calendar which linked the work of the administrative team and the demands this places on academics. The calendar aims to ensure academics are aware of paperwork that is required of them at particular times of the year to ensure smooth running of student services.
The SSNO for this faculty developed an induction guide for Associate Lecturers

Faculty of Creative Industries and Society
A team made up of the administrative managers planned to instigate weekly meetings for representatives of the whole Schools team held at rotating sites. Meetings will have a firm agenda and action points will be noted and circulated immediately after the meeting. Meetings will include updates from each site as well as a chance to highlight issues such as policy or regulation changes
A team of four members of staff devised an approach to ensure any relevant changes in regulations or policy are disseminated in a systematic way round the Schools Team. This dissemination could also be extended to include admin teams notifying lecturers of such changes. This would be in addition (belt and braces) to notifications academics receive from an associate dean
One member of staff considered ways of sharing information about a particularly successful approach to handling academic positioning advice forms
A team of four staff devised a calendar to define key activities through the year for administrative staff (useful for new staff induction). Possibility to extend this to include a section for academics about which documentation administrative staff will need from them.
A team of five introduced bi-monthly meetings with academic teams to facilitate the sharing of information. Also planned attendance for a course support adviser at Programme Leader meetings
Five members of staff piloted the design, use and sharing of a spreadsheet for managing the process of deferrals, withdrawals etc for students
Two staff based at a separate office worked on the collection and presentation of collated and reflective information and data about the process and experience of working in a co-located team with academics

Appendix 2 Student Participation Programme: Project outlines

Class cancellations	Reviewing the current situation with class cancellations across faculties. Looking at how the effect of cancellations on students can be mitigated by streamlining processes for advising students of cancellation and re-scheduling classes
Academic availability	Looking at how administrative teams can help academics and students to make contact with each other outside teaching sessions. Focus on use of electronic diaries to allow administrative teams to give accurate advice to students on how best to access academic support
Induction	Considering how the induction experience might be changed to ensure it is easy for new students to make personal contact with staff for help and support when they first join the University. Measuring the impact of personal contact emails from academic staff and reviewing how this could be used more widely
Period 2 data	Analysing current sources of student data to identify when students are most likely to disengage and consider how to prevent this
Revisiting attendance monitoring	A project to review how administrative staff can provide attendance data to academics in a way that best suits their needs. A consideration of how administrative staff and academics staff can work in partnership to ensure the most effective use of all information about attendance to support student Participation
When and where to seek help—diagnostic	A diagnostic which helps students to recognise when they might need help and how best to access it. Aim of the diagnostic is that it will also be useful to staff to help identify when students need help
Working with Student Union to find out about initial student experience	Using established student contacts to find out about what students find difficult when they start university and what they perceive barriers to participation might be

CHAPTER 13

Factors that Enable Strategic Change and Innovation

Be the change you want to see in the world
Gandhi

VISUALISING ORGANISATIONAL CHANGE

Introduction

The aim of this book is to illuminate and gain deeper insights into the way in which the changes promoted through Southampton Solent University's Strategic Development Programme (SDP) were realised. This chapter tries to make sense of organisational change using the descriptions and narratives of change provided in the previous chapters.

The SDP stimulated two main sorts of change some of which were grown, owned and implemented by individuals and small teams (Chapters 5-11) while other changes, like new business systems were developed by the owners and introduced to the wider community which then had to learn new practices (chapters2 and 12).

This chapter begins by looking at the activity-based perspective that was adopted by the Programme Team and connects the modelling of this back to the level of individuals, who provide the locus for concrete change. The second part looks at the factors that seem to have been important to the people who accomplished change within the SDP and concludes with an examination of twelve organisational factors that appear to be important in strategic change that encourages and supports bottom-up innovation, based on what has been learnt through the SDP.

ACTIVITY-BASED PERSPECTIVE

Underpinning the SDP strategy was a belief that change will only happen if people do new things i.e. change comes from acting, doing and making rather than just thinking and talking about it and thus the Programme Team adopted a pragmatic action—oriented stance towards the change project.

> You have to begin by doing new things and experiment with doing it. *SDP Manager*

Change is brought about through people engaging in activity and the way the SDP worked was to stimulate new activity that would enable the University to achieve its strategic objectives. All SDP proposals were vetted to ensure that the activities proposed were aligned to these purposes and the tools used to monitor and report on progress all focused on the activities being undertaken to accomplish the strategic objectives.

> It's been action orientated, it's not sitting and having lots of ideas and then pick one. It's, "Well, we've got an idea, we think that might go. Let's work it through and see where it goes," so it's action learning. And this is what I've tried to encourage. . . . . "Don't think about it too much, Just try it!" *SDP Programme Director*

According to Engestrom (1987) organisations can be viewed as an activity system or more accurately a constellation of simultaneous, activity systems. Engestrom *(ibid)* developed a model of an activity-based system (reproduced in Figure 13.1) which provides a useful framework for understanding how a wide range of factors work together to influence purposeful activity.

In order to reach an *outcome,* (change), individuals engage in purposeful activity, often working collaboratively with other people to produce certain *objects* (e.g. experiences, knowledge, and physical products).

Activity is shaped by the community working within the organisation's written and unwritten rules and with the tools to achieve needs and ambitions. In engaging in activity to create and implement new practices individuals learn, and the accumulated collective learning of many individuals expands the learning of the organisation.

Figure 13.1 The structure of human activity (Engeström 1987:78)

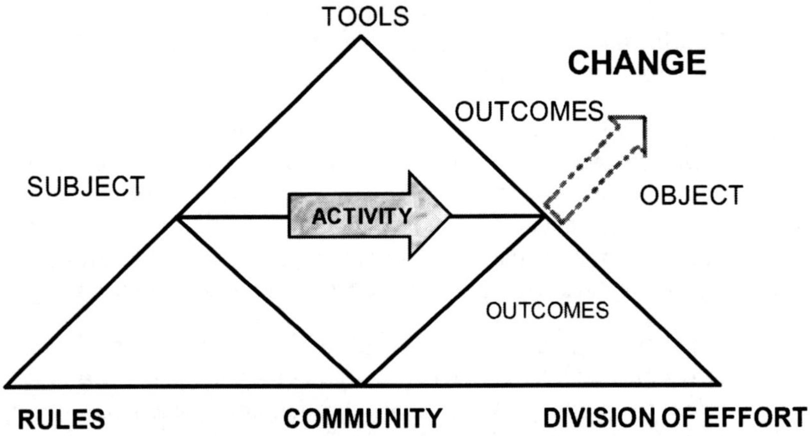

The premise of activity theory is that a collective work activity, with the basic purpose shared by others (community), is undertaken by people (subjects) who are motivated by a purpose or towards the solution of a problem (object), which is mediated by tools and/or signs (artefacts or instruments) used in order to achieve the goal (outcome). The activity is constrained by cultural factors including conventions (rules) and social organisation (division of labour) within the immediate context and framed by broader social patterns (of production, consumption, distribution and exchange). Activity theory provides a conceptual framework from which we can understand the inter-relationship between activities, actions, operations and artefacts, subjects' motives and goals, and aspects of the social, organisational and societal contexts within which these activities are framed.

We can use this descriptive framework to reveal some of the complexity in the activities, interactions and relationships within the SDP strategic change process. For example, Figure 13.2 summarises the pattern of relationships and activities of the SDP team as they encouraged and helped the community to engage with the SDP, provide practical help and emotional support and develop the intelligence needed to keep the project leader and the Management Board informed of progress.

Figure 13.2 Solent University Strategic Development Programme mapped onto Engstrom's (1987:78) activity system diagram

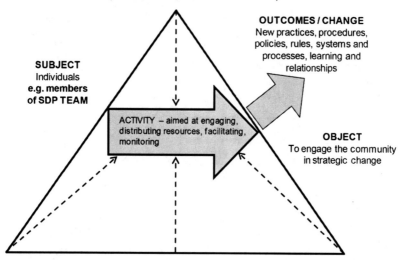

TOOLS (mediating artefacts)
e.g. SDP Business Plan and other plans, progress reports, information, website, promotional films, conferences and workshops

OUTCOMES / CHANGE
New practices, procedures, policies, rules, systems and processes, learning and relationships

SUBJECT
Individuals
e.g. members of SDP TEAM

ACTIVITY – aimed at engaging, distributing resources, facilitating, monitoring

OBJECT
To engage the community in strategic change

RULES & CONVENTIONS
•University Vision, Mission, Objectives
•Rules controlling functional role of SDP Team
•Rules for distributing additional resources (Management Board procedures)
•Operate by persuasion
•Respect autonomy individuals, Schools, Faculties
•Work with those who want to, celebrate achievement, build on success but don't publicly criticise

COMMUNITY
•Vice-Chancellor's Group
•SDP Leader & Team
•University staff responsible for creating, managing and delivering educational opportunities
•University staff who provide professional support or services to support delivery
•University staff who manage external relationships
•Students and potential students who engage with educational activities
•Employers who contribute to the University's educational enterprise

DIVISION OF EFFORT
•Activity towards the SDP strategic objective carried out by whole community.
•Action towards a specific conscious goal by individuals or collaborations
•Actions of the SDP team to engage people, provide help to individuals, monitor and report progress to Management Board

We can extend activity-theory modelling to the level of individuals which provided the locus for concrete change (Figure 13.3).

Figure 13.3 Example of an individual's activity system created through their involvement in the SDP using the framework provided by (Engeström: 1987:78). The innovator whose comments were reported under hard and soft systems thinking (above) is used to model activity.

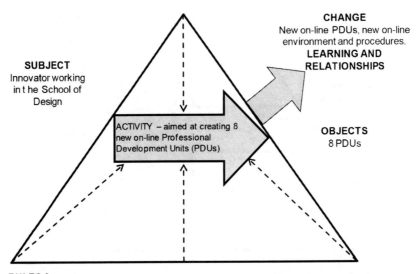

Using the story of one of the innovators in the School of Design we can see that the innovator was guided by the objectives in the School's SDP project plan (School objectives that were aligned to the overall strategic objectives of the programme). Her activities were geared to creating eight new on-line Professional Development Units. Such things did not yet exist so she was in effect breaking new ground and had to invent tools/frameworks in order to achieve her goal. She received little practical help until she had structured her environment for learning and achievement. This involved 1) contracting two external consultants with industry specific knowledge to write the content 2) finding colleagues from the E Development Centre who were expert in the design of on-line learning materials. An example of local contentious practice emerged as the innovator tried to find out how register and secure payment for people wanting to study the PDU's. There was no existing procedure. At the time the innovator was interviewed this was still a source of frustration but over the next six months the matter was resolved. Illustrating how innovators provoke the organisation's established systems to change.

Expanding Initial Change

One measure of transformation is the extent to which new changes that were accomplished through the SDP catalysed further change. While this process has not yet happened in all areas of development there are a sufficient number of examples to show that this is an important process. For example, in the School of Design (chapter 4) several innovators used the metaphor of *growing legs* to explain the widening effects and consequences of the project they had been involved in.

so most of these projects grew legs . . . . I don't suppose we'll ever capture them all now because they've all happened and some of them are embedded and some with just the project, but the legs that grew out of each of these projects was enormous. *Head School of Design (Chapter 5)*

In strategic change processes those sponsoring change assume that those who participate in the change process will continue to participate and embed or adapt the change so that there is continuity and a return on the additional resources invested to bring about change. They also hope that the practice will be diffused or spread beyond the area where new practice was developed thus amplifying the value of the original investment. We might liken this to a change 'chain reaction' occurring in two dimensions— deepening or embedding, and diffusing or spreading (Figure 13.4). In this way the effects of an initial intervention can 'grow legs', and over time a new way of thinking and practising can have a significantly larger effect than could be observed or accounted for at the end of the initial change.

Figure 13.4 Types of change 'chain reaction' associated with strategic change interventions

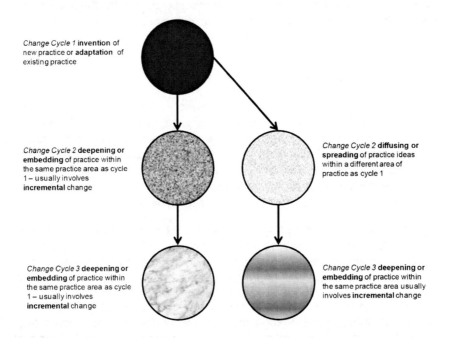

Change Cycle 1 **invention** of new practice or **adaptation** of existing practice

Change Cycle 2 **deepening or embedding** of practice within the same practice area as cycle 1 – usually involves **incremental** change

Change Cycle 2 **diffusing or spreading** of practice ideas within a different area of practice as cycle 1

Change Cycle 3 **deepening or embedding** of practice within the same practice area as cycle 1 – usually involves **incremental** change

Change Cycle 3 **deepening or embedding** of practice within the same practice area usually involves **incremental** change

Expanding Learning

The SDP might be viewed as a management 'tool' to create a new contradiction which created a gap between the educational practice that historically and currently exists in the University, aimed at traditional 18-21 learners, and the ambition of the University to address the needs of non—traditional learners and employers, and the future position it would like to occupy.

> The University is currently very successful in serving the needs of its existing, predominantly young, full-time student cohorts . . . . However, the University acknowledges that it has made less rapid progress in reaching new types of learner, in engaging with employers employers across all vocational areas and in responding with sufficient agility to external change. *Strategic Development Fund Business Plan 2009-13 p4*

The function of SDP was to stimulate and resource activity to engage with and address this contradiction and encourage the growth through experimentation, of new practices consistent with the new context. When viewed from this perspective, people who got involved in SDP change, analysed the implications for their practice of the new context, designed and experimented with new educational practices and created new delivery and support mechanisms. They were also engaging in what Engeström (1987, 2011) calls expansive learning.

> In . . . . *expansive learning* (Engeström, 1987), we meet a kind of learning that goes beyond the dichotomies between formal and informal learning, between individual and organizational learning, and between learning and developmental transformation. To construct an *expanded context*, individuals have to face and articulate the inner contradictions of their organizations and institutions. This requires that they seek and form alliances and initiate joint efforts at analysis, design and experimentation. Such learning is not anymore satisfied with finding the right answers but aimed at grasping why the institution functions as it does and how to go beyond it. Moreover, such expansive learning efforts make use of diverse tools and resources, including informally gained experiences and observations as well as appropriate formal learning opportunities (Engeström, 2011:2).

Organisational change (Figure 13.5) combines and integrates the managed/ planned/deliberate strategy, actions and language (left hand side of figure) with improvised/emergent/strategy, actions and language (right hand side of figure).

Figure 13.5 Multidimensional activity-theoretical approach to organisational change promoted by SDP represented as an interplay of managerial and practitioner thinking, action and creativity that stimulated expansive learning, community building, and process enhancement and the radical expansion of the objects of strategic change. Adapted from Kajamaa (2011:148)

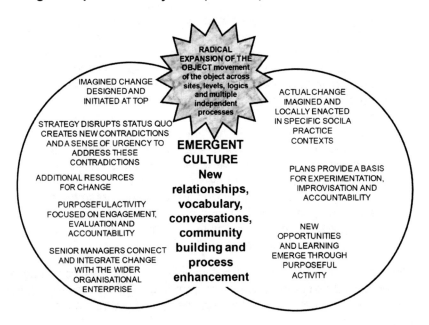

Mostly, organisational change is brought about by the continuous incremental changes made by every member of the organisation as they go about their daily business. The sense of community and purpose is historically constructed around and through these core activities but periodically, the organisation may be 'encouraged' to see and move beyond its current practices through top down initiated and managed interventions. This is the situation with the SDP programme, but the way change actually happens, the way expanded organisational learning actually occurs is captured well by Engeström (2011:13).

> Expansive learning may be started by one person questioning and problematising some aspect of the present practice. This may provoke another person to analyze the problem, and another one to propose a new model for the activity, which the others examine—and so forth. Expansive learning moves like a soccer game in which individuals and sub-groups pass the developing idea through learning actions to one another until a new

model ready to be experimented with has been created and implemented in practice. The dynamics of the collective learning process are created by a trading and negotiation in which the area of mutual interest and a picture of a new shared object of activity begin to take shape gradually, in exchanges in which the participants try to relate their resources and ideas to the other discussants' situation and vice versa (Engeström 2011:13).

Viewed through this lens the SDP is an example of a strategy directed to promoting expansive learning. Its objective was to focus attention on and encourage development of new relationships and forms of education that were relevant to deeper employer engagement, a more flexible, blended e—learning-rich curriculum, increased student employability, and improved progression of students from local FE colleges. These were the objects of change and in terms of expansive learning, the objective of SDP was to 'radically expand these objects'. The case studies reveal how this was realised through the specific projects. What is clear is that without the SDP the sorts of activities that were undertaken to realise the University's strategic objectives would not have been systemic.

INNOVATOR PERCEPTIONS OF CHANGE

So far, this chapter has provided an activity-based perspective on change associated with the SDP. In this section we consider the views of the people responsible for bringing about changes in practice, and consider their perspectives on change.

The views of twenty four people who were involved in significant change within the SDP were canvassed during interview using a simple tool as a prompt. The tool (Table 13.1) was adapted from Trowler et al (2003:7). Interviewees were invited to compare their experiences of bringing about change with short descriptors of change contained in the tool.

Table 13.1 interviewees' views on the appropriateness of five different theories of change (adapted from Trowler et al 2003:7)

Change Theories

A Technical Rational: Positivism works: experts plan and then manage faithful implementation

B Resource Allocation: Rational economic model: allocate additional resources to achieve desired changes

C Diffusionist Clear visible messages are picked up by early adopters. They diffuse according to the fit of message with the audience.

D Continuous quality improvement Change happens because the system gets people to be continuously tinkering looking for ways of doing things better. Change is brought about incrementally.

E Complexity Change cannot be controlled in a top down way. Rather, change sponsors create the conditions in which change of a certain sort is more likely to happen than not because individual agents are empowered to interpret managerial visions and create the changes that they believe are right.

A			√		√						√	√	√
B	√	√	√	√	√	√	√	√	√	√	√	√	√
C	√	√	√	√	√	√	√	√	√	√	√		√
D	√		√			√							√
E		√	√	√		√	√	√	√	√			√
A	√		√	√		√				√		√	
B	√		√	√	√	√	√	√		√	√		√
C	√		√	√	√	√	√	√	√	√	√	√	√
D	√	√	√	√	√	√	√		√		√		√
E	√	√	√	√	√	√	√	√	√	√	√	√	√

58% of interviewees recognised 2 or 3 change theories, 42% recognised 4 or 5 change theories were involved in their SDP change process.

42% of interviewees recognised that technical rational planning followed by faithful implementation was a significant part of their change process. Others recognised that rational plans were made but that implementation had significant elements of making it up as you went along and felt strongly that there had to be flexibility in work plans in order that they can be adapted to situations as they are encountered on the ground. Some responses implicitly incorporated the idea of flexibility into their concept of this view of change.

> *Edward:* I did a plan but being the one and only project leader it was mostly in my head, although I brought in many different people into the plan to help out. It was

a plan for improvisation, rather than a plan that's got everything thought through.

Emma: No we didn't have a linear plan that we followed from start to finish. We have evolved and evolved and evolved. I like the idea of that, that suits my logical brain but no, the plan changed and changed and changed. . . . . so you think of everything all the way through and complete it and meet your objective and it's all done. I didn't find that at all. In many ways that was one of the biggest challenges and will be this year. You can't control it all. The system does what the system does and you have to work on it. So yes, this is a very messy way to achieve change but I actually think it probably does achieve change.

William: I can't really agree with this one, I mean there were experts, you could call us two experts, we were involved but we didn't manage faithful implementation, we managed the implementation to the point where the students wanted it. So it was improvised after a certain point.

Sophie: the closest would be technical rational. It was basically myself and a colleague did a plan for the implementation of the project, we put it on Project Document. We would've been very happy to adapt that plan if it didn't appear to be working and I would not say that we were in any respects experts on chat but as it was, the plan worked and so we didn't really deviate from that plan.

Robert: Well technical rational is how I like to work, certainly, but I've been pulled out of that and not predominantly by SDP but by the changing . . . circumstances

88% of interviewees recognised that their SDP work had required additional resources. However, some people felt that a) they themselves had not benefited directly from accessing the resources or b) that the resources had not been allocated in a rational way, because as the detail of the work emerged and required more resources, these were not forthcoming. In other words resources did not reflect the complexity that emerged during the change process. A rational model of planning and resource allocation depended on being able to plan and implement the plan perfectly or adjust this in a rational way should circumstances warrant. In their view this had not happened.

Nearly all (88%) of interviewees recognised that they themselves were early adopters of change. Indeed, their involvement in the SDP innovation process was because they were good at looking for new opportunities and picking up messages like—'here is a funding opportunity to do something different'. Several participants also recognised that they were working with other enthusiasts or that they sought out other enthusiasts to help propagate what they had achieved.

Just over half the interviewees (53%) could see a component of continuous improvement in their change process either because their innovation had grown from incremental and adaptive change from what had already existed or, more commonly, as a second stage in the innovation process after a significant change had been made. In other words incremental change was generally the natural consequence of refining an innovation.

Finally, 85% of the innovators who brought about significant change felt that the complexity view of change was an important feature of their experience of change.

Much of the variation in responses can be explained by variations in the nature of the individual change projects. At one end of the spectrum are projects which lend themselves to the creation and faithful execution of a plan—where cause and effects are fairly predictable and where the end goal is clear e.g. introduction of a chat software into the library enquiry service.

> I think for this specific project, the closest would be technical rational. It was basically myself and a colleague did a plan for the implementation of the project, we put it on Project Document. We would've been very happy to adapt that plan if it didn't appear to be working and I would not say that we were in any respects experts on chat but as it was, the plan worked and so we didn't really deviate from that plan.

At the other end of the continuum innovators had very different experiences, where the end results emerged through actions that were guided by only a general idea about the final goal and the innovators realised that they, or anyone else could not control change.

> It's very messy but I think that is actually the way things happen. I love the idea of a project plan—so you think of everything all the way through and complete it and meet your objective and it's all done. But I didn't find that at all. In many ways that was one of the biggest challenges and will be as we move it forward this year. You can't control it

all. The system does what the system does and you have to work on it. So yes, this is a very messy way to achieve change but I actually think it does achieve change in the end.

It is more like the idea of *agile software development* which is where you do a little bit, you try it out, you see if it works and adapt it to make it better.

There is a sense that the leaders of complex change projects must be able to integrate all these ways of thinking about change in their strategies for involving people in change.

Outcomes are not predictable although I predicted outcomes but we had lots of richness added to that. So change sponsors create the conditions in which change of a certain sort is more likely to happen than not . . . . but it's the more likely bit, because, in my view, it was going to happen

. . . but then you've got to allow failure to make change of course, but maybe what made this work is we looked at 'work arounds'. So when it looked like something wasn't going to happen, we found another way through it.

WHAT'S IMPORTANT TO INDIVIDUALS?

The second part looks at the factors that seem to have been important to the people who accomplished change within the SDP and concludes with an examination of twelve organisational factors that appear to be important in strategic change that encourages and supports bottom-up innovation, based on what has been learnt through the SDP.

The innovation of professional practice is a highly situated phenomenon. Only the people involved can see the possibilities and turn their imaginations into new practice that has meaning in and beyond their context. One of the important contributions that the innovators can make to organisational learning, is to share their perspectives on the factors that enabled or inhibited change in their particular contexts.

A questionnaire was developed based on the findings of the initial study of SDP-related change at Southampton Solent University (Chapter 5) which revealed a number of factors that seemed to be important in enabling change to happen. These factors showed a remarkable degree of consistency with a recent study conducted by Amabile and Kramer (2012), of factors that influence inner work life, which in turn impact on employee performance and creativity in the work environment. A small number of additional factors were incorporated into the questionnaire from this study. A total of twenty two factors were identified in the questionnaire and twenty one people who were involved in SDP innovations completed it. Their responses are summarised in Table 13.2

Many Factors are Important to Innovators

Nearly all the factors were considered to be important in accomplishing significant change. 21 of the 22 factors scored an average of 4 or more, and 19 factors scored 4.3 or more (max 5.0). The only factor to score less than 4 was (1) Having a clear vision of how the University saw its future and how SDP contributed to that vision.

The highest rated factors scoring 4.5 or higher (max = 5.0) were—

2 My readiness and willingness to get involved in the opportunity provided by SDP

3 My vision of what I wanted to achieve

4 My will/motivation to succeed with something I cared about

12 Having good communication with the people I needed to talk to

13 The active involvement of others—good teamwork

15 Feeling trusted and being allowed to get on with it without interference

16 Feeling that I made good progress within the time available

17 Feeling that what I was doing was valued by my colleagues

Personal characteristics (my will, my vision, my readiness) feature prominently in what is important, together with the way people wanted to be trusted and feel that their contributions would be valued. High value is also placed on communication, the social dimension of work and the need to make progress. The large number of factors innovators believe are involved in enabling innovation to be accomplished is striking and accounts for some of the complexity involved in innovating.

Table 13.2 Innovator ratings (n=21) of the importance of a range of factors in enabling them to accomplish their innovation A) importance to them B) extent to which this factor was realised.

	A Not very important / important					Av	B Not realised / realised					Av
	1	2	3	4	5		1	2	3	4	5	
1 Having a clear vision of how the University saw its future and how SDP contributed to that vision		1	4	12	3	3.7						4.0
2 My readiness and willingness to get involved in the SDP opportunity			1	5	15	4.7			2	8	11	4.4
3 My vision of what I wanted to achieve			2	7	12	4.5		2	4	9	7	4.1
4 My will/motivation to succeed with something I cared about			1	9	12	4.7	1			13	7	4.2
5 Having explicit goals and realistic work plans to achieve my objective		1	1	8	11	4.4	2		8	5	6	3.1
6 Having the autonomy to implement the project as I wanted to		1	2	8	10	4.3	1	1	5	8	6	3.8
7 Having the opportunity to use my personal creativity	1	1	3	5	11	4.1		1	7	8	5	3.8
8 Believing I could take risks without feeling I would be criticised if I wasn't completely successful	1		1	9	10	4.3		3	3	7	8	4.0
9 Having the financial resources I needed when I needed them			1	7	12	4.3	1	2	4	11	3	3.6
10 Having the time I needed to complete the job			1	10	10	4.4	2	4	8	6	1	3.0
11 Being able to find the help I needed when I needed it			2	10	9	4.3	1	1	12	6	1	3.4
12 Having good communication with the people I needed to talk to			1	9	11	4.5		3	7	6	5	3.6
13 The active involvement of others—good teamwork				6	15	4.7			5	11	5	4.0
14 Learning through the experience (learn from problems as well as success)			2	11	8	4.3			3	12	5	3.9
15 Feeling trusted and being allowed to get on with it without interference				7	14	4.7	1		2	10	9	4.4
16 Feeling that I made good progress within the time available			1	8	12	4.5	1	1	4	7	8	4.0
17 Feeling that what I was doing was valued by my colleagues			2	6	13	4.5		1	4	10	6	4.0
18 Feeling that what I was doing was valued by Head of School/Service/Dean			3	7	11	4.4		1	8	8	4	3.7
19 Forming new productive relationships with colleagues in my school or elsewhere in the University	1		3	7	10	4.2			3	10	8	4.2
20 Forming new productive relationships with people outside the University		1	2	8	10	4.3		1	4	8	8	4.1
21 Feeling that the environment encouraged and supported me throughout the process especially when things did not go as planned			2	11	8	4.3	1	3	9	6	2	3.2
22 Feeling my contribution to the SDP has been recognised and appreciated			1	12	8	4.3		2	4	13	2	3.7

Realisation of Factors through SDP

Innovators were invited to consider the extent to which each factor was realised through their particular SDP change project. Eight factors had significantly lower average scores for realisation compared to the average scores for what was believed to be important, namely—

5 Having explicit goals and realistic work plans to achieve my objective (3.1 versus 4.4)

9 Having the financial resources I needed when I needed them (3.6 versus 4.3)

10 Having the time I needed to complete the job (3.3 compared to 4.5)

11 Being able to find the help I needed when I needed it (3.0 versus 4.4)

12 Having good communication with the people I needed to talk to (3.6 versus 4.5)

13 The active involvement of others—good teamwork (4.0 versus 4.7)

18 Feeling that what I was doing was valued by the Head of School/Director of Service or Dean (3.7 versus 4.4)

21 Feeling that the environment encouraged and supported me throughout the process especially when things did not go as planned (3.2 versus 4.3).

These factors boil down to a combination of having the resources to complete the task of innovating, and innovating in an environment that supports and values the efforts of the innovator. In other words there was a consistent pattern of responses that suggests that there is a gap between the type of environment innovators believe is important to bring about innovation successfully and the environment that they experienced while they were innovating. Closing this gap would go a long way to creating an organisational culture that was as supportive of innovation as the innovators would like.

ORGANISATIONAL FACTORS THAT ENCOURAGE BOTTOM-UP INNOVATION AND FACILITATE STRATEGIC CHANGE

The study of strategic change at Southampton Solent University demonstrates the value of bottom-up innovation within a comprehensive and sustained strategic change project. While top down initiatives, like the introduction of new business systems and processes are essential to enabling a university to be more effective, responsive and adaptive in its educational work, it is the innovators who provide the key resource to enact and embody the significant educational changes the University is trying to make. The study reveals that innovators thrive in an organisational culture where leaders and managers are encouraging, supporting and enabling. Where they have the resources—especially time to make change happen. Where the institution's systems and procedures enable rather than hinder progress. Where they have the respect, emotional support and encouragement of managers and colleagues and where they can find help when they need it. Where they feel their efforts have been valued and they have made a positive difference.

It stands to reason that for organisational change to be successful the conditions and situations embodied in the factors that innovators consider to be important in accomplishing significant change (Table 13.2), have to be supported and realised. Twelve factors summarised in Table 13.3 and elaborated below, provide an overarching framework within which bottom-up innovation is more likely to be encouraged, supported and facilitated within a process of strategic change.

Table 13.3 Summary of factors and conditions that encourage, support and facilitate bottom-up innovation within a process of strategic change.

Leadership, management & facilitation of strategic change & bottom up innovation

1 Leadership is shared and distributed throughout the organisation

2 A strategic vision that inspires people to create their own visions for change that they will embody

3 A strategy for both planned and emergent change

4 A strategy that involves the whole socio-cultural environment

5 Involvement of brokers to facilitate change across and between structures, hierarchies and practice domains and between different organisations

6 An effective but flexible approach to managing and accounting for resources

Environmental/cultural factors that encourage, support and enable strategic change and bottom-up innovation

An environment/culture that:

7 promotes effective, honest and meaningful communication

8 recognises and supports resolution of local contentious practice—that facilitates rather than inhibits progress

9 encourages new relationships and collaborations to foster change

10 provides emotional support and celebrates what has been achieved

11 values learning and encourages and enables people to share what they have learnt so that it can be reused or adapted to other contexts

12 encourages people to take risks and harness their creativity to actualise themselves

---

1 Leadership is shared and distributed throughout the organisation

Whole organisation change is led from the top, middle and bottom. Leadership is shared and distributed throughout the organisation and innovators must be viewed as leaders of strategic change.

Leading from the top involves visualising the future and creating the conditions that motivate people to move the organisation in the direction of that future. It requires an integrating style of management able to hold the vision and deliver on commitments. It also requires a management style that is open, flexible and trusting to allow ideas to emerge from the middle and bottom, and enable people to take ownership and exercise their autonomy to create and implement change. And it involves trusting people to create the change once the direction has been set and encouraging and supporting the right sort of changes as they emerge.

> I think the role of SDP leader was integrated into my role as an academic leader . . . . There are so many linkages across and if you are really trying to ensure that a project becomes internalised and part of the University, you have got to be looking for those opportunities all the time, where are the open doors? . . . . it is a very privileged position to be in to be able to see so much of what is going on across the University and to talk to other senior colleagues and get insights into where things are shifting for them as well. I think leadership is about using that opportunity. always looking for where a door is opening, where there is an opportunity, where someone is beginning to do something, being alert and responsive to changing mood.
> *PVC Academic*

Leading from the middle requires managers to accept responsibility for involving their Department, School, Faculty or Service in the strategic change and creating the conditions that encourage and enable their staff to participate in change. Leading from the middle involves translating organisational objectives into objectives that are meaningful in the local socio-cultural practice environment. Leading from the middle does not mean 'go and do it' it means 'we will do it together.'

> my theory of big change is you have to harness your champions and your front [line] leaders and you have to work with them and you have to get your little pots of energy moving ahead . . . . by just getting the energy and moving things forward, that is what change is about for me. . . . . Making them proud to be there, annoying everybody else by letting them know that these people

are moving forward and putting me right in the middle of it as well. A part of it, doing things at the same time. So I am saying as a Dean I am in here. *Dean*

Leading from the bottom involves individuals accepting responsibility to make change happen by adapting existing or inventing new practice that is consistent with the change the institution is seeking to make. The innovators are people who lead change by involving themselves in it and showing others how to accomplish it.

> [Leadership] I think it is about seeing what you want to achieve and getting people to come with you to achieve it. it is not just an individualistic thing. I mean this vision was handed to me, but I shared it. you know, I think this is exactly what we should be doing. This idea of getting education out and making it collaborative and using the theory of how adults learn best, it is the right way to go. It is also much more commercially viable in the new world of higher education. I am very excited about that. So I share that vision, I have got that vision and I can see exactly how we can make it work. So it's kind of getting the conditions around you to be able to . . . I am very keen to make the changes, but I need the sort of conditions to enable that to happen.

> I think it is about inspiring and empowering people and getting everybody on board . . . . I think a big structure like a university finds that extraordinarily difficult to do. Until you get right in the top and you are sort of at the top of the University you can have those thoughts. But when you are actually trying to make it happen lower down it is very hard. *Innovator*

There is one secret to leading organisational change. The leaders at the top and in the middle have to create the conditions in which people at the bottom feel empowered and are enabled to change themselves and their own practices in order to make strategic change happen. This is a shared concept of leadership in which leadership is broadly distributed, such that people within a team and organization lead each other. It is a social, non-hierarchical concept and contrasts with more traditional notions where leadership roles are vested in individuals appointed by management.

These ideas about leadership at all levels are consistent with the concept of shared leadership (Pearce and Conger 2003, Thomas 2006).

> Shared leadership is a helpful idea when considering multiple complementary changes that help whole systems to change. (Thomas 2006:22)

But there is an issue for organisations that embrace these forms of leadership. Having provided opportunities for shared leadership the challenge is will leadership from the bottom continue to be encouraged and supported?

> You push the boundaries, you know, you push the boundaries and that is a hard thing to do. It led me to conclude maybe there has to be created that environment within the University where, if you like, the particular kind of leaders would sprout. We came out of hiding because of this opportunity to come out. We came out of hiding but it doesn't mean we are going to stay in that place. We are like plants, we need to keep growing. So where are we growing to? Maybe we are better off being left as seeds in the Earth. So this has happened now, we have come out, but are we going to end up as a big tree? Is this university going to grow that tree? I think these are questions that we need to ask. We know we have grown, but can the University keep nurturing us in those directions? *Innovator*

2 A strategic vision that inspires people to create their own visions for change that they will embody

An organisational vision for strategic change must encourage and enable people to create their own visions through which they can enact and embody change that they own. The secret of encouraging bottom-up innovation through strategic change requires people to connect their own visions for educational change with the institution's strategic ambition.

Organisational change involves someone with the power and authority to see the direction in which the organisation needs to travel and communicate that through a vision for a different and better world. An organisational vision for strategic change, must encourage and enable people to see things in a different way and inspire them to create their own visions through which they can enact and embody change that they own. A vision at the top is of little value if people at the bottom cannot understand and relate it to their world of everyday practice and the things that they value. Middle managers play an important role in translating high level ideas and engaging their staff in new conversations about the implications of these ideas for their individual and collective practice.

The SDP vision was simple and clear, and consistent with the University's strategic plan. But the vision had to be interpreted and animated through conversation so that new ideas enter the imaginations of individuals. The SDP Team and the SDP Project Leader played an important role in communicating the vision to all parts of the University. Some middle managers were key to translating the vision into ideas that their staff could create meanings that related to their everyday work. For example, the Dean of Learning and Information Services promoted discussions across all Service areas to stimulate thinking about the implications of this strategic vision (chapter 4). The poster that was created through this process contained a wealth of ideas for the practices that would have to be developed and became a key tool for communicating these ideas throughout the services and also to senior managers. This imagining activity resulted in new levels of awareness that eventually resulted in concrete plans for change.

Similarly, the Head of the School of Design embedded her interpretations of the SDP vision in the School's SDP proposal (chapter 5). The vision connected past history and current practice in the School, but created a new sense of direction. Contextual knowledge, effort and imagination are required to translate the high level organisational ambitions into ideas that can be owned and put into practice on the ground. The School's SDP proposal provided the blueprint for strategic change. It encapsulated a coherent vision and a narrative about that vision that made sense to members of the School's community (the social world see below) and connected to the University's strategic intentions. As such it created an important, home grown 'tool' to facilitate the mediation of thinking, discussion and action.

Innovators place high value on their own visions of the changes they were trying to accomplish (Table 13.2). It is these visions and associated convictions that inspire them and fuel their determination to accomplish significant change.

> The vision was to develop a unique umbrella organization for the worldwide commercial yacht sector, and no other organisation in the world today can currently compete with what we are about to launch.

> I guess my belief in it helped though. It would have been easy to park it when I hit various roadblocks along the way but I just kept persevering and the right moment came
> *Innovator*

Sometimes these visions meet resistance and there is conflict that has to be resolved before progress can be made. On other occasions the visions are already aligned to the wider intentions of Schools or Faculty.

> But you see my vision should not be seen as a vision which was outside [the organisation]. My vision was negotiated already in line with what the faculty is trying to do, but maybe they wouldn't see it that way. I think the SDP . . . not just the funds of SDP but the SDP as the idea of trying to bring about change in the University, created an environment where that discussion could happen.
> *Innovator*

The overall process is one of continually aligning personal and organisational visions.

3 A strategy for both planned and emergent change

Strategy needs to balance the needs for planned action determined at the top with the need to create the conditions that encourage an organic and emergent process of change in the practice environment.

The University set out to transform itself through the SDP and investment in and encouragement for bottom-up innovation formed a significant part of the strategy. The architects and managers of the strategy were aligned in their thinking and action was coordinated and sustained in a consistent manner. Furthermore, the vision that was communicated and the support that was given from the top encouraged and enabled people in the middle and bottom of the organisation to interpret the SDP goals in ways that were meaningful to their own contexts and practices.

> You have to balance the pursuit of aspirations and goals with taking advantage of unanticipated opportunities. Managing this part of the strategy process is often the difference between success and failure for companies. (Christensen et al 2012:42)

For a strategy to be successful it needs not only to involve deliberate planned actions to achieve tangible objectives and goals, but also the space to improvise as new and better ideas emerge. It needs to encourage, stimulate and support activity that will lead to change and provide sufficient resources to enable change to happen and ensure that people involved in change have the necessary resources when they need them. This process of connecting top, middle and bottom in this way is more likely to create ownership and responsibility for ideas and actions so that the changes that emerge are owned at all levels of the organisation.

Emergence cannot be controlled, predicted or managed but the leaders, managers and facilitators of organisational change can create conditions that are more likely to lead to changes of a certain type.

> It is the willingness of the Senior Management . . . to work with an emergent process that makes this different. *SDP Programme Director*

The successful management of change combines and integrates managed, purposeful and focused change through planned activities that enable and encourage people to *improvise and discover* the best ways forward for themselves.

> I guess there were objectives coming down but then it is about how individuals take those objectives and interpret them for themselves and motivate themselves to do those things. *Innovator*

> There was a lot of rich detail that came out of the projects and the linkages that wouldn't have otherwise . . . that you could never foresee in an original brief, so you have to let things evolve and then look for the opportunities as they do evolve, . . . The clear goal was there but along the way, the journey brought out a richness that we couldn't have foreseen that we've tried to capture as we've gone through the process. *Innovator*

4 A strategy that involves the whole socio-cultural environment

Strategic change must involve the whole organisation. But how you involve people in change is crucial. It involves working within, across and outside the cultural and practice grains and involves imposing change from the top (like new business systems or procedures) and encouraging bottom-up change—adaptations and inventions—by individuals and groups.

Underpinning the SDP strategy was a belief that change will only happen if people do new things ie change comes from acting, doing and making rather than just thinking and talking about it. Another important belief underlying the strategy was that change must involve most of the people in the organisation. The SDP sought to involve the academic teaching community in all the Faculties and Schools through the funding of innovation through Faculties, Schools and individuals. It engaged Faculty and Service Administrative teams through the Service Plus project that sought to involve administrators in creating solutions to problems and challenges associated with the strategic agenda. Furthermore, by changing a number of business systems that were central to many of the University's operations it involved all staff in fundamentally new practices that were more in tune with the strategic changes the University was seeking.

The feeling that everyone was involved, and change was not just targeted at a specific group of people, was an important factor in accomplishing change at the organisational scale. By offering incentives to stimulate change and innovation within Faculties and Schools the University was seeking to work within the disciplinary cultural grain. By supporting individuals and teams with central expertise, for example in the design of on-line flexible learning, the University facilitated development and innovation in the Schools that was more consistent in its outcomes and quality standards than if development had been entirely from within the School. There are many examples of the University supporting innovation within the cultural grain to achieve the global objectives of the SDP in ways that are appropriate and relevant to the discipline area.

Working across the academic cultural grain has been accomplished through the introduction of new business systems and through the Service Plus project which is increasingly involving teams containing both academics and administrators.

Working outside the existing cultural grain is witnessed in the Foundation Degree in Social and Health Care and more recent spin-offs where University staff are working in partnership with employers who have a very different cultural heritage to that found in the University.

People are more likely to commit themselves to significant change if their will to be involved is driven by their own intrinsic motivations rather than extrinsic forces. Finding and engaging self-motivated enthusiasts who enjoy such challenges is essential in the progression of strategic change.

> you have to harness your champions and your front [line] leaders *Dean*

Innovators are people who create and innovate regardless of whether there is a strategic change initiative they are the key resource for leading bottom-up change and to changing institutional culture. The SDP performed the role of an 'attractor' and people who are naturally innovative will be attracted to such initiatives.

> I always put my hand up for those things because I like doing other things. I mean I love teaching but obviously I like getting involved in other projects. *Innovator*

> I respond to challenges and I am always looking for the next thing, the next idea. I come up with lots of ideas. I like following through with them as much as I can. Obviously

there does need to be support for that, so yeah. I have got involved as much as I can. *Innovator*

People like to invent their own ideas they don't like being given them. For any plan for change to be credible it has to be based mainly on ideas that are familiar and authentic to the people who will turn them into new practice. This is why top down strategy has to enable people to interpret the strategy offered by the top and create their own ideas for change at the bottom.

A strategy that seeks to involve everyone in change invites the innovators and early adopters to lead strategic change through their inventions of new practice and adaptations to existing practice. The insights and new practice models that they provide can then be adapted to other parts of the organisation and change is propagated in this way. The process of disseminating the results of change, for example through the annual Solent Exchange conference, means that large numbers of people in the organisation are exposed to new ideas and ways of doing, and the introduction of new business systems and processes means that most people in the organisation are eventually involved in change.

5 Involvement of brokers to facilitate organisational change across and between structures, hierarchies and practice domains and between different organisations

Changing an organisation as complex and culturally diverse as a university requires capacity for brokering to facilitate exchange and action across and through the structures and cultures.

Brokers perform an important role in enabling change in complex organisational systems (Jackson 2003). They work in collaborative and creative ways with people, ideas, knowledge and resources to enable things to happen that otherwise would not happen. They are a kind of multi-skilled anthropologist who can get inside and comprehend not just needs and desires, but the language, politics, positioning and outlook of the different parties (Barnett 2003: xviii).

> people like me that are sort of in the middle, I suppose I have more inroads to work arounds, or people that can [unblock things], or I have more clout to push things forward . . . whereas people on the . . . chalk face . . . don't know all of that, so that's not an easy place for them to be. So it does mean that there has to be this kind of middle character, I think, to find the work arounds or kind of just divert the end result in some way. *Head of School*

Through their brokerage role the SDP team encouraged and facilitated staff engagement, cultivated relationships, organised activities and monitored and reported on progress. The SDP team's brokerage role might be characterised through the metaphor of gardeners cultivating the conditions for new ideas and practices to grow and helping innovators to flourish.

Overcoming inertia and securing initial engagement is the initial challenge in bringing about change in a university. Like all good gardeners the SDP team were proactive, they 'nudged' people into action and encouraged them to take risks—sometimes in opposition to established procedures. Like good gardeners the SDP Team kept a watchful eye on their garden. They were the eyes and ears of the institution gathering information relevant to accomplishing change and monitoring and documenting progress, and making small interventions where they believed more growth could be nurtured. As some of the case studies reveal, bringing about change, especially when it is on top of an already busy life, can cause anxiety and be very stressful. On occasion members of the SDP Team provided emotional support, 'a shoulder to cry on', or took on a coaching/mentoring role suggesting that they were also involved in the empathetic management of anxieties within the SDP process. The SDP Team was also proactive in sowing new seeds (eg involving new people), propagating ideas and disseminating the results of innovation.

The SDP Team with its overview of the 'Solent garden' and expertise in organisational change was also able to appreciate what was missing. The willingness to try out new techniques and take risks, led to the introduction of entirely new and novel approaches to organisational change, such as the Customer Service programme.

Like all good gardeners the SDP Team accumulated and used the knowledge they had gained about what works or doesn't work. This book is just one example of the concern for consolidating and applying the learning that was gained.

The change programme also utilised brokers who spanned organisations. For example, the secondment of a member of the Southampton Hospital NHS Trust to the University resulted in a number of innovations that would not have been possible without their involvement.

6 An effective but flexible approach to managing and accounting for resources

Changing an organisation requires new resources or the redistribution of existing resources—the most important of which is the time to change.

Resourcing change that is emergent requires a more flexible and adaptive model of distributing resources than is used in more predictable operational processes

> Real strategy in companies and in our lives is created through hundreds of everyday decisions about how we spend our resources. As your living your life from day to day, how do you make sure you are heading in the right direction? Watch where your resources flow. If they're not supporting the strategy you've decided upon, then you are not implementing that strategy at all. (Christensen 2012: 62)

Large scale organisational change requires the distribution of significant new resources. Regardless of whether the funding is externally or internally sourced there needs to be effective mechanisms for assigning and distributing resources, monitoring and accounting for their use. The Solent strategic change programme used a combination of SDP Team procedures and decision making, and the University's Management Board to approve the distribution of resources and account for their use.

While it is a straightforward matter to distribute and account for resources in a system that is operating in a business as usual mode, it is not so easy when the business is change and much of that change appears in an emergent form. The case studies reveal that from the innovators' perspective resourcing mechanisms were not always responsive to the emergent nature of the change process.

Large publicly funded projects in universities are often overseen by a Steering Committee whose purpose is to ensure that there is proper and effective accountability. For the SDP project the decision was taken to use the existing university 'Management Board', the senior collective managerial decision making body of the University to provide the supervisory and project approval function. This governance mechanism was efficient in terms of the use of managerial time and they served the project well: the downside was that SDP was treated as one item in a busy and competing business agenda and the structure did not encourage the growth of new institutional champions beyond the membership of Management Board.

People who were directly involved in change discussed resources in terms of their time and workload, and their ability to manage their time for development work alongside existing teaching and administrative commitments. Being able to manage and juggle time for development and existing commitments is an essential capability for all those involved in change. For academics the additional complication involves managing time within a fairly rigid academic calendar and weekly timetabling of teaching activities.

SDP resources provided additional capacity to employ knowledgeable consultants, or administrative or technical assistance from people within and outside the School. People also talked about resources in terms of funding and physical resources like equipment, the manufacturing of products created through an educational process, and social activity like hosting events and exhibitions for students from local 6th Form Colleges. The Strategic Development Fund was able to support these requirements.

SDP provided a reason and focus for change and through the resources it provided it enabled more ambitious change to occur than would have been possible through the normal incremental change process. It also enabled change to happen more quickly. SDP was able to provide time, support and funding that was not otherwise available, thus acting as a catalyst to enable individuals to actualise their ideas

> I mean bottom line, it gave us the cash, so it bought time and it bought people like the part-time lecturer. We could pay her to undertake that research. We could pay a student to upload, so it gave us the cash and freed up some of our time to get involved with it as well through remission. *Innovator*

The downside of upfront planning and resource allocation is that estimates have to be made in advance of the problems, challenges and opportunities being known. Consequently it is difficult to anticipate needs and match actual requirements particularly in response to the unforeseen challenges of radical change.

> I think . . . . more resources would have been helpful because . . . . they didn't realise how big each project was, so ideally each of those projects should have had an extra person giving their assistance and that would have been very helpful to all of them actually. *Innovator*

While it is a straightforward matter to distribute and account for resources in a system that is operating in a business as usual mode, it is not so easy when the business is change and much of that change appears in an emergent form. The case studies reveal that from the innovators' perspective resourcing mechanisms were not always responsive to the emergent nature of the change process. Designers of strategic change and innovation projects need to design in a significant contingency to deal with the unexpected or develop mechanisms for gaining additional funds as a change process unfolds.

Transparency and fairness in how resources are allocated to where they are needed is an important aspect of involving people in change.

> *Faculty Dean* We had to create a fair system. It was creating that fairness that was the hard bit.

> *Interviewer:* So creating a fair system sounds like an important thing to do when you are trying to get buy-in above and beyond the day job.

> *Faculty Dean:* Hugely, it is massively important to me . . . . The teams know that work with me that I will be awfully fair about sharing out the workload and sharing out the rewards that come from it as well. You do get money that comes in. I have gone over backwards to be transparent about it.

When such transparency is not achieved, and the people involved in bringing about change feel there is a mismatch between what they are being asked to do and the resources that are available to do it, there is dissatisfaction and a loss of morale. As one innovator explained.

> [there was resource, but there wasn't sufficient resource to do what we had to do] It required the goodwill of people like myself and my colleagues to work holidays and not have a break basically, it pushed us to the limit, it really did push us to the limit. So, again, I wouldn't say it was rational because it's about power and politics, you know, it wasn't allocation on the basis of this is what's needed here and that's what's needed there, it was, you know, there were certain things going on at levels I wasn't involved in that meant that it wasn't transparent so I wouldn't say it was rational in a way everyone understood. *Innovator*

7 An environment/culture that promotes effective, honest and meaningful communication

Communication that is honest and meaningful connects the managed, social and individual worlds of change and is the means to overcome the barriers between these different worlds. You cannot change an organisation without changing the conversations within it (Seel 2004).

Communication, more specifically communication that is meaningful to those receiving it, pervades innovators' stories of change. If visions, ideas and invitations to contribute are not communicated in a way that has meaning to those who receive it—nothing will happen.

> I think one of the things this university can do better is communication. I think everybody would acknowledge that we're not great at that and partly at the beginning of the SDP, I think those at the top completely understood what it was about but those down at base level probably didn't really get the picture at all. So I think they have done quite a lot of work to get that out and certainly with people like me, once projects like this became about, SDP is now a language everybody understands *Innovator*

The lesson is clear that just sending information to people who are busy and who have many priorities, will often not cause them to act. What causes them to act is when communication causes them to create their own interpretations and meanings for themselves. Strategic change has to begin somewhere and that is when 'someone chooses to do something and then acts on that decision.' The case of the School of Design provides a good example. The Faculty of Technology had spent a year implementing an SDP project so the Head of School was well aware of the SDP and the opportunities for getting involved but involvement was triggered by a specific event that suddenly created new meaning.

> [it was at] a head's meeting, everyone was talking about it. I suddenly thought, oh, what was going on here? . . . . I . . . sat there listening to what other people were doing and I think I heard that [two Faculties] were developing lots of professional development units . . . . I thought, oh, that's a lot; we're not even doing any. Listening to what other people were talking about I just thought, we need to be doing this, and that was important. That day, I can sort of picture myself in that meeting thinking, I feel like we failed and we need to do something about it. And that, to me, was the day when I decided we would do something about it.

From this story it can be inferred that the decision for the School to be involved in the SDP did not arise from the formal distribution of information about the SDP, rather it emerged through social interaction and conversation—a Head's meeting in which people talked about their involvement in SDP. The change in attitude that resulted in the School becoming involved in the SDP was due to conversations that carried personal meaning and significance, and created feelings of dissatisfaction and a sense that an opportunity was being missed. An opportunity highlighted by what others were managing to achieve. This is a good example of how communication about the SDP became personally meaningful and it was only at the point at which it became meaningful that it became emotionally engaging and change began to happen.

Good and honest communication creates the trust and mutual understandings that are essential when trying to accomplish change. Poor communication or an absence of communication invariably causes problems and a loss of trust. Communication, particularly conversation, lies at the heart of an organisation's culture and its ability to learn and to spread new learning. What the SDP did was to change the nature and pattern of conversations which enabled people to do new things and these activities stimulated different sorts of conversation. What emerged through this process was new learning, new ways of being and doing and the modification of culture in small but measurable ways.

From the organisational perspective, perhaps the most important effect of this meaning making process is the influence it has had on the people who led and managed the project who are in the position to take what has been leant and use it when making decisions in future.

8 An environment that recognises and supports resolution of local contentious practice—an environment that facilitates rather than inhibits progress

Tensions and conflicts often arise when bottom-up innovation meets existing procedures and systems. A system in change needs the awareness, will and capability to facilitate the resolution of local contentious practice. An organisation involved in strategic change needs the awareness, will and capability to facilitate the resolution of local contentious practice. This is another role for organisational brokers.

People working in an organisation (persons in practice) historically constitute their everyday world as they help to make it through their participation in it while being shaped by the world in which they are a part (Holland and Lave 2009). Local contentious practice, and its resolution, lies at the heart of bringing about innovation in an organisation that is full of systems, procedures and traditions. Local practice comes about in the encounters between people as they address and respond to each other while enacting cultural activities under conditions of political-economic and cultural historical conjuncture. Elements of the SDP narrative reveal that when working within their cultural domain (eg their school) innovators have control over what they do. But once they have to relate their innovations to existing business systems there is often conflict between the new practices they were trying to create and practices that already existed within the institutions established systems and processes.

> the University's inbound and outbound logistics are not good at all to work with industry. I know the University is accountable, but it is not like you can just say 'Okay we

have got to have this now'. For example, we needed to get some samples to measure and get the fits correct. Well I wanted to buy some samples and measure them but where does that money come from? You have to put in a purchase order, that takes a couple of weeks. You haven't got a couple of weeks because you are on a critical path that says you need these measurements today and you need to email them through. So how does that work with systems that were not designed for this way of working? *Innovator*

Posing the question 'how can we do this?' challenges existing ways of doing things and the innovator initiates the struggle to resolve the issue. These are the 'pinch points' where innovations can be thwarted and innovators can become demotivated if progress cannot be made towards resolving the problem. These are the areas that organisations involved in strategic change need to pay particular attention to. Relationships and communication between innovators and system owners are crucial to resolving these troublesome areas and when they are good they can greatly facilitate progress.

So that's a problem because they need to come back and enrol and they can't understand [why they can't] . . . . we have met with all the relevant people [in Registry] and said, "How can we get around this in the future because this is going to be happening on a regular basis?"

. . . . I have to say I've been quite impressed with the support that we've had in trying to address things and find ways round problems. *Innovator*

One of the really crucial factors in enabling local contentious practice to be resolved, is for the people who are trying to make change happen to be able to find people who will help them overcome the procedural and decision making barriers between different parts of the organisation. These are the brokers and boundary spanners, that silo'd organisations need in order to unblock things that seem to be frozen.

this morning [I went to see someone] . . . . we have the central university and we have got the faculty. Because this is collaborative provision it tends to sit in central services, and yet everything gets approved through the faculty. There has to be communication between the two. Things were getting sort of passed around between people. So I went to somebody who I respect in the SDP project and I

> said, 'How do I unblock this?' and she has kindly said she
> will go and see if she can *Innovator*

9 An environment that encourages new relationships and collaborations in order to foster change

Organisational change is accomplished through the deepening of existing relationships and the forging of new collaborative partnerships that generate ideas and new opportunities, and provide encouragement, practical help and emotional support.

The SDP study demonstrates the importance to those accomplishing change of new relationships through which ideas were generated, problems were solved and practical and emotional support was given. Such relationships helped innovators to appreciate the value of their own work and efforts, encouraged them to 'go the extra mile' and enabled them to persist especially at the most frustrating and challenging moments.

Forming productive, co-creative and emotionally supportive collaborative working relationships with members of their School or colleagues in central university departments—particularly the Flexible Delivery Team (e-Development and Educational Technology Unit) and Partnerships Office was an important strategy for innovators.

> Once I started working with them [Flexible Delivery Team] everything just fitted together really well and they developed a really strong belief that my units were going to work and that they were going to be understandable for a learner. Their motivation began to help me achieve this because of the relationship that we had built and they could see how much it meant to me and therefore how important it was for me to do this for the school and succeed in this project

> Their time was then really important to the success of the project because without them helping me so much, I wouldn't have achieved the outcomes. Basically I felt like I had made some friends there and they were going to help me get through this if no one else was. So they were incredibly supportive. *Innovator*

Extending existing relationships or building new relationships in the external environment was also a priority in the strategic change process. Relationship building with employers was crucial to the success of several of the innovations. In the case of the Foundation Degree in Health and Social Care the relationship was underpinned by a formal strategic alliance but ultimately it is the interpersonal relationships between the directly involved in change that really matter.

10 An environment/culture that provides encouragement and emotional support, and celebrates what has been achieved

An emotionally nourishing environment helps people deal with the challenges, stresses, anxieties and frustrations of trying to bring about significant change and helps them to remain positive in the face of setbacks. Such an environment recognises the efforts and celebrates the achievements of those who are involved in change.

Stress, anxiety and frustration are often associated with significant organisational change as people encounter problems and setbacks, things do not work out as intended or other situations. Sources of stress, anxiety and frustration encountered in this study included: 1) the competing demands of developing new practices while continuing to teach 2) inadequacy of resources for some projects where the amount of resource was underestimated or could not be estimated in advance, or when there was a lack of transparency as to how resources were being allocated 3) insufficient support when dealing with difficult problems 4) seeming inability of some institutional systems, procedures and infrastructures to adapt to the changes that they were creating. Such adverse psychological impacts could have been reduced if participants had more time particularly at critical moments in the change process, had more resources—not only money but practical help at certain stages of their project and had more support and empathy in resolving difficult problems that blocked progress.

Amabile and Kramer's study of the socio-cultural work environment identified four categories of nourishers (Amabile and Kramer 2011: 131—33) and all seemed to be important to the innovators. They have a significant impact on the way they feel and on their creativity and productivity. These are:

1 Respect—managerial actions determine whether people feel respected or disrespected and recognition is the most important of these actions.

2 Encouragement—for example when managers or colleagues are enthusiastic about an individual's work and when managers express confidence in the capabilities of people doing the work increases their sense of self-efficacy. Simply by sharing a belief that someone can do something challenging and trusting them to get on with greatly increases the self-belief of the people who are engaging with the challenge.

3 Emotional support—People feel more connected to others at work when their emotions are validated. This goes for events at work, like frustrations when things are not going smoothly and little progress is being made, and for significant events in someone's personal life. Recognition of emotion and empathy can do much to alleviate negative and amplify positive feelings with beneficial results for all concerned.

4 Affiliation—people want to feel connected to their colleagues so actions that develop bonds of mutual trust, appreciation and affection are essential in nourishing the spirit of participation. One of the challenges for innovators is that they often feel alone because they are moving into new territory by themselves—where there is no-one they can affiliate with! The role of the SDP team was important here in giving people an affiliation that was purpose—as well as culturally-based.

It is clear from the case studies that innovators thrive and innovation is more likely to happen when the environment is emotionally nourishing in the manner described above. An environment that is respectful, positive, encouraging and emotionally as well as practically supportive. SDP was an important additional element in the institutional climate that contributed to a climate of positivity.

> the way I find the most effective way to get things accomplished is to constantly believe it is possible to have a sort of can-do attitude and to assume other people have also got a can-do attitude and to treat them as if they have. On the whole I find that I get more productive responses if I do that. But it involves huge amounts of diplomacy and of trying to establish and sustain relationships, really. We want the shared goal, don't we? How do we together make that happen? Sometimes you just want to say 'For goodness sake, get on with it and do it.' Yeah, I think its masses of flexibility, respect, grace and diplomacy. *Innovator*

A lack of support might not be due to deliberate interference: rather it might be due to more passive disinterest.

> I think it is largely because people have got enough on their plates. This is something that is different, it demands them to think in a different way, to do things in a different way. With the best will in the world, they are busy enough and I quite understand where they just don't really want to try. *Innovator*

But the case studies also reveal that progress was hindered where there was scepticism about the potential of an idea or where ideas were not respected and someone else's ideas were imposed.

> I think overall, because in some ways it's been a relatively small part of our business up until now, there was some scepticism from a number of people . . . not just here but [higher up] . . . . and probably because they didn't really understand the market, underestimated just what the true potential was. *Innovator*

On the other hand support and encouragement from people outside the immediate work area can also be very valuable to the innovator.

> I've had a lot of support from particular quarters, some negative feedback from other quarters and then some feedback that was indifferent. It was almost a case of okay, well crack on and see how far you get with it. If I'd had really negative feedback from [critical friend] right at the start, then perhaps I wouldn't have taken it much further, or gone back and completely rethought the plan. But because she has a commercial background as well as having worked in academic institutions, I trusted what she said. I think it was really having somebody who doesn't really know anything about [this area], to ask does the business concept make sense? and she got it [whereas] other people didn't seem to get it. *Innovator*

Appreciating and valuing the efforts of innovators and the contributions they have made

Professional satisfaction and a sense of well being through accomplishment in the workplace often derive from the belief that our work and contributions to change are valued by colleagues, managers and students. Recognition, for what they had done and achieved, was very important to the innovators and its absence was a source of unhappiness

The University's annual Solent eXchange conference provided one opportunity for participants to share their innovations and gain recognition from colleagues in other parts of the University. Events that were organised locally like 'Away Days' or talks also provided important opportunities for public recognition.

> It was probably only until the Away Day they really fully understood what we were doing with everything . . . . the Away Day was for the staff in a way. I just wanted everyone to feel part of something good and that we've achieved *Head of School*

Anyone who takes risks to deliver a change he or she feels the organisation is seeking, needs to know whether their efforts have made a real difference but it is surprising how many innovators said they lacked this feedback.

> The problem is that I have never felt comfortable or confident in the University's strategic decision to back this. It's almost been like a, "we'll see how they get on" and there doesn't seem to have been the commitment.

> I just felt for me personally I needed to know that this was the way we were headed and that we weren't just doing this just for a play to see how it would go, because it took so much work and I still don't feel comfortable that I'm hearing that message, this is the way the University is going to go. Well not the whole University obviously, but a significant portion of the University's strategy may be devoted to this type of approach. *Innovator*

The importance of an environment that nourishes the inner work life of people who commit themselves to bringing about change is illustrated by this innovator's story.

> *Innovator:* there were two occasions at which I got to [in] the year when I said 'I have had enough . . . [but] I have a really strong working relationship [with Anna] and her ability to then re-motivate is very good. So she would say 'Okay, well what can we do? How can we find a way through it?' And actually I had the answers myself, it was just a case of actually being able to talk to somebody about it I suppose. So yes, part of that moving on process again was my own personal motivation and the motivation to continue with the projects for Anna.

> *Interviewer:* So her role was to empathize?

> *Innovator:* Yes, and motivate. Re-motivate and motivate and re-motivate.

11 A culture that values learning and an environment that encourages and enables people to share what they have learnt so that it can be reused or adapted to other contexts

If learning to do new and better things is the core enterprise in strategic change it is vital that new knowledge and understanding grown through the change process, is consolidated, made visible and distributed to other members of the organisation in ways that are appropriate and meaningful to them. Only then can what has been learnt be applied in other situations and contexts.

As John Cowan reminds us in his excellent book 'On Becoming an Innovative Teacher' (Cowan 2006), creating a successful innovation requires not only the process of creating new practice, but also the process of evaluating and refining that practice, in the light of experience. The deeper learning and meanings are only gleaned through this reflective and analytical process and these feed into the incremental refinements that ultimately make an innovation far more effective and meaningful. This process of taking stock and appreciating consequences is as important for organisations involved in innovation as it is for individual practitioners and this book and the interview process have provided a means to stimulate this process.

The dissemination of what has been leant remains an important processes in the SDP. Without this process important lessons will not be distributed to the people who need this knowledge.

> I think the reason the barriers are there is because the learning from developing that programme hasn't filtered to as many people as you might have hoped. So people are still saying 'No, you can't do it that way.' Yes we can. I suppose the worry I have is that when somebody new comes into this organization they are being told the old 'you can't do that' story, instead of the, 'yes we can do it' story, which is a bit of a worry really. *Innovator*

During the SDP the annual Solent eXchange conference provided a vehicle for dissemination of information and learning. The design of the conference changed during the course of the three years from an initial focus (Year 1) of trying to get more people involved and showing them how they can get involved, through sharing and celebrating achievements (Year 2 and 3) to focusing on sustaining new practices.

Innovators were also able to share the results of their work at a more local level. For example, the outcomes of the School of Design's SDP work (chapter 5) was shared with other members of the School at the annual School Away Day to which SDP Team members were invited. As a result of this the SDP Team commissioned a film to document and disseminate the results and the film was shown in the opening plenary session at the University's annual Solent Exchange conference—the main dissemination event for the SDP. The School also presented its work as a poster at the conference. In addition, learning gained through the School's involvement in SDP has been incorporated into university standards frameworks and staff have presented their work at Faculty staff development workshops and external conferences.

> I'd been asked by the Dean. to give a number of talks at conferences, again to share this experience and encourage other staff to take it on board. [as a result] A number of people have come to see me, from Film, Music and Journalism courses and they are very keen to run forums and they came back a few times to me to say, "This is how I've set it up. What do you think? What should I do with this?" *Innovator*

This brings us back to the important issue of meaningful communication and the plethora of ways and occasions through which people have formal and informal conversations. Creating opportunity for meaningful communication is as important after change has been accomplished as it is before and during the change process, remembering that to change an organisation you need to change a majority of conversations in the organisation (Seel 2004). The hope is that this book will help continue this organic process.

12 A culture that encourages people to take risks to put themselves in unfamiliar situations where they need to harness their creativity to actualise themselves

Accomplishing change—involves new ideas, new ways of thinking, new practices and new ways of being—it's an inherently creative process and ultimately it involves people becoming different and taking risks in order to achieve their self-determined goals.

Innovators viewed creation in terms of the invention of practice that was entirely new to them or existing practice that was significantly modified. They also recognised creation in new relationships and infrastructures to support new practice, and new policies and procedures to guide future practice. The real value of initiatives like SDP is in enabling people to realise their creative potential to actualise themselves to become who they want to become. Innovators and early adopters thrive in such a culture.

> due to the fact that I was doing something new allowed a level of creativity yes, I think when you are developing any aspect of the curriculum you are being 'creative', you have the feeling that you have the opportunity to 'shape' what is available for people/students to learn and you are 'creating' that learning experience. I personally find that a creative process. It isn't entirely without edges though, there are boundaries and quality considerations to work within but still, there is room within the set frameworks to 'create' the richness of content and the teaching

and learning strategies that encourage an inspirational learning process. *Innovator*

Academics are motivated to innovate by the ideas of helping their students learn, and through this to improve their chances in life. By creating a more imaginative and more effective curriculum they are helping their learners to actualise themselves. In the process of designing and implementing and new curriculum they are actualising themselves.

> I don't really call them students. I think they are designers or photographers or whatever the student is . . . .' You are actually working now, you are part of industry. What you are doing is part of a unit. It sort of carries the same risk as if you are doing it in business. The money is not involved where you could design a collection and it doesn't sell. Well, that is a risk. But the risk they are learning, no, because I think it enriched them. It was exactly the same as what we would do in a [commercial] unit, but we actually went further and actually said we are going to produce these to actually contextualize your whole learning process . . . . People usually stop at the . . . concept [stage]. You do the concept and then you say 'Actually here is what we are handing in on a sheet [of paper] and then it is done.' You don't really get a final outcome. You just sort of maybe theorize the work, but you don't actually actualize the work.

> This project allowed them [the students] to actually reach out and visualize what is possible. It is fantastic for me to . . . . see those students design and then see people wear [their garments] . . . . People are actually paying real money . . . . then it becomes something special, I think. That is my motivation for being in it. That is my motivation for being here, otherwise I would still be working in industry *Innovator*

Underpinning the SDP strategy was a belief that change will only happen if people do new things i.e. change comes from acting, doing and making rather than just thinking and talking about it. Another important belief underlying the strategy was that change must involve most of the people in the organisation.

CONCLUDING THOUGHTS

A self-actualising university

The secret of accomplishing strategic change is to engage and connect the people who want to actualise themselves through their innovations with the strategic changes the organisation wants to make

In trying to answer the question how does a university accomplish strategic change in which a large part of the educational change is brought about through the educational innovations of teachers, we discover that an organisation's strategic ambition and the will and creativity of the individuals who bring about change are intertwined.

In its mission and vision statements a university sets out where it believes its destiny and future identity lie but it is only through the concerted and deliberate actions of individuals and groups of individuals in its community, each of whom is striving to actualise their own vision and destiny, that the University achieves its ambition.

People leading and enacting change appear to be a particular type of person with the will to get involved in something and stay involved until the job is done. Not only do they generate ideas, they also like to actualise these ideas and they do not want to fail so they persist until they are satisfied. The will to complete something is a strong as the will to begin it.

It is the will to be and become a certain sort of person (like a better teacher) or to help others (like enabling students to learn better), or to develop a better system (to improve the support given to students, teachers or perhaps external employers and businesses), that provides the deep motivational force for many of the people who contributed to the Southampton Solent change project. The combination of challenge, personal autonomy, the desire for doing something new and the invention and mastery of new practice, and the belief that people are making a valuable contribution to the educational enterprise of students, were the most important factors that caused deep and sustained engagement in SDP projects.

What comes out of this process is not something that can easily be codified or quantified. What comes out of it are new relationships and new sorts of conversation within and outside the University, new forms of practice and models or approaches that can be re-used and adapted to other contexts, and new ways of seeing and understanding things—in other words culture that is different to what existed before.

> I think it has been very positive actually. Given all of the challenges that we faced with all of the projects I think everyone has faced challenges. It has been a positive

outcome. It has made us realise how much we can achieve when we set our minds to it. It has made us realise that our ideas can become reality and that those ideas can be put in place to actually enhance the students' experience and their learning and how they move on into industry. So I think it has really helped us to see how we can translate ideas into real outcomes that can make a difference to our curriculum and to enhancing the employability of the students. *Innovator*

These reflections provide the most uplifting message to emerge from this study. The idea that people are able to realise their ambitions and to actualise themselves through their work and in this process help their University achieve its strategic ambition.

With a complex story like the SDP there can be no closure because there is always more detail, more perspectives and more understanding to be drawn in to it and from it. This chapter has tried to make sense of SDP organisational change from a number of perspectives.

The consequences of the activity-led approach to change was that people who wanted to, or were persuaded to get involved in the SDP did things. They interacted, had conversations with other people, and built new or deepened existing relationships. They worked collaboratively with people who shared their interests. In short, the SDP engaged people in creating many new social practices. In doing so change became ingrained in local culture. Sites of emerging new practice became the 'battle ground' (local contentious practice) for bringing about change in institutional systems in order to accommodate new practices. Larger scale cultural effects (the way we do things here) are manifest in the preparedness of senior managers and leaders of the institution to think differently because they have new social practice models to work with. These conditions provide the starting point for more pervasive cultural change.

Change has occurred at all scales, at all levels and in all parts of the organisation, and in all forms (simple, complicated, complex and chaotic). The complexity of change can never be fully comprehended and all this book does is provide examples that can be used as a resource to think about change.

CHAPTER 14

Reflections on Leadership

Introduction

It was both daunting and exhilarating to be asked to prepare the bid to the Higher Education Funding Council for England within days of joining the University in October 2007. Here was a major opportunity to lead an ambitious change process which would accelerate our strategic plan and help to shape the future of the University. It was also a rare chance to adopt a holistic approach to change, to provide the time, space and support for genuine innovation and to break down some of the silos which exist in every university.

We all draw on our reserves of experience when faced with a difficult challenge; during my three decades as a lecturer and manager I had become very wary of the apparent reassurance provided by a grand 'masterplan'. The unorthodox behaviour of academics, the constant shifts in funding and the predominance of stewardship over management combine to produce a complex environment in universities. Experience suggested that while the bid needed to be imaginative, realistic and focused on clear outputs it also needed to leave sufficient space for the unexpected outcomes which would prove to be its most striking achievements.

WHAT DID WE LEARN?

During the following four and half years, we learned many valuable lessons about accomplishing complex change in a university. The fact that many of these lessons are simple does not of course mean that the change process was easy: far from it.

Perhaps our first lesson was to have confidence in the creative potential of staff within the University, although it is not always a straightforward matter to translate this belief into successful change. As George Bain's perceptive observation quoted in chapter one shows, universities are full of new ideas but often struggle to convert them into action. We discovered that this reluctance is also context-specific: as one of Britain's newest universities, we seemed to lack confidence in our strengths, capabilities and creativity.

The SDP propelled a wave of confidence through the University as ideas were translated into action and actions delivered results. This was not purely about additional resources but about believing in our collective capacity to tackle the 'wicked challenge' of strategic change.

To achieve this, we had to be prepared to use an approach to change which recognised that the conventional 'technical rational' perspective on change programmes does not fit easily with the structures and cultures of universities, let alone with the tribal disciplinary territories and loyalties of academic staff. We had to resist the powerful temptation to 'master-plan' and to over-bureaucratise the process.

Underpinning Philosophy

The strategic change programme aimed at deep organisational change which covered not only the objectives of our new Strategic Plan—delivering more flexible provision, helping students to succeed, developing new forms of progression and forging innovative partnerships with employers and the wider community—but also required changes to the underpinning infrastructure of quality assurance, business systems and associated organisational development. This holistic approach closely aligned to the Strategic Plan has been a fundamental aspect of our change programme. There was no tension between the two, indeed a clear strength of the Strategic Development Programme was its reinforcement of the core values of the University as embodied in the Strategic Plan—particularly our commitment to students and our concern for social justice. This helped staff to identify with the aspirations of the programme and provides a powerful means to maintain momentum and move further forward.

The central team which managed the project was crucial in conveying the message that this was going to be a different approach. We deliberately established their role as enablers working through the ideas of others rather than implementers of top down ideas, or planners gathering data, identifying specific problems and implementing tightly defined solutions. This was not easy at first, either for members of the SDP team who had come from external commercial organisations or for those established staff who were involved in leading projects. These colleagues struggled initially to let go of well-rehearsed project management techniques and learn to deal with the occasional frustration of unconventional delivery patterns and outcomes that had not been predicted in project bids.

From the outset we were clear that listening, waiting and maximising opportunities as they surfaced would be key to success. Letting go is difficult for many managers and purposeful inaction, in the belief that good things will eventually emerge, is counter intuitive. But both are crucial factors in allowing change to happen. There are echoes throughout the case study accounts in this book from colleagues who achieved change because they felt trusted to interpret our direction of travel and, more importantly, felt able to try to change without fear of blame if they were not successful. In the process, we learned that our approach mirrored theories of change in organisations that behave as complex adaptive systems (CAS). As we reflected on what we were doing, we drew upon the huge literature on complexity in organisations, viewed from the intersection of complexity science and management studies. As the Vice-Chancellor has pointed out in his foreword, we had the same experience as Moliere's character in the 'Le Bourgeois Gentilhomme' who discovered that he had been speaking prose all his life. Our willingness to embrace many perspectives was a key feature of our approach to change; our external evaluators endorsed this approach in their assessment of its effectiveness:

> At Southampton Solent University complex adaptive systems (CAS) has been implemented well, with strong attention being paid to CAS watchwords: broad involvement; shared purpose; low-resolution initial planning; inclusive decision-making; participant engagement; encouragement of challenges to the status quo; high quality information; self-organization; acceptance of diversity; delayed movement to consensus. (Davies and Trowler 2013: 7)

The Value of Conversation

Encouraging conversation was an essential part of our approach. We emphasized the importance of constant dialogue and cross-institutional discussion as a means of engaging an ever-widening circle of participants. This became the powerful theme running through SDP events such as our annual conferences where we used the strapline, 'the value is in the conversation'. These 'Solent eXchange' events were open to all staff across the University and encouraged discussion which crossed the usual faculty or professional service boundaries. Through these conversations we were trying to encourage the idea that the whole organisation was involved in the change process. The results of projects were shared, contributions were invited from staff and students, the perspectives of employers and partner colleges were discussed and, most important, staff began to talk about change. In this way the members of the University were able to progressively share and build their own understandings of how the changes were reshaping the University and what these changes meant for them.

The increasing pace of university life for both academic and professional service staff has reduced opportunities for the type of conversations which encourage collaboration or remove misunderstandings before they become insuperable obstacles. Finance procedures, quality assurance processes and employment policies are often seen as impediments by academic staff. Through the new opportunities for conversation we were able to create, professional service colleagues provided some of the most imaginative solutions to overcoming what staff perceived as obstacles to change. For example, before flexible delivery could become a reality, the University had to devise a quality assurance framework which balanced academic rigour with speed of response to employer demands for short courses. The Professional Development Awards Framework was the creative response of the relevant professional service and this liberated the creativity of academic staff to design entirely new learning opportunities to meet the interests and needs of employers or people in employment.

Liberating Creativity

We learned that creativity is not the preserve of any one part of a university or particular functional roles or individuals. It was evident among all those who championed individual SDP projects, whether large or small, wherever they were based. The success of the programme owed much to the considerable personal investment by these innovators who were 'joining up the strategic dots'. A number of the projects represented in the case studies were led by middle managers, reinforcing our conviction that change is not limited to 'top-down' or 'bottom-up' approaches but can also be 'middle-out'. We also recognised the value of capturing and bringing new structures and ways of doing things into the institution from the world outside ie 'outside-in'.

A certain amount of conflict is inevitable when creativity meets systems and procedures that were not designed to accommodate emerging practice. In such situations good communication between innovators and the central services is essential as is the commitment to finding a way to make it work. As the case studies show this was not always achieved, particularly early on in the project, and it led to frustration. Our lesson for the future is to pay closer attention to these areas of conflict and, where appropriate, to provide support to mediate them.

Importance of Bridge Builders

As the case studies in this volume demonstrate, universities are full of talented and creative people but they often need help to 'bridge' across traditional, vertical hierarchies in order to turn their ideas into reality. Essential to achieving change were the 'bridge-builders', the enablers who worked across the conventional faculty and service silos to engage participants, communicate our shared purpose, overcome barriers and support the early adopters. The small central team was a vital group of bridge-builders led by an exceptionally able Programme Director; the tireless efforts of the team were absolutely critical to the success of the SDP, helping to connect people across the organisation, tackling procedural, structural or managerial obstacles and supporting champions of change at local level. Cultural translation is an important part of the role of the bridge builder, especially where a change programme is seen as yet another 'managerial' initiative. As one colleague noted:

> I have worked here a long time and I knew that the culture of the organisation was such that people resisted the management edict, in common with most HE institutions.

Key members of staff in the core team and middle managers, played an important role in translating and mediating our strategic objectives so that staff could interpret and act on them in their own contexts.

We also realised that we needed bridge-builders who connect us more effectively to the external world to achieve significant change. Their role was to mediate the University's relationship with employers, helping to translate the language and culture of external organisations, such as the National Health Service or national retailers, and in turn connect university staff with external opportunities. Universities have many high-level contacts with external organisations but meaningful connections are difficult to establish on the basis of occasional meetings of senior staff. Secondees from external organisations were key to identifying and nurturing collaborative work across an unimagined range of areas—for example, Fine Art students were able to secure opportunities to display their work to thousands of hospital visitors—and the external bridge-builders helped to shape an innovative move by the University into the congested field of health education.

Academics who have pursued their entire career in universities are not always well placed to judge the interests of employers so we created new posts and recruited people who had already developed strong links with the business community and were able to represent their interests and needs. Through their established contacts they identified potential for collaboration with employers by creating educational programmes that not only met their needs but also validated their own training and education. This gave us important new capacities to meet one of our main strategic goals.

Sensitivity to Context

Within the same university there are many different cultures and ways of working and sensitivity to context was vital. Academic staff in Applied Sport Science, for example, have a strong culture of teamwork while those in Photography or Fashion emphasise individual creativity. The case study of the Design School acknowledged the need for adaptability in dealing with highly creative people; introducing the commercial dimensions of the School's project into an academic environment was described as 'like putting a square into a circle'. The reward for sensitivity to context was seeing most of the projects 'growing legs', because people who were able to see value in a new practice felt able to adapt it to their own context. The net effect was for SDP educational innovations to extend their influence in directions which could never have been anticipated. In this way, the outputs were far more substantial than the specific targets required by HEFCE and sustainability emerged as a natural consequence of the work.

Willingness to Work Flexibly

At a general institutional level, the ebb and flow of the academic calendar is a highly specific characteristic of university life. Annual cycles of admissions, induction, assessment and graduation are firmly understood by the academic or professional services staff whose working patterns are determined by them. Devising rigid project timelines which cut right across these cycles would have alienated staff and jeopardised the outcomes of the programme. The SDP team had to work flexibly around these core business processes. This produced results at every level of the University. For example, one of the most notable meetings during the regular visits of the HEFCE scrutiny team involved a group of early career administrative staff from within a faculty. These junior staff gave an impressively confident presentation of their ideas on improving the experience of students on a blended learning degree, all drawn from their front-line familiarity with the issues. Their project had emerged from SDP support which was carefully wrapped around their working schedules rather than imposing new timescales and commitments which would have cut across their day jobs at peak times. This sensitivity to context had encouraged them to develop their ideas, implement improvements and begin to discuss similar approaches with other faculty teams. Their work has evolved further into partnership working with academic staff around a common interest in improving the student experience.

Resources and Resourcefulness

There is no doubt that the scale, depth and speed of change could not have been accomplished without additional resources. But there is also no doubt that we would have pursued the same strategic objectives had we been entirely reliant on our own ability to fund strategic change. Progress would have been slower but would have been helped by the considerable advantage that neither investment in our business systems nor changes to our quality assurance procedures were ever reliant on SDP funding. Our fall back plan would have involved some tough internal choices, probably curtailing investment in faculties and services to establish the necessary resources. It is important to set SDP in a financial context, however: HEFCE was providing us with approximately £1.3 million per annum after overheads had been deducted, representing the equivalent of 1.3% of our total income.

In fact, almost as crucial as the amount of funding, was the strong sense of external endorsement which came from HEFCE's investment in the SDP. In the same vein, it also became clear to us that legitimising the ideas brought forward by staff as they bid for SDP funds was often as important as offering the resources to support them. The bidding process was of value in saying that the University had trust and confidence in them.

Many of our innovation projects were accomplished for relatively modest sums confirming that creative and resourceful staff can achieve much with little, and a number of innovators drew additional resources into their enterprise. But several case studies show that the resources allocated to projects did not compensate staff for the time they put into the project. With the benefit of hindsight this should have been foreseen. The lesson we have learned is that innovation needs to be funded according to the needs that emerge through the process of invention and not according to an estimation based on a limited appreciation of what the change will actually involve.

Another lesson we have learned is to try to keep bureaucracy to a minimum: short simple proposals and simple reporting procedures both to account for the additional resources and to monitor progress. Academics with heavy teaching loads have little time or inclination to bid for money to undertake a new project if it involves a lot of paper work. The central team was very helpful in facilitating the process by helping individuals formulate their proposals and format bids in ways that met the requirements of the University Management Board overseeing the SDP. The team also facilitated the monitoring process by gathering progress reports through direct conversation with each project leader.

Through our experience we recognised that resources need to be aligned in real-time to the work of our champions—something we did not always resolve satisfactorily over the past three years. Where we did, the benefits far outweighed the costs. We also recognise that to continue the approach we have used to accomplish change, an innovation fund or equivalent source of funding for bottom-up proposals would need to be established.

Evaluation and Accountability

Throughout the three years of the SDP it was important for us to test our ideas and to receive regular feedback from both our internal and external evaluators. Working in an emergent way without the comforting presence of a detailed master plan can lead to moments of doubt and vulnerability. Continuous feedback was vital to know that what we were doing was worth doing and to develop understanding of the overall effects of our approach. We had consciously avoided the establishment of special governance arrangements in an effort to streamline bureaucracy. The University's existing Management Board was used as the programme board for the SDP, receiving regular monitoring reports from the SDP team and overseeing the allocation of funds for larger projects. This provided a means of ensuring that all of the senior managers in faculties and services, including the Vice-Chancellor's Group, were kept abreast of the SDP although pressure of business often led to heavily time-constrained discussion. The tension between breadth of involvement by all members of Management Board and depth of oversight of the programme was never fully resolved but this was outweighed by the value of locating SDP in the mainstream of university life.

The HEFCE regional team maintained careful oversight of the programme with bi-annual visits and regular requests for monitoring reports. The visits provided a particularly useful opportunity for dialogue and a deepened understanding of the programme. Additional useful input was generated by our external evaluators from Lancaster University, an experienced team who agreed to act as critical friends to the SDP and to produce formal qualitative reports for HEFCE. Their final report was to provide us with a clear reflection of our underpinning philosophy, our ongoing challenges and our achievements.

ACHIEVEMENTS

Virtually all the targets that were set out in the SDP Plan around employer engagement, flexible delivery and progression were successfully delivered. The only exception was the target for co-funded provision, which was overtaken by the new tuition fee regime, and the progression routes from the diplomas, which were phased out by the new coalition government. In achieving these targets the University has already established some future development trajectories: for example, the co-designed and delivered courses in health have established a completely new area of provision. Within a year Solent had become the largest provider of the Foundation Degree in Health and Social Care within the NHS Local Education and Training Board for the Wessex Region.

The preparedness of the SDP team to avoid a 'one size fits all' approach to employer engagement allowed staff to interpret this objective in many different ways. The impact of the recession and the predominance of micro-businesses in the creative industries presented particular challenges and led to an imaginative use of live client briefs routed through an internal agency, 'Solent Creatives'. The agency also enabled hundreds of students to gain real work opportunities that were relevant to their career aspirations, and supported students in creating their own businesses. Thus one new organisation has been able to create three totally different ways of engaging employers and connecting students to real world business opportunities.

Again and again, ideas such as this emerged from across the University to populate the list of required outcomes. The fact that these ideas were deeply-rooted in the aspirations of individual staff—such as the Superyacht Academy—or groups of staff—such as the online learning platform developed by the Learning Technologies Team, provided them with powerful currency beyond the life of the programme. The ultimate challenge will be to sustain these innovations if or when the staff responsible for them leave the University.

Some SDP achievements have already gained independent momentum. The Schools and College Sports Partnership programme outlined in one of the case studies has become a key part of the curriculum for Sports Coaching students and is now one of the largest programmes of its kind in the UK. Over 80 hours a week of after-school sports coaching is now offered to pupils across two-thirds of Southampton's schools. The interconnection between the different strands of the SDP is particularly evident in the extent to which this extra-curricular activity raises the educational aspirations of children from some of Southampton's most disadvantaged areas.

The SDP prompted re-alignment of existing structures and procedures to accommodate innovation. The work of the small employer engagement team, for example, was absorbed by a restructured Careers Service, which had in turn responded to the increasing emphasis on student employability by becoming an Employability and Enterprise team. Many of the achievements of the SDP had inbuilt sustainability—they had 'grown legs'—or, as in the case of the Schools and College Sports Partnership, they had become part of the core curriculum. The external evaluation report picked up the theme of an SDP journey and the qualities which will maintain future momentum:

> The SDP had enabled SSU to highlight and then reinforce its strengths. As a whole, it now feels proud about the qualities it actually possesses and anticipates that this greater awareness of its strengths will help it to continue along the path which the SDP started. This was termed its "distinctiveness trajectory" (Davies and Trowler 2013:9)

FUTURE DIRECTIONS

The SDP helped us create a stronger sense of identity and distinctiveness. How much further forward do we need to move on this 'distinctiveness trajectory'? The SDP has left us with another valuable lesson: we need to remain adaptable and flexible, drawing on the insights of our entire community, including our students, and our partner institutions and employers, in order to meet future challenges in the uncertain world of higher education.

The future trajectory is already evident in the business systems strand of the SDP. The work on the business systems was particularly demanding. This was an area where conventional project management was essential. The SDP surfaced the need for more explicit governance arrangements for individual IT projects and has also led to a step-change in our approach to the development of our corporate business systems. The University has recognized that ongoing development of these systems is not optional in a more competitive HE environment and further investment will be needed. To take one example, the attendance monitoring system was always conceptualised as the first stage of a programme focussed on student engagement. This is a multi-faceted programme involving the front-line faculty administrative staff, the Faculty Student Support Network Officers, specialist central services and academic staff. The data on student attendance helps to identify those who are beginning to disengage and allows a co-ordinated approach to student support; the SDP could only begin the work in this area and we now need to accomplish more.

Strategic change is not an event but a continually unfolding and never ending process. The University is in the final year of the strategic plan that created the SDP but continuity will be secured through the new strategic planning process. This will reinforce the culture change which was so fundamental to the long-term sustainability of the achievements of the SDP.

Changing culture

At the heart of our strategic change process lay the ambition to bring about a change in institutional culture. We always recognised that the sustainability of the programme and our ability to be the agile institution we intended to be would depend on the extent to which we could effect cultural change as part of our organisational change project. We learned that observing change in language was a vitally important way of measuring the deep institutional shifts which were occurring during the three years of the programme. As Shotter and Tsoukas (2011) point out in their study of language-based change in organisations:

> Change in language amounts to change in how problems are viewed, experience and managed . . . Generating and managing change is a matter of shifting conversations, since when this happens, people shift to what they talk about and pay attention to . . . . change is change *in* language, rather than change through language . . . In so far as people in organisations tell stories about themselves, change comes about by telling *different* stories, while the work of the change agent is to facilitate the process of story re-telling.(Shotter and Tsoukas 2011: 334-5)

In the early phase of the SDP, the small central team often reported the question 'Am I allowed to . . .' when in discussion with those wanting to take forward projects. Three years later in their final report our external evaluators note the existence of a more 'can do' philosophy across the University:

> By its very nature, organisational culture is intangible, but staff at SSU consistently describe the University as now having more of a 'yes we can' culture where staff are far more comfortable in negotiating the challenges facing the higher education sector (Davies and Trowler 2013:10-11).

Change in language has become apparent in other contexts. One of the key targets of the SDP was to improve the employment prospects of our graduates by ensuring that every student was exposed to work-related experience in their course. Embedding employability in the curriculum is a challenge which mirrors many of the earlier debates around integrating study skills, in particular the reluctance of academic staff to sacrifice disciplinary content for perceived 'extra-curricular' activities. The language of employability has changed at Solent over the last three years. The SDP encouraged relationships with employers, as seen in the case study for the School of Design, and in the work spearheaded by Solent Creatives for embedding live client briefs in the curriculum. The University's existing processes of validation and periodic academic review of the curriculum began to internalise the language of employability and fewer voices now question the role of academics in supporting the drive to improve the employment prospects of our students.

Stronger Sense of Identity

The SDP aimed to create a more distinctive institution with a clear place in the changing HE landscape. When the original bid was devised in 2007-8 Solent was still finding its feet as one of the UK's newest universities. SDP has helped us develop a much stronger sense of who we are and the values that underpin our place in the HE world. As the external evaluators noted:

> SSU had been energised by its recently acquired status as a University, and the SDP was viewed as a means of strengthening it by providing a distinctive portfolio of courses and innovative ways of working with employers and non-traditional student communities. (Davies and Trowler 2013: 1)

In the turbulent environment of contemporary higher education, the tactics previously adopted by many institutions of belonging to an 'undifferentiated centre', covering a wide range of activity and able to move in numerous directions, may have run their course. As Kennie and Price note:

> The new 'battle zone' for HEIs is very much focused around finding ways to redefine priorities so as to avoid trying to be 'all things to all people'. This is not to argue for an oversimplification into 'research-intensive' versus 'teaching-focused' distinctions but to create interesting narratives which reflect the balance and interplay between the different areas of activity which make up a modern HEI and offer adequate differentiation (Kennie and Price 2012:12)

The 2008-13 Strategic Plan offered a clear framework for differentiation; the Strategic Development Programme aimed to accelerate progress towards achieving the plan and, in the process secure both distinctiveness and long-term sustainability. The University has created a new narrative, positioning itself as innovative, willing to take risks and less bound by traditional hierarchies and structures. The SDP has taken the University a long way towards achieving its objectives in a relatively short time. More importantly among the crowd of 'business-facing' universities we intend to remain clearly marked out by aligning our concern for social justice, our commitment to education and our obligations to support our students with the interests of business and the wider community.

Coping with the unexpected

In any large programme there are some intentions that are not fully realised. In the first year of the SDP considerable management time was devoted to a key initiative in securing new forms of progression: a proposed merger with a local FE College. The timing was not right and the merger talks failed. As the higher education landscape becomes more turbulent and competition for students increases, encouraging progression becomes even more critical and mergers are a matter of discussion in the HE press. In their analysis of distinctive models in the future ecosystem of higher education Kennie and Price (2012) identify a 'vertically integrated' structure:

> The 'merged multiversities' might emerge and gain competitive advantage from their ability to build close and sustainable partnerships between part of the school system, the further education college sector involved in higher education delivery and in some cases with limited private sector providers (Davies and Trowler 2012:6).

Any organisation that embarks on a sustained programme of change knows that the world outside will not stand still. The world within and beyond higher education changed dramatically during the life of the Strategic Development Programme. We started writing the bid in 2007 before the onset of the most severe global economic crisis since the Wall Street Crash of 1929. These have been exceptionally tough years for new graduates seeking employment and there are serious and highly-publicised risks of a 'lost generation'. As the recession has deepened it has also become more difficult for those universities trying to work more closely with employers. Much careful preparation for co-funded provision, co-delivery or co-location with employers disappeared almost overnight as businesses collapsed or reined in their 'non-core' activities. To compound the problem for English universities, the current government's response to its fiscal crisis included a radical revision of the funding mechanism for higher education with the cost of tuition transferred from the state to students. This has been accompanied by *ad hoc* policy changes aimed at creating a market in English higher education, initially though a bidding process for additional student numbers, then through the encouragement of lower-cost, private providers and, more recently, through the introduction of unregulated admission for students.

One of the goals of SDP was to enable the University to be more agile, not only to respond to new opportunities but to cope with and quickly adapt to changes in the external environment. The SDP created a framework for more flexible provision, allowing the University to open the new curriculum area of health, to respond to employers' demands for in-company provision and to offer more opportunities for distance and blended learning. Within three years a more diverse student body and the delivery of courses co-designed by employers have both become realities. Keeping pace with these changes, the improvement of the core business systems of the University helps us to face the challenge of an increasingly marketised environment.

AN OPTIMISTIC FUTURE

Organisational change can never be a single story. This book has tried to tell the stories of nearly sixty people who were involved in the Strategic Development Programme. The external evaluators examined some of these interviews and reached the following conclusions about the staff perspective on their future:

> A new culture within SSU was considered to be a somewhat intangible but, nevertheless, vital force that would help sustain change. This new culture was described as confident, willing to take risks, and more likely to adopt an institutional perspective rather than a subject or faculty one. It was also more proactive and accepting of the need to instigate and promote change from different levels of the University rather than have change passed down from senior management. The SDP has been important in changing the culture at SSU and for assisting staff in recognising the qualities the institution possessed which provided it with a strong position within a turbulent policy and funding environment (Davies and Trowler 2013:9).

Perhaps most encouragingly, staff are more confident and realistic about their future.

> . . . they were also conscious of the fact that when SDP funding ceased there needed to be other forces responsible for both maintaining existing developments and identifying the next wave of changes. The principal forces thought likely to fulfil this role were: the new culture at SSU; the scaling up of small changes through the use of exemplars; business systems designed to accommodate and promote rapid and flexible response to opportunities;

and locating SSU on a "distinctiveness trajectory" where the strengths of the institution would shape its future path. (Davies and Trowler 2012:6)

At the heart of the SDP was the wicked challenge confronting all universities: How can we become the University we need to become so that we can enable our students to prepare for a complex, uncertain and sometimes disruptive world? As this book shows, through the resourcefulness, inventiveness and hard work of our staff, we have engaged purposefully and imaginatively with this challenge and in the process we have gained confidence in the value of a different approach to university leadership in the twenty-first century.

References

Davies, P. and Trowler, P. (2013) 'Southampton Solent University Strategic Development Programme: Final Evaluation', unpublished report for the Higher Education Funding Council, January 2013.

Kennie, T. and Price, I (2012) *Disruptive innovation and the higher education ecosystem post-2012* Leadership Foundation for Higher Education, Stimulus Paper

Shotter, J. and Tsoukas, H. (2011) 'Complex Thought, Simple Talk: An Ecological Approach to Language-Based Change in Organizations', in P. Allen, S.Maguire and B. McKelvey (eds), *The Sage Handbook of Complexity and Management*

REFERENCES

Alderfer, C. P. (1980) The Methodology of Organizational Diagnosis, *Professional Psychology*, 11: 459-68.

Avey, J.B., Avolio, B., Crossley, C. Luthans, F. (2009) Psychological Ownership: Theoretical Extensions, Measurement, and Relation to Work Outcomes. Nebraska University Management Department Faculty Publications. Paper 18. http://digitalcommons.unl.edu/managementfacpub/18

Bain, G. (2004) Leading and Managing Universities. European University Association/EFMD Workshop Paper available on-line at: http://www.eua.be/eua/jsp/en/upload/Bain_Keynote.1096538364192.pdf

Bain, G. (2007) Leading Universities. In B. Conraths and A. Trusso (ed) Managing the University Community: Exploring Good Pratice. European University Association Case Studies Brussels 13-15

Becher, T. (1989), *Academic Tribes and Territories*, Buckingham, SRHE &Open University Press.

Becher, T. (1994), 'The significance of disciplinary differences', *Studies in Higher Education* 19, 2, 151-161.

Belk, R. W. (1988). Possessions and the extended self. Journal of Consumer Research, 15, 139-168.

Belmont. N. (2012) Knowledge Economy 2.0: Fulfilling the needs of the modern-day workforce. Stanford Social Innovation Review. Available on—line at http://www.ssireview.org/blog/entry/knowledge_economy_2.0

Blackler, F. Crump, N. and McDonald, S. (2000), 'Organizing Processes in Complex Activity Networks,' *Organization*, 7, 2, 277-300.

Bore, A. and Wright, N. (2009) The wicked and complex in education: developing a transdisciplinary perspective for policy formulation, implementation and professional practice. Journal of Education for Teaching, 35, 3, 241-256

Braxton, J. M. (1995), 'Disciplines with an affinity for the improvement of undergraduate education,' in Hativa, N. and Maarincovich, M. (eds) *Disciplinary Differences in Teaching and Learning: Implications for Practice,* San Francisco, Jossey-Bass, 59-64.

Camillus, J.C. (2008) Strategy as a Wicked Problem, Harvard Business Review. Available at: http://hbr.org/2008/05/strategy-as-a-wicked-problem/ar/1

Capra, F. (1997) The Web of Life: A New Synthesis of Mind and Matter. London: Flamingo

Cashin, W. E. and Downey, R. G. (1995), 'Disciplinary differences in what is taught', in: Hativa, N. and Marincovich, M. (eds). *Disciplinary Differences in Teaching and Learning: Implications for Practice*, Jossey-Bass: San Francisco 59-64.

Christensen, C. M. and Eyring, H.J. (2011) The Innovative University: Changing the DNA of Higher Education from the Inside Out. Jossey—Bass: San Fancisco

Christensen, C. Allworth, J. and Dillon, K. (2012) How Will You Measure Your Life? Boston: *Harvard Business Review.*

Cresswell, J. W. and Roskens, R. W. (1981), 'The Biglan studies of differences among academic areas', *Review of Higher Education* 4, 3, 1-16.

Deal, T. E. and Kennedy, A. A. (1982*), Corporate cultures, The rites and rituals of corporate life.* Reading MA, Addison-Wesley.

Deci, E. L. and Ryan, R. M. (2000) The 'What' and 'Why' of Goal Pursuits: Human Needs and the Self-determination of Behavior, *Psychological Inquiry*, 11: 227-68.

Dittmar, H. (1992). The social psychology of material possessions: To have is to be. New York: St. Martin's Press.

Dobson, S. and McNay, I. (1996), 'Organizational culture', in D. Warner and D. Palfreyman (eds.) *Higher Education Management*, Buckingham, SRHE & Open University Press 16-32.

Engeström, Y. (1987) Learning by Expanding: An activity-theoretical approach to developmental research, Helsinki: Orienta-Konsultit Oy.

Eraut, M. (2009) How Professionals Learn through Work. In N. Jackson (ed.) *Learning to be Professional through a Higher Education.* Online at http://learningtobeprofessional.pbworks.com/How-professionals-learn-through-work (accessed 03/01/11).

Ewell, P. (2004) Across the Grain: Learning from Reform Initiatives in Undergraduate Education. Change Academy Handbook Higher Education Academy available at: www.heacademy.ac.uk/assets/documents/

resources/database/id548_co   mplex_change_in_heis_paper3.doc
accessed 14/09/12

Fullan, M. (1993), *The New Meaning of Educational Change*, London: Cassell.

Fullan, M. (1999), *Change Forces the Sequel*, Falmer Press.

Fullan, M. (2003a) Change Forces: With A Vegeance London RoutledgeFalmer

Fullan M (2003b) Education in Motion. Leading in a Culture of Change Michael Fullan Handbook: UK and Ireland Workshop Tour May 2003

Gibbs, G. (2000), 'Are the pedagogies of the disciplines really different?', in Rust, C. (ed.) *Improving student learning through the disciplines*, Oxford Centre for Staff and Learning Development.

Hannan, A. and Silver, H. (2000), *Innovating in Higher Education*. Buckingham, SRHE & Open University Press.

Hativa, N. (1997), 'Teaching in a research university: Professor's conceptions, practices and disciplinary differences', Paper presented at the Annual Meeting of the American Educational Research Association Chicago March 1997.

Hativa, N. and Marincovich, M. (eds.) (1995), *Disciplinary Differences in Teaching and Learning: Implications for Practice*, Jossey-Bass: San Francisco.

Heifetz R and Linsky M (2002) Leadership on the line. Boston: Harvard Business School Press.

HEFCE (2006) Strategic Development Fund. HEFCE May 2006/15.

Available on-line at: http://www.hefce.ac.uk/pubs/hefce/2006/06_15/ Higgins, E. T. (1997). Beyond pleasure and pain. American Psychologist, 52, 1280-1300.

Higgins, E. T. (1998). Promotion and prevention: Regulatory focus as a motivational principle. In M. P. Zanna (Ed.), Advances in experimental social psychology, Vol. 30, (1-46). New York: Academic Press.

Holland, J.H. (1992) In M. Waldrop (ed) Complexity: The Emerging Science at the Edge of Order and Chaos. Simon and Schuster, New York.

Jackson, N. J. (2002) The Complexity and Messiness of Change, In N. J Jackson (ed) Engaging and Changing Higher Education through

Brokerage. Ashgate Press available on line at: http://www.amazon.com/ Engaging-Changing-Education-Brokerage--Monitoring/dp/0754631486 accessed 14/09/12

Kark, R., & Van Dijk, D. (2007). Motivation to lead, motivation to follow: The role of the self regulatory focus in leadership processes. Academy of Management Review, 32, 500-528.

Pierce, J. L., Kostova, T., & Dirks, K. T. (2001). Toward a theory of psychological ownership in organizations. Academy of Management Review, 26, 298-310.

Pierce, J. L., Kostova, T., & Dirks, K. T. (2003). The state of psychological ownership: Integrating and extending a century of research. Review of General Psychology, 7, 84-107.

Pierce, J. L., O'Driscoll, M. P., & Coghlan, A. M. (2004). Work environment structure and psychological ownership: The mediating effects of control. Journal of Social Psychology, 144, 507-534.

Kanter, R. M. (1992), *The change masters: corporate entrepreneurs at work*, Routledge.

Kasper, G. and Clohsey, S (2008) Intentional Innovation: How getting more systematic about innovation could improve philanthropy and increase social impact. Kellogg Foundation Report available at: http://www. clohesyconsulting.com/PDFfiles/kellog_full_report.pdf accessed 14/09/12

Kaufman, J.C., and Beghetto, R.A. (2009) Beyond Big and Little: The Four C Model of Creativity. *Review of General Psychology* 13, 1, 1-12.

Kenny, J. (2003). A research based model for managing strategic educational change and innovation projects. Research and Development in Higher Education, Vol. 26, pp.333-342. Proceedings of HERDSA Conference (2003), Christchurch, New Zealand. http://surveys.canterbury. ac.nz/herdsa03/pdfsref/Y1102.pdf

Knight, P. T. and Trowler, P. R. (2000), 'Department-level cultures and improvement of learning and teaching', *Studies in Higher Education,* 20, 69-83.

Kolb, D. A. (1981), 'Learning styles and disciplinary differences', in Chickering, A. (ed.) *The Modern American College*, San Francisco, Josey-Bass.

Maslow, A. H. (1943) Theory of Human Motivation, *Psychological Review*, 50: 370-96.

Mulgan G, Wilkie N, Tucker S, Rushanara A, Davis F and Liptrot T (2006) Social Silicon Valleys: a manifesto for social innovation: what it is, why it matters and how it can be accelerated The Young Foundation Available at: http://www.youngfoundation.org/files/images/SocialSiliconValleys_06. pdf accessed 13/09/12

Neumann, R (2001), 'Disciplinary differences and university teaching', *Studies in Higher Education*, 26, 2, 135-146.

Pearce, C. L. and Conger, J. A. (2003) Shared Leadership—Reframing the Hows and Whys of Leadership Sage: Thousand Oaks California

Phills, J. A. Jr., Deiglmeier, K., and Miller, D.T. (2008) Rediscovering Social Innovation Stanford Social Innovation Review. Available on-line at: http://www.ssireview.org/articles/entry/rediscovering_social_innovation Accessed 26/10/12

Ritchie T (2011) Wicked Problems: Structuring Social Messes with Morphological Analysis Swedish Morphological Society. Available at: *http://www.swemorph.com/pdf/wp.pdf*

Rittel, H., and M. Webber (1973) Dilemmas in a General Theory of Planning. Policy Sciences, Vol. 4, 155-169

Rogers, E.M. (1995). Diffusion of innovations. 4th Edition. The Free Press, Simon & Schuster, New York.

Ryan, R. M. and Deci, E. L. (2000). Self-determination Theory and the Facilitation of Intrinsic Motivation, Social Development, and Well-being, *American Psychologist*, 55: 68-78.

Sawhney, M, Wolcott, R.C. and Arroniz, I (2011) The 12 different ways for companies to innovate. MITSloan Management Review Winter 2011 available at sloanreview.mit.edu/files/2011/06/INS0111-Top-Ten-Innovation.pdf accessed 13/09/12

Seel, R. (2000), "Complexity and Culture: New Perspectives on Organisational Change", *Organisations & People*, Vol. 7 No. 2, pp. 2-9. (Also Seel 2004 at: http://www.new-paradigm.co.uk/culture-complex. htm) Seel, R. (2004) The Nature of Organisational Change. HE Academy/ Leadership Foundation Change Academy Handbook also http://www.new-paradigm.co.uk/articles.htm

Smelby, J. (1996), 'Disciplinary differences in university teaching', *Studies in Higher Education* 21, 1, 69-79.

Snowden, D. (2000) Cynefin: A Sense of Time and Space, the Social Ecology of Knowledge Management. In C. Despres and D. Chauvel (eds) *Knowledge Horizons: The Present and the Promise of Knowledge Management,* Boston: Butterworth Heinemann.

Snowden, D. J. and Boone, M. (2007) A Leader's Framework for Decision Making. *Harvard Business Review,* November: 69-76.

Soares and Morgan 2011).

Speirn S, Mosle A and Reis T (2008) Foreword in G. Kasper and S, Clohsey Intentional Innovation: How getting more systematic about innovation could improve philanthropy and increase social impact. Kellogg Foundation Report available at:

http://www.clohesyconsulting.com/PDFfiles/kellog_full_report.pdf accessed 14/09/12

Stacey, R. D. (1996) Strategic management and organizational dynamics. 2nd edition London, Pitman.

Stacey, R. D. (2000) Strategic Management and Organisational Dynamics: the Challenge of Complexity. London: Routledge.

Stacey, R. D., Griffin, D. and Shaw, P. (2000), *Complexity and Management: fad or radical challenge to systems thinking?,* London: Routledge.

Stephenson, J. (1998) The Concept of Capability and Its Importance in Higher Education. In J. Stephenson and M. Yorke (eds) *Capability and Quality in Higher Education,* London: Kogan Page.

Thomas, P. (2006) Integrating Primary Health Care: Leading, Managing and Facilitating. Oxford: Radcliffe Publishing

Trowler, P. (1998), *Academics Responding to Change: new higher education frameworks and academic cultures,* Buckingham, SRHE & Open University Press.

Trowler, P. and Knight, P. T. (2001), 'Social Practice Policy Innovations: exploring the implementation gap', in P. Trowler, (ed.) *Higher Education Policy and Institutional Change: intentions and outcomes in turbulent environments,* Buckingham, SRHE & Open University Press.

Trowler, P., Saunders, M. and Knight, K (2003) Change Thinking Change Practices. Gloucester: Higher Education Academy.

Van Dyne, L., & Pierce, J. L. (2004). Psychological ownership and feelings of possession: Three field studies predicting employee attitudes and organizational citizenship behaviours. Journal of Organizational Behaviour, 25, 439-459.

Wai, C. (2011) There Are Three Types Of Innovation. Here's How To Manage Themhttp://www.fastcodesign.com/1665186/there-are-three-types-of-innovation-heres-how-to-manage-them

Weik, K. (1976), 'Educational organizations as loosely coupled systems', *Administrative Science Quarterly*, 21 (1). Reprinted in A. Westoby (1988) *Cultures and Power in Educational Organizations*, Buckingham, SRHE & Open University Press.

Wenger, E. (2000), 'Communities of practice and social learning systems', *Organization*, 7, 2, 225-246.

West MA and Farr JL (1990) Innovation and Creativity at Work Psychological and Organisational Strategies, Oxford John Wiley & Sons

Zuber-Skerritt, O. (2000). Action learning, action research and process management: Theory, practice and praxis. Action Research Unit, Faculty of Education, Griffith University, Brisbane, Australia.